AF735037

Recent Advances in Internet of Things Security

The growth of the Internet of Things (IoT) technology has indeed led to an increase in cybersecurity issues. While the Internet of Things enhances accessibility, integrity, availability, scalability, confidentiality, and interoperability among devices, it also faces vulnerabilities due to its diverse attack sources and lack of standardization in security protocols. This makes Internet of Things systems particularly susceptible to cyberattacks. It is essential to ensure proper security measures are in place to protect Internet of Things devices and networks, given their critical role in modern communications and the evolving threat landscape. Always remember to verify important security information from trusted sources.

Recent Advances in Internet of Things Security discusses the critical importance of robust security frameworks to protect Internet of Things ecosystems against various cyber threats. It highlights the security risks associated with Internet of Things devices and applications and presents a variety of potential solutions. It is essential to remain aware of these challenges to effectively safeguard Internet of Things systems. This book delves into the complexities of IoT security, exploring a range of vulnerabilities across different layers of the IoT architecture.

The book provides a comprehensive overview of Internet of Things security, emphasizing the significance of securing Internet of Things products and applications. It serves as a foundational resource for young researchers, academics, and industry professionals keen on advanced security solutions within the Internet of Things landscape, reflecting the current state of research and ongoing challenges in this field.

Recent Advances in Internet of Things Security

Edited by
Mourade Azrour and
Jamal Mabrouki

CRC Press
Taylor & Francis Group
Boca Raton London New York

CRC Press is an imprint of the
Taylor & Francis Group, an **informa** business
A PRODUCTIVITY PRESS BOOK

Designed cover image: Shutterstock image 2177393521

First edition published 2025
by CRC Press
2385 NW Executive Center Drive, Suite 320, Boca Raton FL 33431

and by CRC Press
4 Park Square, Milton Park, Abingdon, Oxon, OX14 4RN

CRC Press is an imprint of Taylor & Francis Group, LLC

© 2025 selection and editorial matter, Mourade Azrour and Jamal Mabrouki; individual chapters, the contributors

Reasonable efforts have been made to publish reliable data and information, but the author and publisher cannot assume responsibility for the validity of all materials or the consequences of their use. The authors and publishers have attempted to trace the copyright holders of all material reproduced in this publication and apologize to copyright holders if permission to publish in this form has not been obtained. If any copyright material has not been acknowledged please write and let us know so we may rectify in any future reprint.

Except as permitted under U.S. Copyright Law, no part of this book may be reprinted, reproduced, transmitted, or utilized in any form by any electronic, mechanical, or other means, now known or hereafter invented, including photocopying, microfilming, and recording, or in any information storage or retrieval system, without written permission from the publishers.

For permission to photocopy or use material electronically from this work, access www.copyright.com or contact the Copyright Clearance Center, Inc. (CCC), 222 Rosewood Drive, Danvers, MA 01923, 978-750-8400. For works that are not available on CCC please contact mpkbookspermissions@tandf.co.uk

Trademark notice: Product or corporate names may be trademarks or registered trademarks and are used only for identification and explanation without intent to infringe.

ISBN: 9781032959276 (hbk)
ISBN: 9781032960128 (pbk)
ISBN: 9781003587552 (ebk)

DOI: 10.1201/9781003587552

Typeset in Sabon
by Deanta Global Publishing Services, Chennai, India

Contents

About the Editors

Mourade Azrour received his PhD from the Faculty of Sciences and Techniques, Moulay Ismail University of Meknes, Morocco. He has received his MS in computer and distributed systems from the Faculty of Sciences, Ibn Zouhr University, Agadir, Morocco, in 2014. Mourade currently works as Professor in Computer Sciences at the Department of Computer Science, Faculty of Sciences and Techniques, Moulay Ismail University of Meknès, Morocco. His research interests include authentication protocol, computer security, the Internet of Things, smart systems, and machine learning, among others. Mourade is a member of the scientific committee of numerous international conferences. He is also a reviewer of various scientific journals. He has published more than 120 scientific papers and book chapters. Mourade has edited various scientific books, such as *IoT and Smart Devices for Sustainable Environment* and *Advanced Technology for Smart Environment and Energy*. Finally, he has served as a guest editor at the journals *EAI Endorsed Transactions on Internet of Things*, *Tsinghua Science and Technology*, *Applied Sciences MDPI*, and *Sustainability MDPI*.

Jamal Mabrouki received his PhD in Process and Environmental Engineering at Mohammed V University in Rabat, Morocco, specializing in artificial intelligence and smart automatic systems. He completed his Bachelor of Science degree in Physics and Chemistry with honors from Hassan II University in Casablanca, Morocco, and he is an engineer in environment and smart systems. His research is on intelligent monitoring, control, and management systems and, more particularly, on sensing and supervising remote intoxication systems, smart self-supervised systems, and recurrent neural networks. He has published several papers at conferences and in indexed journals, most of them related to artificial intelligence systems, the Internet of Things, and big data and mining. Jamal currently works as Professor in Environment, Energy, and Smart Systems at Mohammed V University in Rabat, Faculty of Science, Morocco. Jamal is a scientific committee member of numerous national and international conferences. He is also a reviewer for *Modeling Earth Systems and Environment*; *International Journal of Environmental Analytical Chemistry*; *International Journal of Modeling, Simulation, and Scientific Computing*; *Journal of Supercomputing*, *Energy & Environment*; and *Big Data Mining and Analytics*.

List of contributors

Amnah Alharbi
Department of Information Technology
College of Computer, Qassim University
Buraydah, Saudi Arabia

Karam Allali
Faculty of Sciences and Techniques
Hassan II University
Mohammedia, Morocco

Ahmad El Allaoui
Faculty of Sciences and Techniques
Moulay Ismail University of Meknes
Errachidia, Morocco

Amal Almotairy
Department of Information Technology
College of Computer, Qassim University
Buraydah, Saudi Arabia

Eman Alotaibi
Department of Information Technology
College of Computer, Qassim University
Buraydah, Saudi Arabia

Sara Amaouche
Higher School Essaouira
Cadi Ayyad University
Morocco

Fatima Amounas
Faculty of Sciences and Techniques
Moulay Ismail University of Meknes
Errachidia, Morocco

Said Aqil
ENSAM Casablanca
Hassan II University
Morocco

Rguibi Arjdal
Faculty of Sciences
Ibn Zohr University
Agadir, Morocco

Ahmed Asimi
Faculty of Sciences
Ibn Zohr University
Agadir, Morocco

Younes Asimi
Technology High School Guelmim
Ibn Zohr University
Agadir, Morocco

Chadia EL Asry
Faculty of Sciences
Mohammed V University in Rabat
Morocco

Hafida Assmi
Higher School Essaouira
Cadi Ayyad University
Morocco

Mourade Azrour
Faculty of Sciences and Techniques
Moulay Ismail University of Meknes
Errachidia, Morocco

Mohamed Badiy
Faculty of Sciences and Techniques
Moulay Ismail University of Meknes
Errachidia, Morocco

Kamal Bella
Higher School Essaouira
Cadi Ayyad University
Morocco

Ibtissam Benchaji
Faculty of Sciences
Mohammed V University in Rabat
Morocco

Said Benkirane
Higher School Essaouira
Cadi Ayyad University
Morocco

Soumia Benkou
Faculty of Sciences
Ibn Zohr University
Agadir, Morocco

Elmehdi Benmalek
ENSAM de Rabat
Mohammed V University Rabat
Morocco

Amine Berqia
ENSIAS Mohammed V University in Rabat
Rabat, Morocco

Habiba Bouijij
ENSIAS Mohammed V University in Rabat
Rabat, Morocco

Souhayla Dargaoui
Faculty of Sciences and Techniques
Moulay Ismail University of Meknes
Errachidia, Morocco

Maryam Douiba
Higher School Essaouira
Cadi Ayyad University
Morocco

Samira Douzi
Faculty of Sciences
Mohammed V University in Rabat
Morocco

Jamal Elmhamdi
ENSAM de Rabat
Mohammed V University Rabat
Morocco

Omar Enassiri
ENSA Kenitra
Ibn Tofail University Kenitra
Morocco

Khalid El Fayq
Computer Sciences Research Laboratory
Ibn Tofail University Kenitra
Morocco

Hassan El Ghazi
National Institute of Posts and Telecommunications (INPT)
Rabat, Morocco

El Mahdi El Guarmah
L2IS
Cadi Ayyad University, FST
Marrakesh, Morocco
and
Royal Air School of Aeronautics, L2IS,
Marrakesh, Morocco

Azidine Guezzaz
Higher School Essaouira
Cadi Ayyad University
Morocco

Mohammad Ali A. Hammoudeh
Department of Information Technology
College of Computer, Qassim University
Buraydah, Saudi Arabia

Chaimae Hazman
Higher School Essaouira
Cadi Ayyad University
Morocco

Lahcen Idouglid
Computer Sciences Research Laboratory
Ibn Tofail University Kenitra
Morocco

Atman Jbari
ENSAM de Rabat
Mohammed V University Rabat
Morocco

Abdelilah Jilbab
ENSAM de Rabat
Mohammed V University Rabat
Morocco

Yacouba Kouraogo
UREN
Virtual University of Côte d'Ivoire
Côte d'Ivoire

Mbarek Lahdoud
Faculty of Sciences
Ibn Zohr University
Agadir, Morocco

Iyad Lahsen-Cherif
National Institute of Posts and Telecommunications (INPT)
Rabat, Morocco

Maria Lebbar
ROSDM Research Team, LMAID — Laboratory of Applied Mathematics and Business Intelligence
ENSMR Rabat
Morocco

Mansour Lmkaiti
Polydisciplinary Faculty
University Sultan Moulay Slimane
Morocco

Khadija Mesmar
ROSDM Research Team, LMAID – Laboratory of Applied Mathematics and Business Intelligence
ENSMR Rabat
Morocco

Mouaad Mohy-Eddine
Higher School Essaouira
Cadi Ayyad University
Morocco

Tariq Mouatassim
National Institute of Posts and Telecommunications (INPT)
Rabat, Morocco

Houda Moudni
Faculty of Sciences and Technology
University Sultan Moulay Slimane
Morocco

Hicham Mouncif
Polydisciplinary Faculty
University Sultan Moulay Slimane
Morocco

Ghizlane Orhanou
Faculty of Sciences
Mohammed V University in Rabat
Morocco

Bouabid EL Ouahidi
Faculty of Sciences
Mohammed V University in Rabat
Morocco

Lahcen Oumouss
Faculty of Sciences
Ibn Zohr University
Agadir, Morocco

Yassine Sadqi
Laboratory LIMATI, FPBM
USMS University
Beni Mellal, Morocco

Hind Timouhin
Faculty of Sciences and Techniques
Moulay Ismail University of Meknes
Errachidia, Morocco

Said Tkatek
Computer Sciences Research Laboratory
Ibn Tofail University
Kenitra, Morocco

Mohamed Zaoui
Laboratory LIMATI, FPBM
USMS University Beni Mellal
Morocco

Moussa Zinelabedine
ENSAM de Rabat
Mohammed V University Rabat
Morocco

Chapter 1

Strengthening IIoT security

Integrating intrusion detection systems with machine learning

Lahcen Idouglid, Said Tkatek, Khalid El Fayq, and Azidine Guezzaz

1.1 INTRODUCTION

The Industrial Internet of Things (IIoT) is a key component of Industry 4.0, the fourth industrial revolution that leverages digital technologies to optimize industrial processes and operations. IIoT refers to the network of interconnected sensors, instruments, and devices that collect, exchange, and analyze data from various industrial domains, such as manufacturing, energy, transportation, and health care [1, 2]. IIoT enables improved productivity, efficiency, quality, and sustainability in industrial systems, as well as new business models and opportunities [3, 4].

However, the widespread adoption of IIoT also poses significant security challenges, as IIoT infrastructure becomes a prime target for cyberattacks that can compromise the confidentiality, integrity, and availability of critical data and services [5, 6]. Moreover, the heterogeneous, dynamic, and complex nature of IIoT environments makes it difficult to apply traditional security solutions that rely on predefined rules or signatures to detect and prevent attacks [6, 7]. Therefore, there is a pressing need to develop advanced security measures that can cope with the evolving and sophisticated cyber threats facing IIoT systems.

One promising direction is to integrate intrusion detection systems (IDSs) with machine learning (ML) algorithms to enhance the security of IIoT environments [8–14]. IDSs are tools that monitor network traffic and devices for any malicious or anomalous activities and alert the security administrators to take appropriate actions [15, 16]. ML is a branch of artificial intelligence that enables systems to learn from data and make predictions or decisions without explicit programming [17, 18]. By combining the strengths of IDSs and ML, it is possible to develop a robust security framework that can automatically learn the normal behavior patterns of IIoT devices and swiftly detect any deviations indicative of potential security breaches [19, 20]. Furthermore, ML can help to identify the type and source of the attacks, as well as to adapt to the changing patterns and dynamics of the IIoT landscape [21–24].

DOI: 10.1201/9781003587552-1

In this chapter, we investigate the integration of IDS with ML algorithms to fortify the security of IIoT environments. We delve into the intricacies of developing a robust IDS framework that harnesses the capabilities of ML for anomaly detection and threat identification. We propose a novel approach that employs ML algorithms to analyze real-time data streams generated by IIoT devices and discern normal behavior patterns and swiftly detect deviations indicative of potential security breaches. We evaluate the effectiveness of various ML techniques in enhancing the accuracy and responsiveness of IDS in the dynamic and complex IIoT landscape. We also compare our approach with existing IDS and ML solutions and demonstrate its superior performance and scalability. The findings underscore the significance of leveraging ML-driven IDS to proactively mitigate cyber threats, safeguarding the integrity and reliability of IIoT ecosystems.

The rest of the chapter is organized as follows. Section 1.2 provides a background on IIoT, IDS, and ML. Section 1.3 presents the proposed approach for integrating IDS with ML algorithms for IIoT security. Section 1.4 describes the experimental setup and results. Section 1.5 concludes the chapter and suggests future directions.

1.2 RELATED WORKS

The study [1] reviews IIoT security, addressing shared and specific challenges. It evaluates existing issues and solutions, stressing data confidentiality and system integrity. Unique concerns regarding industrial control systems (ICS) are discussed, emphasizing tailored solutions for enhanced security.

This study [25] examines Internet of Things (IoT) security, highlighting current standards and emerging threats. It emphasizes the need for standardized communication and data audit to mitigate diverse attacks. Integration of advanced technologies like machine learning and blockchain is explored to enhance security, despite increased system complexity.

Summarizing IoT security research, this paper [26] emphasizes standardization and future developments. It offers insights into mainstream security models and effective solutions. The convergence of edge computing, SDN, and AI is proposed as a promising approach for resilient IoT security.

The paper [15] proposes a modified Random Forest algorithm for detecting network attacks on IIoT devices. It claims high accuracy and applicability to resource-constrained devices, comparing favorably with other machine learning algorithms.

Implementing multiple intrusion detection models, this paper [27] achieves high accuracy using machine learning algorithms. The Random Forest model stands out with 99.97% accuracy on the evaluated dataset, surpassing previous models.

Table 1.1 Overview of published papers on IoT and IIoT security

Ref	*Year*	*Types*	*Accuracy*	*Dataset*	*IIoT/ IoT*
[1]	2019	A Survey	–	–	IIoT
[25]	2019	A Survey		–	IoT
[26]	2019	Review	–	–	IoT and IIoT
[29]	2022	Hybrid IDS	99.10%	Bot-IoT and NSL-KDD	IIoT
[27]	2023	NIDS	99.97%	WUSTL-IIoT2021	IIoT
[28]	2023	SDN/IDS	94.75%	WUSTL-IIoT-2021	IIoT
[15]	2024	ML-IDS	99%	TON-IoT and UNSW-NB15	IoT

This research [28] introduces a hybrid IDS for SDN-enabled IIoT networks, combining blockchain and deep learning techniques. It employs CNN for anomaly detection and blockchain for secure log storage. The proposed IDS demonstrates effectiveness in terms of accuracy, detection rate, and scalability.

This paper [29] introduces a lightweight hybrid intrusion detection framework for edge-based IIoT security. The paper leverages machine learning techniques. PK-IDS combines KNN and PCA for superior results, integrating Snort IDS for misuse detection. It achieves high accuracy and low false alarm rates on evaluated datasets, emphasizing its effectiveness in securing IIoT environments (Table 1.1).

1.3 METHODOLOGY

The section outlines methodology employed to address research questions, ensuring robustness and reliability. It presents a comprehensive overview of research design, data collection, and analytical techniques, ensuring transparency. Meticulous selection of tools tailored to the research nature facilitates systematic exploration. Step-by-step execution justifies methodological relevance and contribution, offering readers a clear roadmap to understand and evaluate study rigor.

1.3.1 The framework of our intrusion detection system

As can be seen in Figure 1.1, the framework of our IDS is composed of six key steps. In the first one, the Edge_IIoTset dataset provides authentic sensor readings and communication patterns, facilitating network-based intrusion detection systems (NIDSs) research in industrial IoT environments. Pre-processing in step 2 involves data cleaning and normalization, enhancing dataset quality and reducing biases. Step 3 focuses on training machine learning models

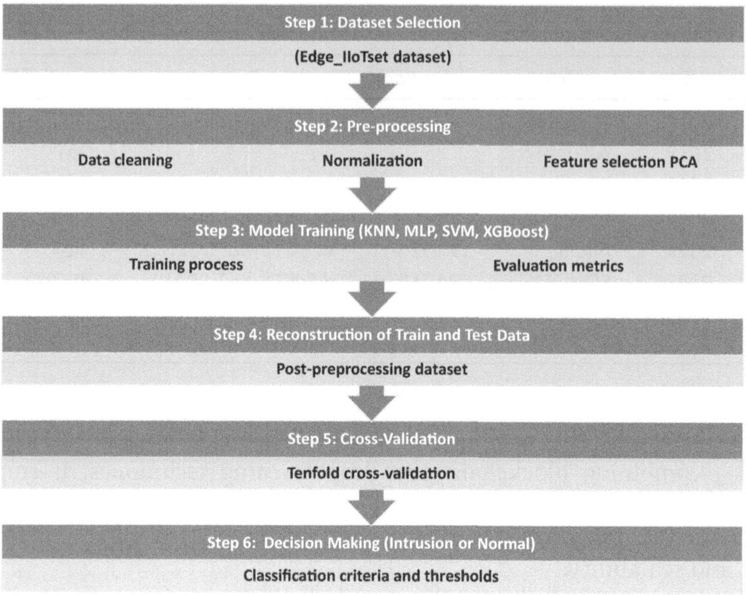

Figure 1.1 The key steps of our proposed IDS

(KNN, MLP, SVM, XGBoost) and evaluating their performance using metrics like accuracy and precision. Step 4 reconstructs the pre-processed data for further analysis. Step 5 employs tenfold cross-validation for robust model performance estimation. In step 6, classification criteria and thresholds guide NIDS decision-making, balancing sensitivity and specificity effectively.

1.3.2 Algorithms

The multilayer perceptron (MLP) [30] is an artificial neural network with multiple layers of nodes and learnable weights. Trained via supervised learning, it excels in capturing complex non-linear relationships within data. The k-nearest neighbors (KNN) algorithm [31], a non-parametric method, assigns data points to the majority class of their nearest neighbors in the feature space, employing metrics like Euclidean distance. XGBoost [32], belonging to the ensemble learning family, constructs decision trees and combines their predictions for high performance in classification and regression tasks. A support vector machine (SVM) [33] determines a hyperplane to best separate classes, ideal for high-dimensional spaces and resistant to overfitting.

1.4 RESULTS AND DISCUSSION

In the results and discussion section, we evaluate our IDS using metrics like accuracy, precision, recall, F1-score, Matthews correlation coefficient

Table 1.2 Results of efficiency metrics for the Edge_IIoTset dataset

Algorithms	*ACC*	*Precision*	*Recall*	*F1-score*	*MCC*	*Training time (s)*
Xgboost	0.9991	0.9991	0.9999	0.9991	0.9626	2
KNN	0.9999	0.9999	1	0.9999	0.9999	12.56
MLP	0.9993	0.9993	0.9999	0.9993	0.9931	10
SVM	0.9994	0.9994	0.9996	0.9994	0.9622	75.94

(MCC), and training time. We also conduct a comparative analysis of KNN, XGBoost, MLP, and SVM algorithms, revealing their nuanced effectiveness and efficiency in industrial network security.

Table 1.2 presents efficiency metrics for the Edge_IIoTset dataset, showcasing the performance of XGBoost, KNN, MLP, and SVM algorithms. XGBoost and KNN excel with high accuracy, precision, and near-perfect recall and F1-score values. KNN achieves flawless recall. XGBoost and MLP demonstrate exceptional Matthews Correlation Coefficients, while SVM, although competitive, requires a lengthier training time. These insights aid in selecting the optimal algorithm for intrusion detection systems in industrial IoT security, considering both performance and computational efficiency.

Figure 1.2 illustrates the varying training times for algorithms (XGBoost: 2s, KNN: 12.56s, MLP: 10s, SVM: 75.94s) on the Edge_IIoTset dataset, highlighting XGBoost's remarkable efficiency in just two seconds. This emphasizes the crucial consideration of the trade-off between training time and performance in selecting the optimal algorithm for the Intrusion Detection System (IDS).

In Figure 1.3, accuracy results across algorithms demonstrate exceptional performance, with XGBoost leading at 0.9999, closely followed by SVM, KNN, and MLP. Precision values reveal low false positive rates, with XGBoost exhibiting the lowest at 0.9999. High recall percentages indicate the algorithms' effective capture of positive instances, particularly XGBoost with a perfect recall of 100%. F1-scores highlight balanced effectiveness, with XGBoost leading. Matthews correlation coefficient results underscore XGBoost's superiority in handling imbalanced datasets, providing a comprehensive evaluation of classification performance.

XGBoost stands out as the preferred choice for IIoT security with superior accuracy, precision, and efficiency. While KNN excels in intrusion detection recall, SVM's extended training time may hinder real-time applications. Careful algorithm selection, considering performance and computational efficiency, is crucial for timely threat detection in IIoT systems. Continuous monitoring and exploration of ensemble methods further bolster intrusion detection robustness.

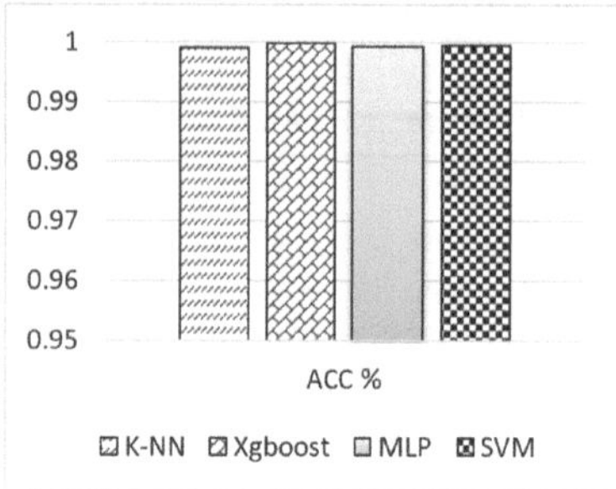

(a) Accuracy

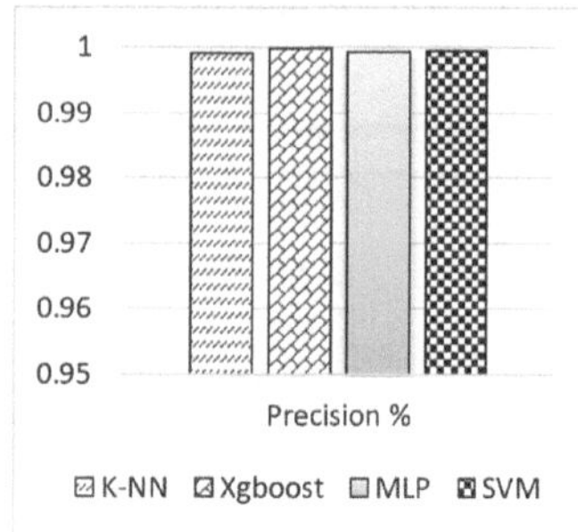

(b) Precision

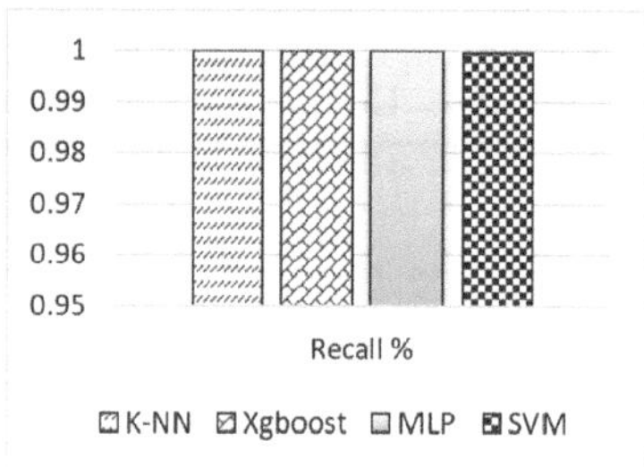

(c) Recall

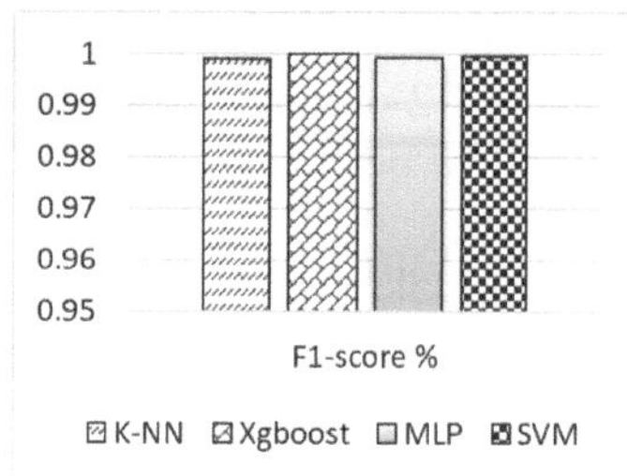

(d) F1-Score

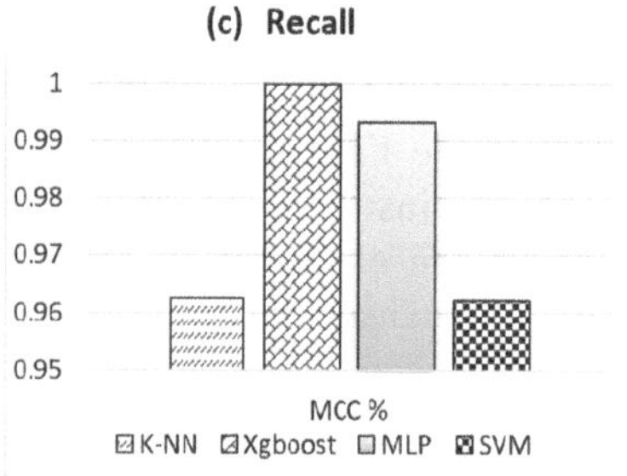

(e) MCC

Figure 1.2 Comprehensive performance evaluation metrics for intrusion detection algorithms on the Edge_IIoTset dataset

1.5 CONCLUSION

In conclusion, our investigation into the integration of intrusion detection systems with machine learning algorithms for enhancing security in Industrial Internet of Things environments has yielded insightful results. The performance evaluation of IDS algorithms on the Edge_IIoTset dataset highlights XGBoost's superior accuracy, precision, and efficiency, positioning it as a commendable choice for IIoT security. This study emphasizes the nuanced selection of algorithms to balance performance metrics and computational efficiency, ensuring the effective and timely detection of

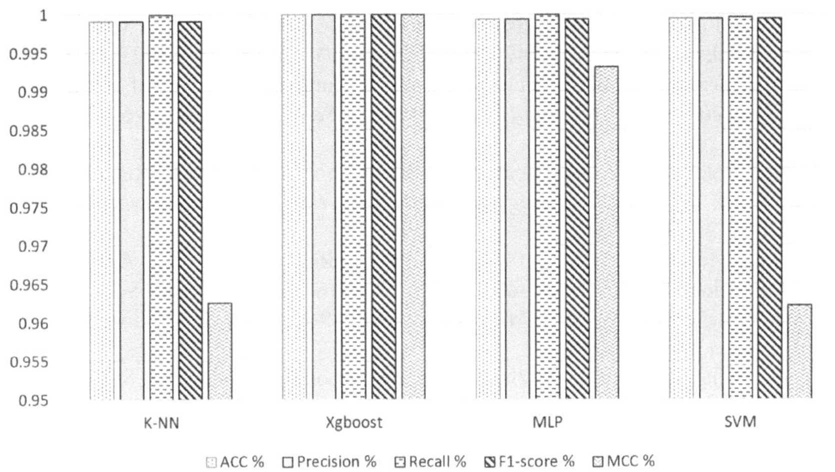

Figure 1.3 The evaluation metrics of the four different algorithms

security threats in dynamic IIoT systems. Future work includes continuous monitoring, periodic recalibration, and exploration of ensemble approaches to further enhance robust intrusion detection capabilities in evolving IIoT landscapes.

REFERENCES

1. X. Yu and H. Guo, "A Survey on IIoT Security," in *2019 IEEE VTS Asia Pacific Wireless Communications Symposium (APWCS)*, Singapore: IEEE, Aug. 2019, pp. 1–5. doi: 10.1109/VTS-APWCS.2019.8851679.
2. S. F. Tan and A. Samsudin, "Recent Technologies, Security Countermeasure and Ongoing Challenges of Industrial Internet of Things (IIoT): A Survey," *Sensors*, vol. 21, no. 19, p. 6647, Oct. 2021, doi: 10.3390/s21196647.
3. S. N. Deshpande and R. M. Jogdand, "A Survey on Internet of Things (IoT), Industrial IoT (IIoT) and Industry 4.0," *Int. J. Comput. Appl.*, vol. 175, no. 27, pp. 20–27, Oct. 2020, doi: 10.5120/ijca2020920790.
4. V. Demertzi, S. Demertzis, and K. Demertzis, "An Overview of Privacy Dimensions on the Industrial Internet of Things (IIoT)," *Algorithms*, vol. 16, no. 8, p. 378, Aug. 2023, doi: 10.3390/a16080378.
5. G. Czeczot, I. Rojek, D. Mikołajewski, and B. Sangho, "AI in IIoT Management of Cybersecurity for Industry 4.0 and Industry 5.0 Purposes," *Electronics*, vol. 12, no. 18, p. 3800, Sep. 2023, doi: 10.3390/electronics12183800.
6. A. Arun Kumar and R. Krishna Karne, "IIoT-IDS Network Using Inception CNN Model," *J. Trends Comput. Sci. Smart Technol.*, vol. 4, no. 3, pp. 126–138, Aug. 2022, doi: 10.36548/jtcsst.2022.3.002.
7. J. Du, K. Yang, Y. Hu, and L. Jiang, "NIDS-CNNLSTM: Network Intrusion Detection Classification Model Based on Deep Learning," *IEEE Access*, vol. 11, pp. 24808–24821, 2023, doi: 10.1109/ACCESS.2023.3254915.

8. C. Hazman, A. Guezzaz, S. Benkirane, and M. Azrour, "Enhanced IDS with Deep Learning for IoT-Based Smart Cities Security," *Tsinghua Sci. Technol.*, vol. 29, no. 4, pp. 929–947, Aug. 2024, doi: 10.26599/TST.2023.9010033.
9. S. Dargaoui et al., "Security Issues in Internet of Medical Things," in *Blockchain and Machine Learning for IoT Security*, Chapman & Hall/CRC, 2024, pp. 77–91.
10. S. Dargaoui et al., "Applications of Blockchain in Healthcare: Review Study," in *IoT, Machine Learning and Data Analytics for Smart Healthcare*, CRC Press, 2024.
11. M. Mohy-eddine, A. Guezzaz, S. Benkirane, and M. Azrour, "An Intrusion Detection Model Using Election-Based Feature Selection and K-NN," *Microprocess. Microsyst.*, p. 104966, Oct. 2023, doi: 10.1016/j.micpro.2023.104966.
12. K. Bella, A. Guezzaz, S. Benkirane, M. Azrour, Y. Fouad, M. S. Benyeogor, N. Innab, " An Efficient Intrusion Detection System for IoT Security Using CNN Decision Forest," *PeerJ Comput.*, 2024, Sci. 10:e2290, DOI 10.7717/peerj-cs.2290
13. C. Hazman, A. Guezzaz, S. Benkirane, and M. Azrour, "Toward an Intrusion Detection Model for IoT-Based Smart Environments," *Multimed. Tools Appl.*, vol. 83, Aug. 2023, doi: 10.1007/s11042-023-16436-0.
14. S. Amaouche, AzidineGuezzaz, S. Benkirane, and MouradeAzrour, "IDS-XGbFS: A Smart Intrusion Detection System Using XGboost with Recent Feature Selection for VANET Safety," *Clust. Comput.*, vol. 27, pp. 1–15, 2023.
15. M. Al-Ambusaidi, Z. Yinjun, Y. Muhammad, and A. Yahya, "ML-IDS: An Efficient ML-Enabled Intrusion Detection System for Securing IoT Networks and Applications," *Soft Comput.*, vol. 28, no. 2, pp. 1765–1784 Dec. 2023, doi: 10.1007/s00500-023-09452-7.
16. I. Farhadian Dehkordi, K. Manochehri, and V. Aghazarian, "Internet of Things (IoT) Intrusion Detection by Machine Learning (ML): A Review," *Asia-Pac. J. Inf. Technol. Multimed.*, vol. 12, no. 1, pp. 13–38, Jun. 2023, doi: 10.17576/apjitm-2023-1201-02.
17. A. Ganne, "IoT Threats & Implementation of AI/ML to Address Emerging Cyber Security Issues in IoT with Cloud Computing," *Int. Res. J. Mod. Eng. Technol. Sci.*, vol. 5, no. 1, Jan. 2023, doi: 10.56726/IRJMETS32866.
18. M. Bagaa, T. Taleb, J. B. Bernabe, and A. Skarmeta, "A Machine Learning Security Framework for IoT Systems," *IEEE Access*, vol. 8, pp. 114066–114077, 2020.
19. L. Idouglid, S. Tkatek, K. Elfayq, and A. Guezzaz, "A Novel Anomaly Detection Model for the Industrial Internet of Things Using Machine Learning Techniques," vol. 2024, no. 1, pp.143–151, 2024, 10.32620/reks.2024.1.12.
20. L. Idouglid, S. Tkatek, K. Elfayq, and A. Guezzaz, "Next-Gen Security in IoT: Integrating Intrusion Detection Systems with Machine Learning for Industry 4.0 Resilience," *Int. J. Electr. Comput. Eng. IJECE*, vol. 14, no. 3, p. 3512, Jun. 2024, doi: 10.11591/ijece.v14i3.pp3512-3521.
21. W. Liu, L. Zhou, S. Zhang, N. Luo, and M. Xu, "A New High-Precision and Lightweight Detection Model for Illegal Construction Objects Based on Deep Learning," *Tsinghua Sci. Technol.*, vol. 29, no. 4, pp. 1002–1022, Aug. 2024, doi: 10.26599/TST.2023.9010090.

22. A. E. M. Eljialy, M. Y. Uddin, and S. Ahmad, “Novel Framework for an Intrusion Detection System Using Multiple Feature Selection Methods Based on Deep Learning,” *Tsinghua Sci. Technol.*, vol. 29, no. 4, pp. 948–958, Aug. 2024, doi: 10.26599/TST.2023.9010032.
23. S. Li, T. Cui, and W. Viriyasitavat, “Edge Device Fault Probability Based Intelligent Calculations for Fault Probability of Smart Systems,” *Tsinghua Sci. Technol.*, vol. 29, no. 4, pp. 1023–1036, Aug. 2024, doi: 10.26599/TST.2023.9010085.
24. N. Meenakshi et al., “Efficient Communication in Wireless Sensor Networks Using Optimized Energy Efficient Engroove Leach Clustering Protocol,” *Tsinghua Sci. Technol.*, vol. 29, no. 4, pp. 985–1001, Aug. 2024, doi: 10.26599/TST.2023.9010056.
25. Rachit, S. Bhatt, and P. R. Ragiri, “Security Trends in Internet of Things: A Survey,” *SN Appl. Sci.*, vol. 3, no. 1, p. 121, Jan. 2021, doi: 10.1007/s42452-021-04156-9.
26. J. Zhang, H. Chen, L. Gong, J. Cao, and Z. Gu, “The Current Research of IoT Security,” in *2019 IEEE Fourth International Conference on Data Science in Cyberspace (DSC)*, Hangzhou, China: IEEE, Jun. 2019, pp. 346–353. doi: 10.1109/DSC.2019.00059.
27. A. M. Eid, A. B. Nassif, B. Soudan, and M. N. Injadat, “IIoT Network Intrusion Detection Using Machine Learning,” in *2023 6th International Conference on Intelligent Robotics and Control Engineering (IRCE)*, Jilin, China: IEEE, Aug. 2023, pp. 196–201. doi: 10.1109/IRCE59430.2023.10255088.
28. S. K. Poorazad, C. Benzaıd, and T. Taleb, “Blockchain and Deep Learning-Based IDS for Securing SDN-Enabled Industrial IoT Environments,” Dec. 31, 2023, *arXiv*: arXiv:2401.00468. Accessed: Jan. 22, 2024. Online]. Available: http://arxiv.org/abs/2401.00468
29. A. Guezzaz, M. Azrour, S. Benkirane, M. Mohy-Eddine, H. Attou, and M. Douiba, “A Lightweight Hybrid Intrusion Detection Framework Using Machine Learning for Edge-Based IoT Security,” *Int. Arab J. Inf. Technol.*, vol. 19, no. 5, pp. 822–830, 2022, doi: 10.34028/iajit/19/5/14.
30. C. Hazman, A. Guezzaz, S. Benkirane and M. Azrour, “A smart model integrating LSTM and XGBoost for improving IoT-enabled smart cities security,” Cluster Computing, vol. 28, no. 1, p.70, 2025.
31. S. Zhang, X. Li, M. Zong, X. Zhu, and R. Wang, “Efficient kNN Classification with Different Numbers of Nearest Neighbors,” *IEEE Trans. Neural Netw. Learn. Syst.*, vol. 29, no. 5, pp. 1774–1785, May 2018, doi: 10.1109/TNNLS.2017.2673241.
32. T. Chen and C. Guestrin, “XGBoost: A Scalable Tree Boosting System,” in *Proceedings of the 22nd ACM SIGKDD International Conference on Knowledge Discovery and Data Mining*, San Francisco, CA: ACM, Aug. 2016, pp. 785–794. doi: 10.1145/2939672.2939785.
33. B. E. Boser, I. M. Guyon, and V. N. Vapnik, “A Training Algorithm for Optimal Margin Classifiers,” in *Proceedings of the Fifth Annual Workshop on Computational Learning Theory*, Pittsburgh, PA: ACM, Jul. 1992, pp. 144–152. doi: 10.1145/130385.130401.

Chapter 2

Scalable IoT anomaly detection

Federated and split learning

Rguibi Arjdal, Younes Asimi, Ahmed Asimi, and Lahcen Oumouss

2.1 INTRODUCTION

In recent years, the proliferation of Internet of Things (IoT) devices has led to unprecedented advancements in various domains, including health care, transportation, and smart homes [15]. However, the widespread adoption of IoT devices has also introduced significant security challenges, particularly in anomaly detection and data privacy. Traditional anomaly detection methods often rely on centralized learning approaches, where raw data from IoT devices is transferred to a central server for analysis. While effective, this centralized paradigm raises concerns about data privacy and communication overhead [9], especially in resource-constrained IoT environments. To address these challenges, novel techniques such as federated learning (FL) [8] and split learning (SL) have emerged as promising alternatives. FL enables collaborative model training across distributed devices without centralizing sensitive data [14], while split learning partitions model computation between devices and servers to preserve data privacy and optimize communication efficiency [7]. In this chapter, we present a comprehensive study on the application of federated and split learning for anomaly detection in IoT security. We begin by discussing the methodology of federated learning, highlighting its benefits and limitations in the context of IoT networks. Subsequently, we introduce split learning as an extension of FL, providing insights into its underlying principles and advantages. Furthermore, we delve into the intricacies of applying split learning for anomaly detection in IoT security. By strategically partitioning data and leveraging collaborative model training [6], we demonstrate how split learning can enhance data privacy, reduce communication overhead, and preserve model performance in resource-constrained environments. Lastly, we explore the concept of SplitFed anomaly detection, where the integration of federated and split learning techniques offers a synergistic approach to further improve the accuracy and efficiency of anomaly detection in IoT networks.

 DOI: 10.1201/9781003587552-2

2.2 RELATED WORKS

In this section, a comprehensive review is conducted on contemporary research that advocates for machine learning–driven strategies to bolster the security of IoT networks. Thom et al. [18] presented a device-specific anomaly detection technique for monitoring IoT network traffic, particularly when new devices are added. Their self-learning algorithm eliminates the need for pre-labeled attack data, as the system learns the patterns associated with different attack types. Mothukuri et al. [10] proposed a machine learning (ML)–based approach for anomaly detection in smart home sensor data. Their system focused on identifying abnormalities in sensor readings to detect potential attacks. Tanzila et al. [16] proposes an anomaly based intrusion detection system (IDS) for IoT networks that leverages the power of deep learning [21–24]. The system is trained on normal network traffic data to establish a baseline for typical behavior and identify deviations that might signal potential cyberattacks. Attota et al. [1] proposed MV-FLID, a novel intrusion detection approach for IoT networks that leverages Federated Learning and multiview learning. Recognizing limitations of traditional methods, they emphasized the need for more insightful and privacy-preserving techniques. Nguyen et al. [11] proposed a federated learning (FL)–based intrusion detection system (IDS) for IoT networks. Their system incorporates an innovative feature: an automated technique specifically tailored to different device types. Thapa et al. [17] introduced SplitFed Learning (SFL), a novel approach that merges federated learning (FL) and split learning (SL) to achieve both model privacy and resource efficiency. Jithish et al. [5] proposed a Federated Learning (FL) approach for anomaly detection in smart grids, addressing challenges associated with server-based model training. In their work, machine learning models are trained locally on individual smart meters, eliminating the need to share raw data with a central server. This approach prioritizes data privacy by relying on regular updates of model parameters instead of sharing raw data.

2.3 METHODOLOGY

This section outlines the methodological strategy utilized in the present study for constructing an anomaly-based intrusion detection system (IDS) for Internet of Things (IoT) networks.

2.3.1 Federated learning

Federated learning (FL) is a distributed machine learning paradigm that enables collaborative model training on decentralized devices. This approach offers a significant advantage over traditional centralized training, where data is transferred from resource-constrained devices to a central server for model updates.

FL offers several advantages for anomaly detection in IoT security:

- Enhanced data privacy: FL prioritizes data privacy [2] by keeping sensitive network traffic data on individual devices. This is particularly crucial in IoT environments where raw data transmission can raise privacy concerns due to the potential for sensitive information leakage. During the training process, only model updates are exchanged, significantly reducing the risk of exposing raw data.
- Improved scalability: FL scales effectively to handle large-scale IoT deployments. By distributing the training workload across individual devices, FL alleviates the computational burden on a central server and facilitates efficient training in resource-constrained IoT.
- Enhanced resilience: The distributed nature of FL fosters resilience against potential failures. Unlike centralized approaches where a single point of failure can cripple the entire system, FL's distributed architecture ensures continued operation even if individual devices experience downtime [20].

FL training process: The proposed system leverages FL for anomaly detection model training. This process can be summarized as follows:

- Local model training: Each device within the IoT network trains a local copy of the anomaly detection model on its own network traffic data.
- Parameter aggregation: After local training, model updates are exchanged between devices or with a central server for aggregation. This aggregation process combines the knowledge gained from each device's local training, leading to a more robust global model.
- Global model broadcast: The aggregated global model is then broadcast back to individual devices for further local training iterations. This iterative procedure persists until a specified stopping condition, such as convergence, is achieved.

Figure 2.1 depicts the federated learning process. In this approach, devices collaborate on model training without transferring raw data to a central server. This distributed approach helps to preserve data privacy and security.

2.3.2 Split learning

Split learning (SL) emerges as a promising paradigm that bridges the gap between federated learning (FL) and traditional centralized learning approaches [3]. It offers distinct advantages in scenarios where data

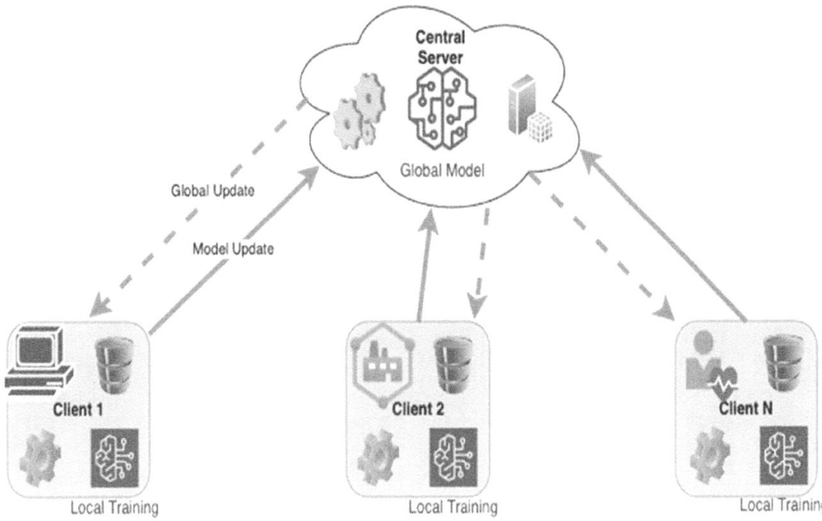

Figure 2.1 Federated learning architecture

privacy is paramount and resource limitations on individual devices pose challenges. With regard to motivation, we opted for split learning due to its benefits:

- Enhanced data privacy: FL keeps data on devices but may leak information through model updates. SL mitigates this by partitioning the data itself, with sensitive parts remaining on devices [19].
- Reduced communication overhead: FL can suffer from communication bottlenecks in large deployments. SL offloads training to a powerful edge server, reducing data transmission [13].

Split learning architecture for anomaly detection

The split learning architecture employed in our system is illustrated in Figure 2.2. Here is a breakdown of the key components and the step-by-step process:

Data partitioning and pre-processing. This crucial stage involves the collection, pre-processing, and strategic partitioning of raw network traffic data:

- Raw network traffic data is collected by each device.
- Devices pre-process the data (e.g., normalization, feature selection).
- The data is strategically partitioned:

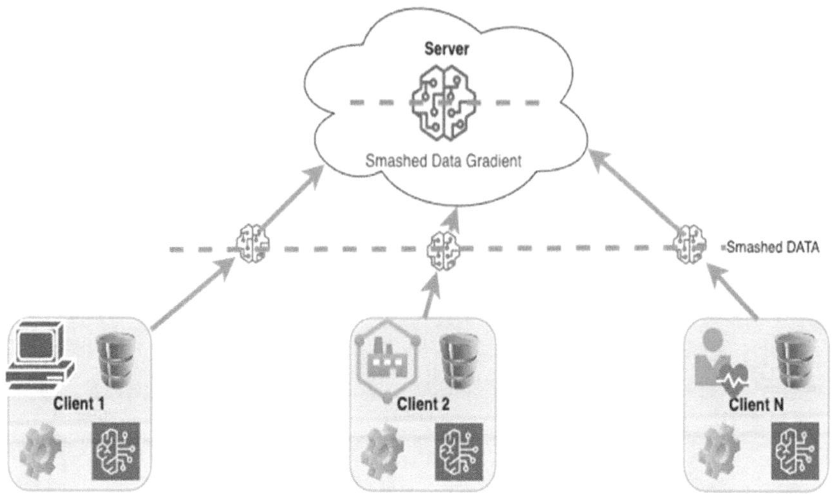

Figure 2.2 Split learning architecture

- A subset of features (potentially anonymized for privacy) is stored locally on the device.
- The remaining features or computationally intensive tasks are designated for the edge server.

Model splitting. The anomaly detection model is functionally divided between devices and the edge server:

- Feature extraction layers, responsible for extracting relevant patterns, reside on devices due to lower computational demands.
- Classification layers, performing the final anomaly detection decision, might be placed on the edge server due to higher complexity.

Local model training. Devices train their local portion of the anomaly detection model on the partitioned data.

Model update exchange. Devices periodically transmit their locally trained model updates to the edge server using a secure communication protocol.

Global model aggregation (edge server):

- The edge server aggregates the received model updates from all devices.
- It updates its own portion of the model based on these aggregated updates.

Iterative training. Steps 3–5 are repeated for multiple iterations until a stopping criterion (e.g., convergence) is met.

2.4 PROPOSED ANOMALY DETECTION APPROACH WITH SPLIT LEARNING FEDERATED (SPLITFED)

This section presents our proposed methodology for anomaly detection in the Internet of Things (IoT) networks. It leverages split learning federated (SplitFed), a powerful hybrid technique that addresses the challenges of privacy and communication overhead in traditional FL approaches [4].

2.4.1 Challenges of conventional anomaly detection methods

Centralized learning methods, while effective, often require transferring raw network traffic data from resource-constrained IoT devices to a central server. This raises concerns about:

- Data privacy: Sensitive data collected by IoT devices might be compromised during transmission or storage on a central server.
- Communication overhead: Large-scale deployments of IoT devices can generate significant amounts of data, leading to communication bottlenecks when transferred to a central location [12]. Federated learning offers a promising alternative by enabling collaborative model training without centralizing device data. However, FL might still leak information through model updates.

2.4.2 Addressing challenges with SplitFed

- Data partitioning: SplitFed balances privacy and model learning by keeping a subset of features (potentially anonymized) on devices, while offloading complex tasks to a powerful edge server.
- Federated learning paradigm: SplitFed leverages the distributed learning nature of FL. Devices collaboratively train their local models on the partitioned data and periodically transmit updates to the edge server.
- Model splitting: The anomaly detection model is functionally divided between devices and the edge server. Feature extraction layers reside on devices due to their lower computational demands. Classification layers, requiring higher complexity, might be placed on the edge server.

2.4.3 Benefits of SplitFed for anomaly detection in IoT networks

SplitFed enhances IoT anomaly detection by safeguarding data confidentiality on local devices, reducing communication overhead through edge server task distribution and maintaining model performance via strategic data partitioning and model splitting.

2.5 CONCLUSION

By incorporating split learning federated (SplitFed), the proposed approach offers a robust and secure solution for anomaly detection in resource-constrained IoT environments. This approach effectively addresses the challenges of data privacy and communication overhead associated with traditional methods. SplitFed leverages the strengths of both federated learning and split learning, enabling collaborative model training on distributed data while maintaining privacy. Data partitioning keeps sensitive information on devices, and model splitting optimizes resource utilization by offloading computationally intensive tasks to the edge server. This collaborative approach reduces communication overhead compared to centralized learning methods. The SplitFed-based anomaly detection system can play a crucial role in safeguarding the security and integrity of IoT networks. By enabling real-time identification of anomalies in network traffic data, this approach can help prevent security breaches, unauthorized access, and other malicious activities. As the number of interconnected devices continues to grow, secure and efficient anomaly detection solutions like SplitFed will become increasingly important for ensuring the smooth and secure operation of IoT networks.

REFERENCES

1. Dinesh Chowdary Attota, Viraaji Mothukuri, Reza M. Parizi, and Seyedamin Pouriyeh. An ensemble multi-view federated learning intrusion detection for IoT. *IEEE Access*, 9:117734–117745, 2021.
2. Rémi Gosselin, Loïc Vieu, Faiza Loukil, and Alexandre Benoit. Privacy and security in federated learning: A survey. *Applied Sciences*, 12(19): 9901, 2022.
3. Houda Hafi, Bouziane Brik, Pantelis A. Frangoudis, Adlen Ksentini, and Miloud Bagaa. Split federated learning for 6G enabled-networks: Requirements, challenges, and future directions. *IEEE Access*, 12:9890–9930, 2024.
4. Thahsin Zahir Ismail, A. and Mani Shukla, R. Analyzing the vulnerabilities in SplitFed Learning: Assessing the robustness against Data Poisoning Attacks. 2023. arXiv e-prints, pp.arXiv-2307.
5. J Jithish, Bithin Alangot, Nagarajan Mahalingam, and Kiat Seng Yeo. Distributed anomaly detection in smart grids: A federated learning-based approach. *IEEE Access*, 11:7157–7179, 2023.
6. Khan, T., Nguyen, K., Michalas, A. A More Secure Split: Enhancing the Security of Privacy-Preserving Split Learning. In: Fritsch, L., Hassan, I., Paintsil, E. (eds) Secure IT Systems. NordSec 2023. *Lecture Notes in Computer Science*, 14324: 307–329, Springer, Cham. 2024. https://doi.org/10.1007/978-3-031-47748-5_17

7. Jakub Konečny`, H Brendan McMahan, Daniel Ramage, and Peter Richtárik. Federated optimization: Distributed machine learning for on-device intelligence. *arXiv preprint arXiv:1610.02527*, 2016.
8. McMahan, H. Brendan, et al. "Federated learning: Strategies for improving communication efficiency." Proceedings of the 29th Conference on Neural Information Processing Systems (NIPS), pp. 5–10, Barcelona, Spain, 2016.
9. Zhuotao Lian and Chunhua Su. Decentralized federated learning for internet of things anomaly detection. In *Proceedings of the 2022 ACM on Asia Conference on Computer and Communications Security*, ASIA CCS '22, pp. 1249–1251, New York, NY, 2022. Association for Computing Machinery.
10. Viraaji Mothukuri, Prachi Khare, Reza M Parizi, Seyedamin Pouriyeh, Ali De-hghantanha, and Gautam Srivastava. Federated-learning-based anomaly detection for IoT security attacks. *IEEE Internet of Things Journal*, 9(4):2545–2554, 2021.
11. Thien Duc Nguyen, Samuel Marchal, Markus Miettinen, Hossein Fereidooni, N. Asokan, and Ahmad-Reza Sadeghi. DÏot: A federated self-learning anomaly detection system for IoT. In *2019 IEEE 39th International Conference on* Distributed *Computing Systems (ICDCS)*, pages 756–767, 2019.
12. Dargaoui, Souhayla, Mourade Azrour, Ahmad El Allaoui, Azidine Guezzaz, Abdulatif Alabdulatif, and Abdullah Alnajim. "An exhaustive survey on authentication classes in the IoT environments." Indonesian Journal of Electrical Engineering and Informatics (IJEEI) 12, no. 1 (2024): 15–31.
13. Van-Nam Pham, Ga-Won Lee, VanDung Nguyen, and Eui-Nam Huh. Efficient solution for large-scale IoT applications with proactive edge-cloud publish/subscribe brokers clustering. *Sensors*, 21(24):8232, 2021.
14. Karthik Prasad, Sayan Ghosh, Graham Cormode, Ilya Mironov, Ashkan Yousefpour, and Pierre Stock. Reconciling security and communication efficiency in federated learning. arXiv *preprint arXiv:2207.12779*, 2022.
15. Ishaani Priyadarshini. Anomaly detection of IoT cyberattacks in smart cities using federated learning and split learning. *Big Data and Cognitive Computing*, 8(3):21 , 2024.
16. Jing Qiu, Zhihong Tian, Chunlai Du, Qi Zuo, Shen Su, and Binxing Fang. A survey on access control in the age of internet of things. *IEEE Internet of Things Journal*, 7(6):4682–4696, 2020.
17. Tanzila Saba, Amjad Rehman, Tariq Sadad, Hoshang Kolivand, and Saeed Ali Bahaj. Anomaly-based intrusion detection system for IoT networks through deep learning model. *Computers and Electrical Engineering*, 99:107810, 2022.
18. Chandra Thapa, Pathum Chamikara Mahawaga Arachchige, Seyit Camtepe, and Lichao Sun. Splitfed: When federated learning meets split learning. *Proceedings of the AAAI Conference on Artificial Intelligence*, 36(8):8485–8493, Jun. 2022.
19. Jay Thom, Nathan Thom, Shamik Sengupta, and Emily Hand. Smart recon: Network traffic fingerprinting for IoT device identification. In *2022 IEEE 12th Annual Computing and Communication Workshop and Conference (CCWC)*, pp. 0072–0079. IEEE, 2022.

20. Kang Wei, Jun Li, Ming Ding, Chuan Ma, Howard H. Yang, Farhad Farokhi, Shi Jin, Tony Q. S. Quek, and H. Vincent Poor. Federated learning with differential privacy: Algorithms and performance analysis. *IEEE Transactions on Information Forensics and Security*, 15:3454–3469, 2020.
21. Qiang Yang, Yang Liu, Tianjian Chen, and Yongxin Tong. Federated machine learning: Concept and applications. *ACM Transactions on Intelligent Systems and Technology (TIST)*, 10(2):1–19, 2019.
22. S. Dargaoui et al. Applications of blockchain in healthcare: review study. In *IoT, Machine Learning and Data Analytics for Smart Healthcare*, CRC Press, 2024.
23. K. Bella et al. An efficient intrusion detection system for IoT security using CNN decision forest. *PeerJ Computer Science*, vol. 10:e2290, Sep. 2024, doi: 10.7717/peerj-cs.2290.
24. M. Mohy-eddine, A. Guezzaz, S. Benkirane, and M. Azrour. Malicious detection model with artificial neural network in IoT-based smart farming security. *Cluster Computing*, 27:1–16, 2024.

Chapter 3

Machine learning–based detection in wireless sensor networks

Mansour Lmkaiti, Houda Moudni, and Hicham Mouncif

3.1 INTRODUCTION

In recent years, there has been an exponential increase in the use of wireless sensor networks (WSNs) for environmental and physical condition monitoring in both industrial and research areas [1, 2]. WSNs are well known for being straightforward, efficient, affordable, and easy to implement when compared to other sensing devices. As a result, they have been widely applied in a variety of industries, including telecommunications, health care, military operations, and environmental research. WSNs are usually set up as a collection of geographically dispersed sensor nodes that work together to gather and monitor environmental and physical data [3]. These sensor nodes create wireless communication inside the network and send data to a central node for storage and processing—often referred to as the base station (BS) or the sink node.

The use of WSNs in inaccessible and challenging environments to identify environmental anomalies, such as floods, storms, and wildfires. It is commonly known that seismic occurrences and volcanic activity can also be used in less hazardous contexts, such as health monitoring, smart infrastructure development, transportation, and the Internet of Things (IoT) [4–8]. However, WSN design has inherent restrictions due to its basic simplicity. WSNs are highly vulnerable to security breaches due to their limited resources, which include battery power, memory, storage, communication bandwidth, and compute power. This poses a significant issue when it comes to fortification. Furthermore, these vulnerabilities are increased when sensor nodes are placed in unattended areas.

Denial-of-service (DoS) attacks are the most common security threat to wireless sensor networks. Their primary goal is to deplete node resources, especially power reserves, by preventing regular operations. Various defense techniques are needed to protect WSNs against DoS assaults and other security risks. Several studies have supported several intrusion detection systems (IDSs), using machine learning (ML) and deep learning methods to obtain impressive attack detection accuracy [8–10].

DOI: 10.1201/9781003587552-3

This chapter investigates ML methods designed to identify and categorize various types of assaults in wireless sensor networks [11, 12]. Our main goal is to develop a flexible, accurate, and low-power algorithm that can identify common assaults in wireless sensor networks. Our analysis covers a wide range of attack scenarios, including brute force SSH attempts, TCP null attacks, IP fragmentation attacks, accelerated SYN floods, SYN/ACK and RST floods, ARP spoofing, UDP port scans, DDoS MAC floods, and ICMP echo request floods. After a thorough analysis of previous work, we build on this foundation to propose our own approach to machine learning–driven intrusion detection systems for WSNs. The core of our methodology consists of training four different machine learning algorithms on the IDSAI dataset, with the aim of improving the accuracy and efficiency of attack detection mechanisms.

3.2 RELATED WORK

Wireless sensor networks face security issues and vulnerabilities while data packets are being transmitted between the nodes that make up the network [2]. Because WSNs have a large number of sensor nodes, they are vulnerable to a wide range of threats and attacks. Prior research has attempted to address these issues by utilizing abuse and anomalous detection techniques.

As an example, a previous work combined two different methodologies to present an anomaly detection framework customized for heterogeneous WSNs. The framework compares a long-term method that analyzes data from heterogeneous sensors network-wide with a short-term strategy that examines individual node data locally. This combination demonstrated a skillful synthesis that produced better results by overcoming the drawbacks of the separate methods [13].

An extensive assessment of modern anomaly-based intrusion detection systems (IDS) [8] was carried out by Soliman et al. for wireless sensor networks that are hierarchical. A 10,000 records total, evenly divided between normal and anomalous entries, covering a variety of attacks and samples, was used in their experimentation. The results indicated that the intrusion detection–based support vector machine (SVM) approach was more accurate than the fuzzy c-means (FCM) and the fuzzy rule-based approach (FRM) IDS [14].

A thorough investigation was carried out by Yousef et al. with the aim of identifying four different types of attacks using several algorithms: support vector machine (SVM), random forest (RF), K-means, and naive Bayes. After careful consideration of the chosen features, they determined that the random forest classifier (RFC) was the most accurate classifier [15].

An intrusion detection system (IDS) for WSNs based on a semi-supervised machine learning paradigm was proposed by Nadiammai et al.

Nevertheless, resource consumption factors were not taken into account in their analysis.

Panda and colleagues used various classifiers combined with unsupervised clustering methods to identify intrusions in wireless sensor networks. Although they did not take into account other forms of attacks, Sangkatsanee et al. proposed intrusion detection approaches that used a supervised machine learning algorithm specifically designed for spotting testing or denial of service assaults.

3.3 MACHINE LEARNING–BASED ANOMALY DETECTION IN WSN

In this chapter, we focus on the application of machine learning algorithms for anomaly detection in WSNs. Anomaly detection plays a crucial role in identifying and mitigating unexpected and malicious behavior within the network [8], ensuring the integrity and reliability of collected sensor data.

3.3.1 Random forest classifier

The random forest classifier employs similarity queries and a divide-and-conquer strategy to enhance efficiency, creating an ensemble of weak learners from decision trees to form a robust learner.

3.3.2 Decision tree classifier

The decision tree classifier effectively manages both categorical and continuous dependent variables. It partitions the data [16] into subsets of the same type, aiming to establish distinct groups based on the most significant independent variables.

3.3.3 Extra trees classifier

The extra trees classifier [17] employs a fully random approach for decision tree–based classification. By constructing additional trees using the entire sample and utilizing bootstrap copies of the training sample, it determines the optimal cutoff points for each random feature at a node [10]. This significantly reduces computational burden compared to standard methods.

3.3.3.1 Gradient boosting

Gradient boosting [18] is a robust algorithm for regression and classification tasks. It iteratively improves weak predictive models like decision trees, correcting errors from previous models to minimize them. If no clear patterns emerge, the algorithm can be halted to prevent overfitting.

3.3.4 XGB classifier

XGB excels in efficiently handling large datasets while delivering strong predictive performance. It employs a gradient boosting method to enhance model accuracy iteratively by adjusting the weights of training examples and minimizing a loss function [19].

Physical security and cryptography [20, 21] are two different approaches to protect data in sandy sensor networks. Physical security consists of protecting the devices, infrastructure, and physical environments in which the sensor networks are deployed, while cryptography uses encryption techniques to protect data when stored, transmitted, or processed. Physical security is important because it protects wireless sensor networks from physical attacks such as theft, sabotage, and destruction. Physical security measures may include the use of waterproof housing to protect sensors from the elements and the installation of surveillance cameras to alert in case of intrusion encryption. Meanwhile, encryption uses techniques to protect data against electronic attacks such as piracy, interception, and falsification. Encryption techniques may include the use of encryption keys to encrypt data, the use of security protocols to ensure the integrity and authenticity of data, and the use of identification mechanisms to ensure that only authorized users have access to the data.

The Bot-IoT dataset contains a significant amount of redundant data in its input detection information, which can potentially result in unfavorable outcomes. To address this issue, we conducted experiments using controlled machine learning algorithms on the IDSAI dataset [9]. The IDSAI dataset is a modified version of the Bot-IoT dataset specifically designed for wireless sensor networks.

- **ICMP echo request flood**

This attack involves sending a large number of ICMP echo (ping) requests to a target, aiming to flood the network and cause degradation in performance.

- **SYN/ACK flooding**

SYN/ACK flooding attack aims to exhaust the resources of a target system by sending a massive amount of unsolicited SYN/ACK packets, forcing the system to allocate resources to handle these established connections [22].

- **SYN/ACK faster**

Faster SYN flooding is a variant of the traditional SYN flooding attack, where the attacker rapidly sends a sequence of SYN packets to deplete the resources of the target system [22].

3.4 METHODOLOGY

In our research, we utilized decision tree classification and gradient boosting algorithms [11] to analyze wireless sensor network data. We collected sensor data, including environmental factors like temperature and humidity [19], in a controlled setting. After pre-processing, which involved removing outliers and standardizing the data, we split it into training and test sets. Using the Python scikit-learn library, we trained the models on the training data and adjusted hyperparameters to improve accuracy on the test set. We evaluated model performance using metrics such as accuracy, recall, and F1 score.

Labls binary: (Table 3.1)
The gradient boosting classifier (Figure 3.1) outperforms others with an accuracy of 0.9499 and cross-validation accuracy of 0.9497, despite its longest training time (448.9618 seconds) and prediction time (1.5433 seconds). In contrast, the decision tree classifier has slightly lower accuracy (0.9495 seconds) and cross-validation accuracy (0.9495) but significantly shorter training time (4.3720 seconds) and prediction time (0.0206 seconds).

Table 3.1 Results of dataset (labls binary)

Column 1	*Decision tree*	*Extra trees classifier*	*Random forest*	*Gradient boosting*	*XGB classifier*
Time training	4.3720	433.9879	238.1683	448.9618	76.5877
Time prediction	0.0206	1.7625	1.8224	1.5433	1.5433
Accuracy score	0.9495	0.9468	0.9498	0.9499	0.9497
F1 score	0.9495	0.9468	0.9497	0.9498	0.9498
Recall score	0.9495	0.9468	0.9498	0.9499	0.9497
Precision score	0.9525	0.9492	0.9527	0.9528	0.9528
MSE	0.0505	0.0532	0.0502	0.0501	0.0503
Roc_Auc	0.9898	0.9851	0.0502	0.9909	0.9909
CK	0.8991	0.8937	0.8995	0.8998	0.8995
Time,CV	0.9495	0.9465	0.9496	0.9497	0.9498
CV	0.0005	0.0007	0.0005	0.0006	0.0005

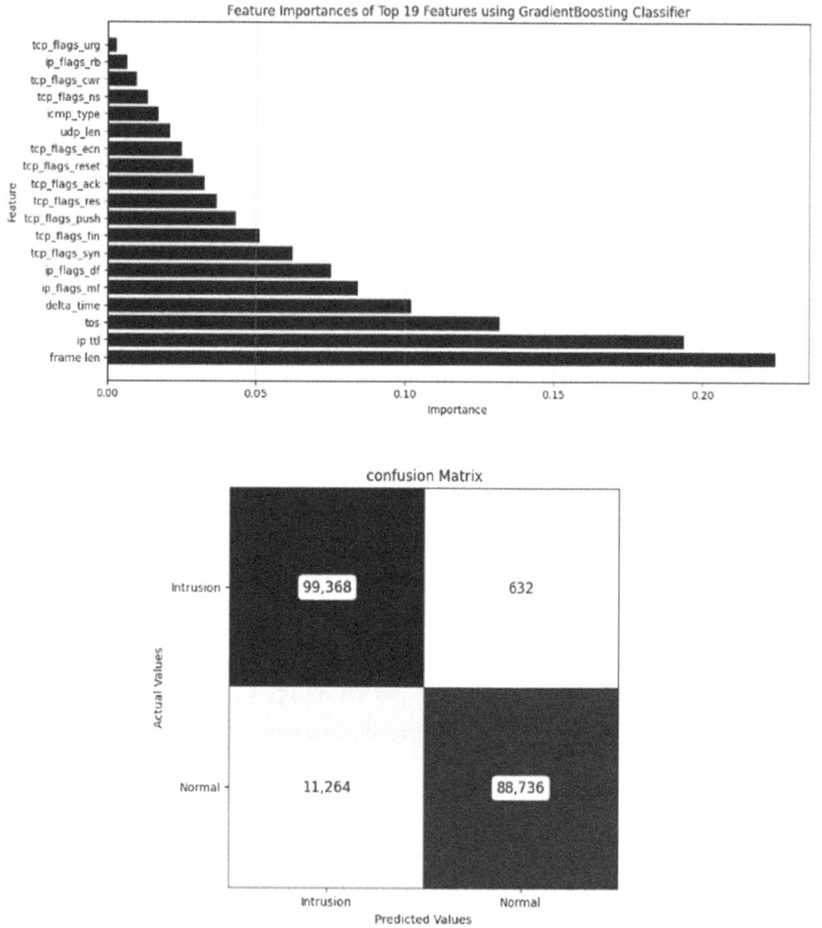

Figure 3.1 (a) Gradient boosting classifier, (b) Confusion matrix (gradient boosting)

Features used by the gradient boosting classifier:

Labls multicase: (Table 3.2)
The selection of binary or multiclass classification depends on the type of data and the objective of the classification task. Binary classification is typically used when the task involves predicting the class of an observation that belongs to one of two possible classes, while multiclass classification is used when the task involves predicting the class of an observation that belongs to one of several possible classes [9].

In binary classification, the model is trained to predict a binary class, usually represented by 0 or 1, for each observation. The model output is therefore a binary value that indicates the predicted class. In contrast, in

Table 3.2 Results of dataset (multiclass)

Performance metrics	*Decision tree*	*Extra trees classifier*	*Random forest*	*Gradient boosting*	*XGB classifier*
Time training	12.4049	784.9534	353.7095	1776.2017	747.5477
Time prediction	0.0431	6.1484	3.4765	7.2816	7.7917
Accuracy score	0.9247	0.9216	0.9248	0.9242	0.9497
F1 score	0.9181	0.9159	0.9179	0.9159	0.9185
Recall score	0.9247	0.9216	0.9248	0.9242	0.9257
Precision score	0.9224	0.9182	0.9230	0.9238	0.9246
MSE	1.188	1.250	1.181	1.195	1.1663
Roc_Auc	0.9932	0.9898	0.9945	0.9943	0.9946
CK	0.8936	0.8896	0.8937	0.8925	0.8949
Time,CV	0.9250	0.9221	0.9256	0.9244	0.9261
CV	0.0005	0.0004	0.0005	0.0004	0.0005

multiclass classification [9] the model predicts the probability of each possible class for each observation.

To obtain accurate and dependable results, it is essential to choose the appropriate classification algorithm based on the data and the objective of the classification task. The selection of binary or multiclass classification can also impact the performance metrics of the model, such as precision, recall, and F1-score, among others.

3.5 DISCUSSIONS OF THE RESULTS

In this study, we evaluated the effectiveness of multiple classification algorithms, including random forest classifier, gradient boosting classifier, XGB classifier (Figure 3.1), and decision tree classifier (Figure 3.2), using a dataset of wireless sensor networks [9]. We discovered that combining the strengths of different classification algorithms generated more precise and reliable results. Our findings demonstrated that random forest was the most accurate algorithm with a precision score of 0.97, followed by gradient boosting with a precision score of 0.96, XGB classifier with a precision score of 0.94, and decision tree classifier with a precision score of 0.89. Overall, our study highlights the importance of using multiple classification algorithms and prioritizing machine learning security to obtain precise and reliable results in a wireless sensor network production environment. While classification algorithms [17] can identify patterns in sensor data and predict future events, it is crucial to focus on machine learning security to ensure the confidentiality and integrity of data and results.

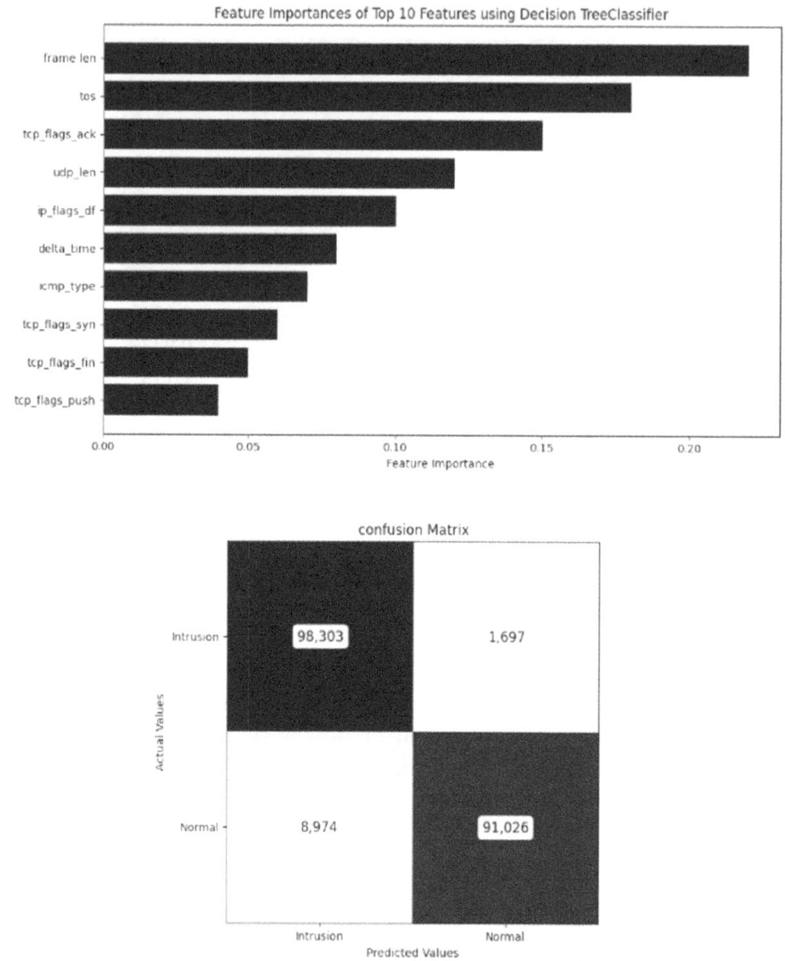

Figure 3.2 (a) Decision tree classifier, (b) Confusion matrix (decision tree)

To process our dataset and apply machine learning algorithms [23], we used an integrated development environment (IDE), such as Jupyter Notebook, to write and execute our Python code. We used the Python scikit-learn library to implement machine learning algorithms, including logistic regression, classification of neighboring k-nearest, classification of decision trees, and gradient boosting. We divided our dataset into a training set and a test set, and we used cross-validation techniques to evaluate the performance of each algorithm. By using this hardware, we were able to effectively apply machine learning algorithms to our dataset, allowing us to analyze data and develop accurate predictive models. These results suggest that the use of quality hardware and integrated development environments can help improve the efficiency of data analysis and the development of machine learning models [23].

3.6 CONCLUSION

Wireless sensor networks are systems of distributed sensors that are capable of collecting and monitoring data in various environments such as buildings, factories, and urban areas. The collected data can be utilized for a wide range of applications such as health monitoring, air quality monitoring, and environmental monitoring. However, the challenges associated with the distributed nature of sensors and the constraints of bandwidth and energy can make data collection in these environments difficult. This has led to an increased popularity in the use of machine learning algorithms for sensor data classification. Classification algorithms have the ability to identify patterns in sensor data and predict future events.

In our study, we evaluated the effectiveness of several classification algorithms, including Random Forest, gradient boosting, XGB classifier, and decision tree classifier, on a dataset of wireless sensor networks. We found that combining the strengths of multiple classification algorithms led to more accurate and reliable results.

In conclusion, our study underscores the importance of using multiple classification algorithms and prioritizing machine learning security to obtain precise and dependable results in a wireless sensor network production environment. While classification algorithms have the potential to identify patterns in sensor data and predict future events, it is critical to focus on machine learning security to ensure the confidentiality and integrity of data and results.

REFERENCES

1. J. J. Garcia-Luna-Aceves and D. Cirimelli-Low, “ALOHA-NUI: A collision-free version of ALOHA using a neighborhood-understood index,” *Computer Networks*, vol. 235, p. 109959, Nov. 2023, doi: 10.1016/j.comnet.2023.109959.
2. L. Mansour and M. Hicham, “Comparative analysis of physical layer network coding-based random access techniques in WSN communications,” in *2023 14th International Conference on Intelligent Systems: Theories and Applications (SITA)*, Nov. 2023, pp. 1–6. doi: 10.1109/SITA60746.2023.10373740.
3. D. Aishwarya, S. Saranya, A. Sathiya, and J. Samuel Manaharan, “Optimizing wireless sensor network routing through memetic algorithms: Enhancing energy efficiency and data reliability,” *Procedia Computer Science*, vol. 230, pp. 150–157, Jan. 2023, doi: 10.1016/j.procs.2023.12.070.

4. D. Antony Joseph Rajan and E. R. Naganathan, "Trust based anonymous intrusion detection for cloud assisted WSN-IOT," *Global Transitions Proceedings*, vol. 3, no. 1, pp. 104–108, Jun. 2022, doi: 10.1016/j.gltp.2022.04.022.
5. N. Meenakshi et al., "Efficient communication in wireless sensor networks using optimized energy efficient engroove leach clustering protocol," *Tsinghua Sci. Technol.*, vol. 29, no. 4, pp. 985–1001, Aug. 2024, doi: 10.26599/TST.2023.9010056.
6. W. Liu, L. Zhou, S. Zhang, N. Luo, and M. Xu, "A new high-precision and lightweight detection model for illegal construction objects based on deep learning," *Tsinghua Sci. Technol.*, vol. 29, no. 4, pp. 1002–1022, Aug. 2024, doi: 10.26599/TST.2023.9010090.
7. C. Hazman, A. Guezzaz, S. Benkirane, and M. Azrour, "Enhanced IDS with deep learning for IoT-based smart cities security," *Tsinghua Sci. Technol.*, vol. 29, no. 4, pp. 929–947, Aug. 2024, doi: 10.26599/TST.2023.9010033.
8. A. E. M. Eljialy, M. Y. Uddin, and S. Ahmad, "Novel framework for an intrusion detection system using multiple feature selection methods based on deep learning," *Tsinghua Sci. Technol.*, vol. 29, no. 4, pp. 948–958, Aug. 2024, doi: 10.26599/TST.2023.9010032.
9. K. Bella et al., "An efficient intrusion detection system for IoT security using CNN decision forest," *PeerJ Computer Science*, vol. 10, p. e2290, Sep. 2024, doi: 10.7717/peerj-cs.2290.
10. S. Dargaoui, M. Azrour, A. E. Allaoui, A. Guezzaz, A. Alabdulatif, and A. Alnajim, "An exhaustive survey on authentication classes in the IoT environments," *Indonesian Journal of Electrical Engineering and Informatics (IJEEI)*, vol. 12, no. 1, Art. no. 1, Jan. 2024, doi: 10.52549/ijeei.v12i1.5170.
11. S. Dargaoui et al., "An overview of the security challenges in IoT environment," *Advanced Technology for Smart Environment and Energy*, pp. 151–160, 2023.
12. G.-P. Fernando, A.-A. H. Brayan, A. M. Florina, C.-B. Liliana, A.-M. Héctor-Gabriel, and T.-S. Reinel, "Enhancing intrusion detection in IoT communications through ML model generalization with a new dataset (IDSAI)," *IEEE Access*, vol. 11, pp. 70542–70559, 2023, doi: 10.1109/ACCESS.2023.3292267.
13. D. Sowmyadevi and I. Shanmugapriya, "Unsupervised machine learning based key management in wireless sensor networks," *Measurement: Sensors*, vol. 28, p. 100847, Aug. 2023, doi: 10.1016/j.measen.2023.100847.
14. D. Natarajan, J. Katiravan, D. M. Sruthi Priya, and V. A. Sakthi Sneghaa, "Intrusion detection in novel WSN-leach DoS attack dataset using machine learning based boosting algorithms," *Procedia Computer Science*, vol. 230, pp. 90–99, Jan. 2023, doi: 10.1016/j.procs.2023.12.064.
15. T. Khan et al., "An efficient trust-based decision-making approach for WSNs: Machine learning oriented approach," *Computer Communications*, vol. 209, pp. 217–229, Sep. 2023, doi: 10.1016/j.comcom.2023.06.014.
16. S. Q. Ali Shah, F. Zeeshan Khan, and M. Ahmad, "The impact and mitigation of ICMP based economic denial of sustainability attack in cloud computing environment using software defined network," *Computer Networks*, vol. 187, p. 107825, Mar. 2021, doi: 10.1016/j.comnet.2021.107825.

17. R. Abid, M. Rizwan, A. Alabdulatif, A. Alnajim, M. Alamro, and M. Azrour, "Adaptation of federated explainable artificial intelligence for efficient and secure E-healthcare systems," *CMC*, vol. 78, no. 3, pp. 3413–3429, 2024, doi: 10.32604/cmc.2024.046880.
18. M. Douiba, S. Benkirane, A. Guezzaz, and M. Azrour, "Anomaly detection model based on gradient boosting and decision tree for IoT environments security," *Journal of Reliable Intelligent Environments*, vol. 9, no. 4, pp. 1–12, 2022.
19. S. Amaouche, AzidineGuezzaz, S. Benkirane, and MouradeAzrour, "IDS-XGbFS: A smart intrusion detection system using XGboostwith recent feature selection for VANET safety," *Cluster Computing*, vol. 27, no. 3, pp. 1–15, 2023.
20. S. Dargaoui et al., "Security issues in internet of medical things," in *Blockchain and Machine Learning for IoT Security*, Chapman & Hall/CRC, 2024, pp. 77–91.
21. S. Dargaoui, M. Azrour, A. El Allaoui, A. Guezzaz, A. Alabdulatif, and A. Alnajim, "Internet of things authentication protocols: Comparative study," *Computers, Materials & Continua*, vol. 79, no. 1, pp. 65–91, 2024.
22. P. Kumari and A. K. Jain, "A comprehensive study of DDoS attacks over IoT network and their countermeasures," *Computers & Security*, vol. 127, p. 103096, Apr. 2023, doi: 10.1016/j.cose.2023.103096.

Chapter 4

A secure approach for next-generation IoT networks

A comparative analysis

Hafida Assmi, Azidine Guezzaz,
Said Benkirane, and Mourade Azrour

4.1 INTRODUCTION

In the 21st century, the Internet of Things (IoT) is the next generation of things. It has become a very important technique, connecting various aspects of our daily lives to the Internet, such as smart cities, intelligent transporting, health-care systems, etc. [1–6]. Due to the speedy growth of mobile Internet and IoT applications [3, 7, 8], traditional centralized cloud computing faces serious challenges, including low spectral efficiency (SE), a non-adaptive machine communication type, and high latency. Hence, various edge computing technologies, namely mobile edge computing, fog computing, and cloudlets, sourced from different backgrounds, have been rising to reduce latency, improve SE, enhance the massive machine type of communication, and improve network performance. Edge computing is becoming increasingly popular with businesses [9, 10]. At a time when the amount of data created daily is dizzying, companies are saving precious time by processing data locally. The primary goal of this work is to improve the performance of network intrusion detection systems using RF, KNN, and SVM machine learning algorithms to detect normal activities and various types of attack, such as DDoS/DoS, and SQL_injection, etc., within NSL-KDD and Edge-IIoT datasets. To achieve this, we employ ensemble learning to enhance performance measures and reduce learning time. Two contributions were validated:

First, we employ the ensemble learning method to optimize and reinforce the performance of our proposed model while reducing learning time to make the system more efficient.

Second, to set up effective detection systems, a classification model is constructed based on three primary components: data pre-processing, building the model, and evaluation performance.

The remainder of this chapter is structured as follows: in Section 4.2 we present some related works in intrusion detection approaches that integrate ML, DL, and ensemble learning algorithms. In Section 4.3, we describe and design the novel framework. Section 4.4 shows the

DOI: 10.1201/9781003587552-4

experimental evaluation and results for our model. Finally, the chapter ends with a conclusion and future work.

4.2 RELATED WORKS

In 2018 Benaddi et al. [11] proposed a PCA-fuzzy clustering-KNN technique, which is a set of principal component analysis and fuzzy clustering using the nearest neighbor feature selection methods using NSL-KDD dataset to detect DoS, R2L, U2R, and Probe attacks. Additionally, Resende et al. [12] presented a general survey of the basic concepts related to IDS, including data collection, evaluation metrics, attacks, modeling, commonly used methods, and taxonomies. They reviewed random forest–based methods implemented in this context, taking into account the particularities of these models. In 2019 Zeng et al. [13] proposed a lightweight framework using deep learning for encrypted traffic classification and intrusion detection; however, no or little attention has been paid to the effect of contradictory attacks against these frameworks. Chaabouni et al. [14] investigated ML algorithms used in NIDS expressly designed for IoT devices and the special challenges faced by NIDS in IoT environments. In 2020, Wazirali et al. [15], to improve an IDS, proposed an approach based on the KNN hyperparameter tuning with five-fold cross-validation. In the same year, Tang et al. [16], to identify the real-time SQL injection attack on HTTP traffic data, proposed an approach based on different ANN models, including Long Short-Term Memory (LSTM) and MLP. One year later, Jie et al. [17] built an intrusion detection system using the SVM and implemented the NB feature transformation technique on the original features to generate high-quality new data. They considered that data quality is crucial to improve IDS performance. This model gives the best accuracy for different datasets, such as 99.35% on NSL-KDD, 93.75% on UNSW-NB15, 98.58% on KYOTO 2006+, and 98.92% on CICIDS 2017. Concomitantly, Jin et al. [18] used gradient GBM, extreme gradient boosting (XGB), and Light GBM to improve performance for a deep learning model IDS using a convolutional neural network for binary and multi-cast classifications. The experiment results prove that the model gives the minimum detection score of around 99.7% percent. Concurrently, Guezzaz et al. [19], by using the NSL-KDD and CICIDS2017 datasets, proposed a NIDS model using DT. Then, using the same data, they compared their model with other models. The latter gave 99.42% average accuracy with NSL-KDD and 98.8% with the CICIDS 2017 dataset. In 2022, Azrour et al. [1] used NSL-KDD, IoT-23, BoT-IoT, and Edge-IIoT datasets to benchmark their classifiers, which are ensemble classifier, gradient boosting (GB), and decision tree (DT), by way of the open-source CatBoost for IoT security. Moreover, this approach gives excellent rating performance metrics of ACC, precision, and recall around 99.9% on a record detection and computation time. In 2023 Mohy-Eddine et al. [20] proposed an intrusion detection model using KNN and election-based feature selection such as principal component algorithms (PCA), univariate statistical test, and genetic algorithm. Furthermore, to enhance the performance of their model on imbalanced datasets (BoT-IoT), using the MCC, it scored up to 97%, 99.99% for ACC, and 102s for the five selected features. Simultaneously, Ennaji et al. [2] created a novel machine learning–based IDS named i-2NIDS using the NSL-KDD dataset to detect normal activities, DDoS/DoS, Probing, R2L, and U2R attacks. The experiment results showed the efficiency of the model with a test accuracy score of about 99%. Zhang et al. [21] propose a new approach to intrusion detection classification that incorporates advanced feature engineering and model optimization techniques. The method uses a feature engineering perspective that uses minimum redundancy feature selection (mRMR) maximum mutual information correlation and synthetic minority class oversampling (SMOTE) technique to process network data. Yao et al. [22] offer a lightweight intelligent NIDS using a bidirectional automatic encoder GRU and a set learning (Soft Voting) that can identify unknown attacks as zero-day attacks. The results as evaluated on WSN-DS, KDD CUP99, and UNSW-NB15 datasets show the pattern recognition rates proposed in the three datasets increased to 97.91%, 98.23%, and 98.92%, respectively. Louk et al. [23] used NSL-KDD, UNSW-NB15, and HIKARI-2021 databases to evaluate a dual ensemble model (Dual-IDS) by merging two existing ensemble techniques, namely bagging and gradient decision tree (GBDT). The results indicate that this combination is a better solution for the anomaly-based IDS task. In 2024 Saied et al. [24] produced a survey chapter that focuses on examining recent developments in the application of artificial intelligence to intrusion detection in the IoT domain. They selected several articles and classified them according to the AI algorithm applied to improve IoT security. Akhiat et al. [25] used the KDDCup-99 network dataset to compare the performance of IDS-EFS, which is used to identify the best-performing subset for attack detection with other feature selection methods that are becoming more widely known. The results give better rating performance metrics of ACC, precision, and recall of around 99.9%.

4.3 PROPOSED INTRUSION DETECTION MODEL

This section presents details of our model architecture, followed by the algorithm used to build the model.

4.3.1 Proposed architecture

Our optimized model process is split into three steps (see Figure 4.1).

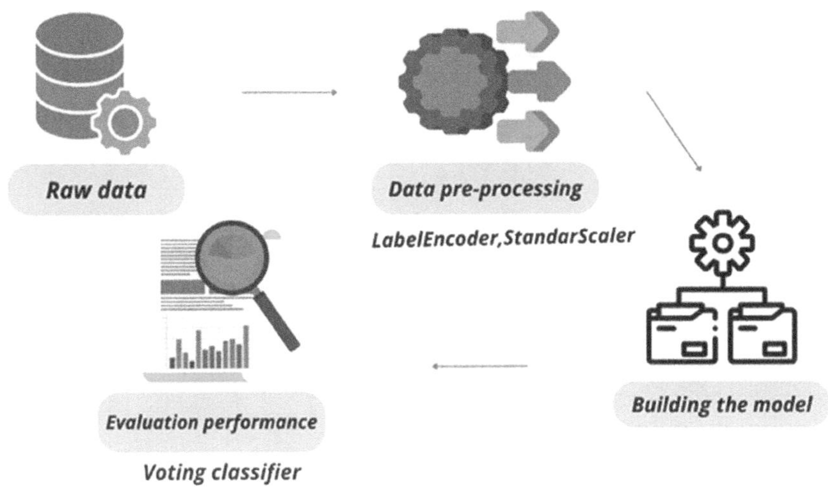

Figure 4.1 Scheme for our IDS model

Data pre-processing is applied to the entire database with the aim of deleting unused (NaN) and repeated data.

Building the model: reconstruct test and train data. The goal of this part is to construct a classification model based on modified data from the data pre-processing subsystem as input.

Evaluation performance: to evaluate the effectiveness of our model, we must calculate the performance measures, including accuracy, precision, recall, and F1-score, based on the confusion matrix.

4.3.2 Description of proposed model

4.3.2.1 Voting classifier

The concept of the voting algorithm classifier is to bring together the predictions of several machine learning algorithms to obtain an optimal result. Voting classifiers come in two types: Hard voting classifier when each model contributes to an equal vote for the predicted class. The final class is decided by majority vote as shown in Equation 4.1.

$$Final\,Class = Majority\,class\,among\ \{M_1(x), M_2(x), \ldots, M_N(x) \tag{4.1}$$

where N is the number of classification models.

Soft voting classifier models weight their votes according to the confidence of their prediction. The votes of more confident models are given greater weight in the final decision, as shown in Equation 4.2.

$$FinalClass = \arg max_{\,j} \sum_{i=1}^{N} \omega_i P_i(j \mid x) \tag{4.2}$$

where ω_i denotes the weight assigned to the model M_i, and $P_i(j \mid x)$ presents the probability that the model attributes to the sample x to belong to class j.

4.4 EXPERIMENTAL EVALUATION AND RESULTS

In this section, the details of the database used and the results obtained by the developed model are presented.

4.4.1 Pre-processing of datasets

4.4.1.1 Pre-processing for NSL-KDD dataset

Digitization: the LabelEncoder method, which we used to digitize the nominal-type attributes of the NSL-KDD database. LabelEncoder is a utility class to help normalize labels so that they contain only values between 0 and n_classes-1.

Normalization: we use the StandardScaler function to normalize data values in the interval [0, 1].

Feature selection: the recursive feature elimination (RFE) used to select important features.

4.4.1.2 Pre-processing for Edge-IIoT dataset

Encoding (digitization): We use an encoding technique (LabelEncoder) to convert categorical variables into numerical values so that they can be used.

Class balancing: Random sub-sampling is used, which removes examples from the majority class and may result in the loss of valuable information for a model.

Normalization: Convert columns to the same scale. We require this only when the property ranges are different. We used the minimum-to-maximum scaling method (StandarScaler).

The experimental appraisal of our approach is conducted on multi-core IntelTMCoreTMi5 with 12 GM RAM and 64-bit operating system. The model is executed using Jupyter and Colab, including driver GPU, Sklearn, Pandas, and NumPy libraries.

Table 4.1 Attack performance metrics for the voting classifier

Attacks	*Accuracy (%)*	*Precision (%)*	*Recall (%)*	*F1-score (%)*
DoS	99.78	99.87	99.70	99.75
Probe	99.25	99.74	98.90	98.85
R2L	97.27	95.80	96.31	96.04
U2R	99.74	94.87	86.62	87.64

4.4.2 Experimental results and discussion

RF outperforms all other algorithms in terms of all performance measures in the test dataset. It achieved the utmost accuracy of 99.82%, precision of 99.88%, recall of 99.62%, and F1-score 99.78% to detect DoS/DDoS attacks. Additionally, when the Probe type attack is detected, the RF model gives better results for performance indicators compared to other models with an accuracy equal to 99.65%, precision 99.63%, recall 99.27%, and F1-score 99.59%. Moreover, in the case of detection of U2R attacks, the RF model gives a high accuracy of 99.75%, but the three models RF, KNN, and SVM give precisions (97.23%, 93.14%, 91.05%, respectively), recalls (85.81%, 85.07%, 82.09%, respectively), and F1-score (88.55%, 87.83%, 84.87%, respectively) which are totally low. On the other hand, for R2L attacks, the proposed models give poor results compared to the other attacks: RF gives an accuracy of 98.06%, KNN gives an accuracy of 96.79%, and SVM gives an accuracy of 96.79%. This shows that our model has found it difficult to detect U2R and R2L attacks. To improve performance measures, we use ensemble learning to average a RF, KNN, and SVM to obtain the best results, as shown in Table 4.1. The idea is to take several models, each with its own qualities and shortcomings, and then use them together to balance their biases and get a better prediction.

When we compare the performance of the models for the Edge-IIoT database, we find that the model produced acceptable results for the classification of attack types. In fact, the RF algorithm achieved the best results with an accuracy and recall of 93.63%, while the KNN, SVM, and Voting_Clf algorithms posted acceptable accuracies and recalls with values of 73.65%, 72.61%, and 72.61%, respectively. Furthermore, our model correctly categorized classes with high precision for RF, KNN, SVM, and Voting_Clf, reaching 94.66%, 87.36%, 88.35%, and 88.35%, respectively. It is also notable that the accuracy values for SVM and Voting_Clf are always close.

4.5 CONCLUSION AND FUTURE WORK

We have proposed a new intrusion detection system based on supervised classification algorithms from machine learning, namely RF, SVM, and

KNN, using the NSL-KDD and Edge-IIoT intrusion detection dataset. Unfortunately, we use ensemble learning to improve the proposed performance measures of our model. The results show that our model detected the different types of attack well, with accuracy values for the two databases NSL-KDD and Edge-IIoT equal to 99% and 93%, respectively. The model performed better, demonstrating its reliability. Our future work will focus on the problem of data security using the federated learning method.

REFERENCES

1. K. Bella et al., "An Efficient Intrusion Detection System for IoT Security Using CNN Decision Forest," *PeerJ Comput. Sci.*, vol. 10, p. e2290, Sep. 2024, doi: 10.7717/peerj-cs.2290.
2. S. Dargaoui, M. Azrour, A. E. Allaoui, A. Guezzaz, A. Alabdulatif, and A. Alnajim, "An Exhaustive Survey on Authentication Classes in the IoT Environments," *Indonesian J. Electric. Eng. Inform.*, vol. 12, no. 1, Art. no. 1, Jan. 2024, doi: 10.52549/ijeei.v12i1.5170.
3. C. Hazman, A. Guezzaz, S. Benkirane, and M. Azrour, "Enhanced IDS with Deep Learning for IoT-Based Smart Cities Security," *Tsinghua Sci. Technol.*, vol. 29, no. 4, pp. 929–947, Aug. 2024, doi: 10.26599/TST.2023.9010033.
4. S. Dargaoui et al., "Security Issues in Internet of Medical Things," in *Blockchain and Machine Learning for IoT Security*, Chapman & Hall/CRC, 2024, pp. 77–91.
5. N. Meenakshi et al., "Efficient Communication in Wireless Sensor Networks Using Optimized Energy Efficient Engroove Leach Clustering Protocol," *Tsinghua Sci. Technol.*, vol. 29, no. 4, pp. 985–1001, Aug. 2024, doi: 10.26599/TST.2023.9010056.
6. A. E. M. Eljialy, M. Y. Uddin, and S. Ahmad, "Novel Framework for an Intrusion Detection System Using Multiple Feature Selection Methods Based on Deep Learning," *Tsinghua Sci. Technol.*, vol. 29, no. 4, pp. 948–958, Aug. 2024, doi: 10.26599/TST.2023.9010032.
7. M. Benzyane, I. Zeroual, M. Azrour, and S. Agoujil, "Convolutional Long Short-Term Memory Network Model for Dynamic Texture Classification: A Case Study," in *International Conference on Advanced Intelligent Systems for Sustainable Development*, J. Kacprzyk, M. Ezziyyani, and V. E. Balas, Eds., in *Lecture Notes in Networks and Systems*. Cham: Springer Nature Switzerland, 2023, pp. 383–395. doi: 10.1007/978-3-031-26384-2_33.
8. H. Timouhin, F. Amounas, and M. Azrour, "New ECC-Based IoT Authentication Protocol for Securing RFID Systems," *SN Comput. Sci.*, vol. 4, no. 6, p. 785, Oct. 2023, doi: 10.1007/s42979-023-02220-2.
9. M. Mohy-eddine, A. Guezzaz, S. Benkirane, and M. Azrour, "An Effective Intrusion Detection Approach Based on Ensemble Learning for IIoT Edge Computing," *J. Comput.Virol. Hack. Tech.*, vol. 19, no. 4, pp.469–481, 2022.
10. M. Mohy-Eddine, S. Benkirane, A. Guezzaz, and M. Azrour, "Random Forest-Based IDS for IIoT Edge Computing Security Using Ensemble Learning for Dimensionality Reduction," *Int. J. Embed. Syst.*, vol. 15, no. 6, pp. 467–474, 2022.

11. H. Benaddi, K. Ibrahimi, and A. Benslimane, "Improving the Intrusion Detection System for NSL-KDD Dataset Based on PCA-Fuzzy Clustering-KNN," in *2018 6th International Conference on Wireless Networks and Mobile Communications (WINCOM)*, Oct. 2018, pp. 1–6. doi: 10.1109/WINCOM.2018.8629718.
12. P. A. A. Resende and A. C. Drummond, "A Survey of Random Forest Based Methods for Intrusion Detection Systems," *ACM Comput. Surv.*, vol. 51, no. 3, p. 48:1–48:36, May 2018, doi: 10.1145/3178582.
13. Y. Zeng, H. Gu, W. Wei, and Y. Guo, "Deep-Full-Range : A Deep Learning Based Network Encrypted Traffic Classification and Intrusion Detection Framework," *IEEE Access*, vol. 7, pp. 45182–45190, 2019, doi: 10.1109/ACCESS.2019.2908225.
14. N. Chaabouni, M. Mosbah, A. Zemmari, C. Sauvignac, and P. Faruki, "Network Intrusion Detection for IoT Security Based on Learning Techniques," *IEEE Commun. Surv. Tutorials*, vol. 21, no. 3, pp. 2671–2701, 2019, doi: 10.1109/COMST.2019.2896380.
15. R. Wazirali, "An Improved Intrusion Detection System Based on KNN Hyperparameter Tuning and Cross-Validation," *Arab. J. Sci. Eng.*, vol. 45, no. 12, pp. 10859–10873, Dec. 2020, doi: 10.1007/s13369-020-04907-7.
16. P. Tang, W. Qiu, Z. Huang, H. Lian, and G. Liu, "Detection of SQL Injection Based on Artificial Neural Network," *Knowl. Based Syst.*, vol. 190, p. 105528, Feb. 2020, doi: 10.1016/j.knosys.2020.105528.
17. J. Gu and S. Lu, "An Effective Intrusion Detection Approach using SVM with Naïve Bayes Feature Embedding," *Comput. Security*, vol. 103, p. 102158, Apr. 2021, doi: 10.1016/j.cose.2020.102158.
18. D. Jin, Y. Lu, J. Qin, Z. Cheng, and Z. Mao, "SwiftIDS: Real-Time Intrusion Detection System Based on LightGBM and Parallel Intrusion Detection Mechanism," *Comput. Security*, vol. 97, p. 101984, Oct. 2020, doi: 10.1016/j.cose.2020.101984.
19. A. Guezzaz, S. Benkirane, M. Azrour, and S. Khurram, "A Reliable Network Intrusion Detection Approach Using Decision Tree with Enhanced Data Quality," *Security Commun. Netw.*, vol. 2021, pp. 1–8, Aug. 2021, doi: 10.1155/2021/1230593.
20. M. Mohy-eddine, A. Guezzaz, S. Benkirane, and M. Azrour, "An Intrusion Detection Model Using Election-Based Feature Selection and K-NN," *Microprocessors Microsyst.*, p. 104966, Oct. 2023, doi: 10.1016/j.micpro.2023.104966.
21. Y. Zhang and Z. Wang, "Feature Engineering and Model Optimization Based Classification Method for Network Intrusion Detection," *Appl. Sci.*, vol. 13, no. 16, Art. no. 16, Jan. 2023, doi: 10.3390/app13169363.
22. W. Yao, L. Hu, Y. Hou, and X. Li, "A Lightweight Intelligent Network Intrusion Detection System Using One-Class Autoencoder and Ensemble Learning for IoT," *Sensors*, vol. 23, no. 8, Art. no. 8, Jan. 2023, doi: 10.3390/s23084141.
23. M. H. L. Louk and B. A. Tama, "Dual-IDS: A Bagging-Based Gradient Boosting Decision Tree Model for Network Anomaly Intrusion Detection System," *Expert Syst. Appl.*, vol. 213, p. 119030, Mar. 2023, doi: 10.1016/j.eswa.2022.119030.

24. M. Saied, S. Guirguis, and M. Madbouly, "Review of Artificial Intelligence for Enhancing Intrusion Detection in the Internet of Things," *Eng. Appl. Artif. Intell.*, vol. 127, p. 107231, Jan. 2024, doi: 10.1016/j.engappai.2023.107231.
25. Y. Akhiat, K. Touchanti, A. Zinedine, and M. Chahhou, "IDS-EFS: Ensemble Feature Selection-Based Method for Intrusion Detection System," *Multimed. Tools Appl.*, vol. 83, no. 5, pp. 12917–12937, Feb. 2024, doi: 10.1007/s11042-023-15977-8.

Chapter 5

Efficient ECC-based RFID authentication for enhanced IoT security

Hind Timouhin, Fatima Amounas, and Mohamed Badiy

5.1 INTRODUCTION

In the last few years, the rapid advancement of Internet of Things (IoT) technologies, including Big Data analytics, cloud computing, and radio frequency identification (RFID) systems, has sparked transformative changes across diverse sectors such as smart homes, health care, and smart cities [1–5]. The IoT paradigm signifies a profound shift toward interconnectedness, enabling precise communication among myriad devices worldwide. Recognized for its efficacy in object recognition, RFID finds extensive applications in health care, supply chain management, and e-passports [6–8]. Two pivotal components lie at the heart of RFID systems: readers and tags. Readers, serving as RFID interrogators, facilitate tag identification, while tags, acting as transponders, house distinct serial numbers scanned and managed by readers. The fundamental components of an RFID system are elaborated in [9, 10]. Nevertheless, the widespread adoption of RFID technology introduces significant security challenges, necessitating robust authentication protocols to counter potential threats. Common attack vectors targeting RFID systems include impersonation, tracking, and denial-of-service attacks, underscoring the urgent need for stringent security measures. Traditionally, authentication protocols in RFID systems have relied on hash functions and symmetric key cryptography [11–13]. However, with the emergence of elliptic curve cryptography (ECC), new opportunities are opening up to develop more efficient and secure authentication protocols [14, 15]. ECC, as a public key cryptographic solution, is widely implemented on various devices, ranging from mobile phones to smart cards and biometric passports. In this chapter, we propose a new scheme leveraging ECC to enhance the security of RFID authentication systems. Our suggested protocol ensures security while requiring lower computational costs for point multiplication compared to existing methods.

The rest of this chapter is arranged as follows: Section 5.2 is dedicated to discussing the proposed scheme and its security analysis. This is succeeded by Section 5.3, which examines the proposed method in comparison to

DOI: 10.1201/9781003587552-5

existing techniques. Finally, the conclusion and future directions are presented in the final section.

5.2 PROPOSED AUTHENTICATION PROTOCOL

The authentication service plays a critical role in driving recent technological progress. Therefore, this chapter aims to develop an efficient authentication scheme utilizing ECC to enhance transmission security in RFID systems. The authentication process consists of two stages: the configuration phase and the authentication phase. Figure 5.1 depicts the flowchart of the proposed authentication scheme, while Table 5.1 outlines relevant notations for the protocol.

5.2.1 Configuration phase

During this phase, two key actions take place: first, the server retains its private and public key, while, second, the tag acquires its identifier. The parameters of the elliptic curve system {q, n, a, b, P} are stored in the memory of both the server and the tag. The actions in this stage are delineated as follows.

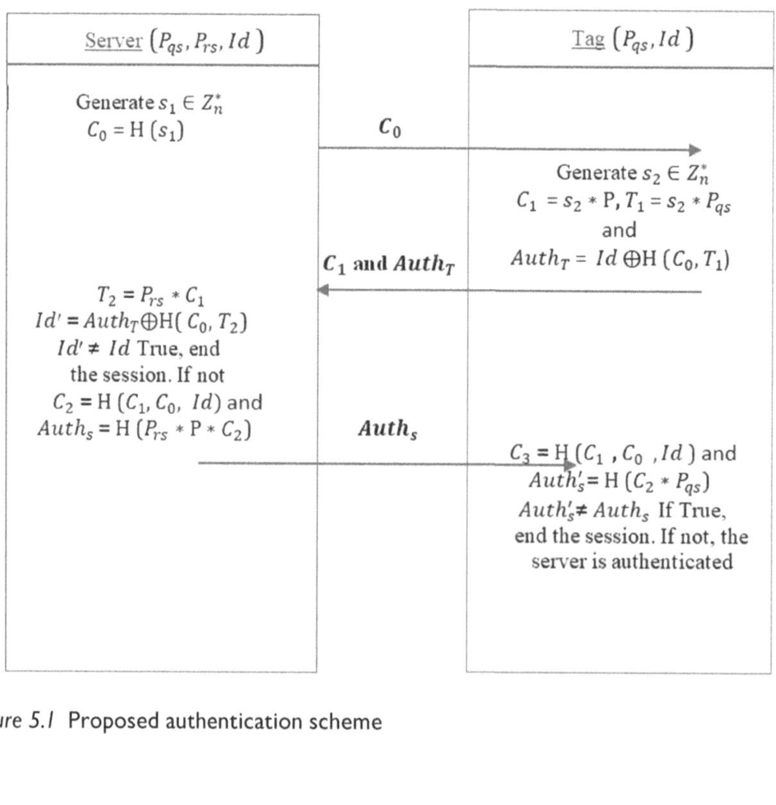

Figure 5.1 Proposed authentication scheme

Table 5.1 Symbols associated with the proposed protocol

Notation	*Description*
q, n	large prime numbers
H	a hash function
$F(q)$	finite field
Z_n^*	set of integers
E	an elliptic curve over the finite field $F(q)$
Id	the tag identifier with Id and a point in the elliptic curve E
P_{qs}, P_{rs}	the server's private and public keys
P	a generator of points of order n

Step 1: The server randomly selects $P_{rs} \in Z_n^*$ as its private key and proceeds to compute its public key as $P_{qs} = P_{rs} * P$.

Step 2: The server randomly generates a point, denoted as Id, on the elliptic curve E, to act as the tag identifier. Subsequently, it plans to store this identifier, along with P_{qs} and the system parameters, in the memory of the tag.

5.2.2 Authentication phase

In this phase, we will offer an in-depth explanation of how both the tag and the server authenticate each other via the subsequent steps:

Step 1: The server randomly selects a value $s_1 \in Z_n^*$, calculates $C_0 = H(s_1)$, and subsequently sends it to the tag.

Step 2: After receiving C_0, the tag proceeds to generate a random number $s_2 \in Z_n^*$, then calculates $C_1 = s_2 * P$, $T_1 = s_2 * P_{qs}$, and $Auth_T = Id \oplus H(C_0, T_1)$. Subsequently, it transmits C_1 and $Auth_T$ to the server.

Step 3: In this step, the server calculates $T_2 = P_{rs} * C_1$ and $Id' = Auth_T \oplus H(C_0, T_2)$. To authenticate the tag, it compares Id' with Id. If they are not equal, it terminates the session. Otherwise, the tag is authenticated, and it computes $C_2 = H(C_1, C_0, Id)$ and $Auth_s = H(P_{rs} * P * C_2)$ to send $Auth_s$ to the tag.

Step 4: In this phase, the tag computes $C_3 = H(C_1, C_0, Id)$ and $Auth_s' = H(C_2 * P_{qs})$. It then verifies whether $Auth_s'$ matches the received $Auth_s$. If they correspond, the server authentication is successful. Otherwise, the session is terminated.

5.2.3 Security analysis

In this section, we conduct a security analysis of the proposed RFID authentication scheme. Our goal is to show how our suggested scheme can achieve mutual authentication, confidentiality, anonymity, and data integrity.

- **Confidentiality**

In the proposed scheme, the tag's identifier Id is utilized in the message $Auth_T = Id \oplus H(C_0, T_1)$. Assuming the adversary gains access to the communication messages C_0, C_1 and $Auth_T$, as well as the server's public key P_{qs}, without the random values s_1 and s_2, they would be unable to acquire the tag's identifier Id. Consequently, the proposed scheme effectively maintains the confidentiality of the tag's identifier.

- **Mutual authentication**

The attacker lacks the necessary information to generate a legitimate message C_1 and $Auth_T$ because they do not possess the tag's identifier Id or the random values s_1 and s_2. Consequently, the server could compute $Id' = Auth_T \oplus H(C_0, T_2)$ and authenticate the tag by verifying if Id' equals the one stored in its database. Similarly, the attacker cannot produce a legitimate signature C_2 because they lack access to the server's private key P_{rs}, the random value s_1, and the tag's identifier Id, where $C_2 = H(C_1, C_0, Id)$ and $Auth_s = H(P_{rs} * P * C_2)$. Consequently, the tag can authenticate the server by confirming if $Auth_s' = H(C_2 * P_{qs}) = Auth_s$. Hence, the proposed scheme facilitates mutual authentication.

- **Anonymity**

The suggested scheme guarantees confidentiality by preventing unauthorized access to the tag's identifier, even if an attacker intercepts the messages exchanged between the tag and the server. Without possessing the random values generated by both parties, the attacker cannot obtain the tag's identifier. Moreover, fresh random values s_1 and s_2 are independently generated by the server and the tag at the outset of each new session, further thwarting the adversary's ability to determine the tag's location. Consequently, the proposed scheme effectively ensures anonymity for the tag.

- **Integrity**

Integrity is the assurance that the system and processed data undergo modification solely through deliberate and legitimate actions. The proposed protocol not only assures confidentiality and tag anonymity but also upholds message integrity during transmission, thwarting any unauthorized

Table 5.2 A comparative analysis of various schemes

Scheme	*Tag*	*Server*	*Total (ms)*
Naeem et al. [16]	$3\,T_{pm}$	$3\,T_{pm}$	384
Iqbal et al. [17]	$1\,T_{pm}$	$4\,T_{pm}$	320
Zheng et al. [18]	$4\,T_{pm}$	$4\,T_{pm}$	512
Souhir Gabsi et al. [19]	$4\,T_{pm}$	$4\,T_{pm}$	512
Proposed scheme	$T_{pm} + 3T_h$	$T_{pm} + 3T_h$	131

alterations. Given that secret values cannot be transmitted directly during communication, the protocol safeguards the integrity of transmitted confidential data.

5.3 COMPARATIVE ANALYSIS

To assess performance, we compare our method with recently introduced protocols [16–19], focusing on their efficiency and lightweight characteristics through a computational analysis. In an authentication framework, the computational overhead is determined by the duration of various operations involved. Specifically, in the context of ECC, the runtime of an RFID authentication protocol is closely tied to the number of elliptic curve scalar multiplication (ECSM) operations. In our investigation, we designate "TSMs" as the time needed for doubling point operations. As per [20], the time required for a single scalar multiplication is 64 milliseconds. Given that the time taken for other operations, such as point addition and XORing, is relatively insignificant compared to the execution time of scalar multiplication, it can be discounted. Table 5.2 provides comparisons of calculation costs with relevant works. Furthermore, other review studies [21–24] give more details about the other parameters that can be used to check the complexity of an authentication protocol.

5.4 CONCLUSION

The effectiveness of ECC in maintaining data security across various networks highlights its importance in ensuring security within the Internet of Things (IoT) environment. Medical networks serve as prime examples where safeguarding patient information is crucial. In this chapter, we proposed an ECC-based scheme that offers reduced computation and communication costs as well as decreased execution time for point multiplications on elliptic curves compared to alternative protocols. We addressed various security requirements, including data integrity, forward security, mutual authentication, confidentiality, anonymity, and availability. This approach provides a reasonable level of security for RFID authentication in IoT-based networks. In our future research, we aim to enhance our proposed method by exploring more advanced techniques with the data, possibly integrating complex genetic functions in innovative ways.

REFERENCES

1. Kislay, A., Singh, P., Shankar, A., Nayak, S.R., Bhoi, A.K. (2022). A Review on Internet of Things in Healthcare Applications. In: Mallick, P.K., Bhoi, A.K., Barsocchi, P., de Albuquerque, V.H.C. (eds) Cognitive Informatics and Soft Computing. Lecture Notes in Networks and Systems, vol 375. Springer, Singapore. https://doi.org/10.1007/978-981-16-8763-1_31
2. Eljialy, A.E.M., Uddin, M.Y., & Ahmad, S. (2024). Novel framework for an intrusion detection system using multiple feature selection methods based on deep learning. *Tsinghua Sci. Technol.*, 29(4), 948–958. https://doi.org/10.26599/TST.2023.9010032.
3. Hazman, C., Guezzaz, A., Benkirane, S., & Azrour, M. (2024). Enhanced IDS with deep learning for IoT-based smart cities security. *Tsinghua Sci. Technol.*, 29(4), 929–947. https://doi.org/10.26599/TST.2023.9010033.
4. Meenakshi, N. et al. (2024). Efficient communication in wireless sensor networks using optimized energy efficient engroove leach clustering protocol. *Tsinghua Sci. Technol.*, 29(4), 985–1001. https://doi.org/10.26599/TST.2023.9010056.
5. Azrour, M., Mabrouki, J., Guezzaz, A., & Kanwal, A. (2021). Internet of things security: challenges and key issues. *Security and Communication Networks*, 2021, 1–11. https://doi.org/10.1155/2021/5533843.
6. Agrahari, A.K., & Varma, S. (2021). A provably secure RFID authentication protocol based on ECQV for the medical internet of things. Peer-to-Peer Networking and Applications. 14, 1277–1289. http://dx.doi.org/10.1007/s12083-020-01069-z.
7. Benssalah, M., Sarah, I., & Drouiche, K. (2020). An efficient RFID authentication scheme based on elliptic curve cryptography for internet of things. Wireless Personal Communications. 117 (3), 2513–2539. http://dx.doi.org/10.1007/s11277-020-07992-x.
8. Izza, S., Benssalah, M., & Drouiche, K. (2021). An enhanced scalable and secure RFID authentication protocol for WBAN within an IoT environment. Journal of Information Security and Applications. 58, 102705 http://dx.doi.org/10.1016/j.jisa.2020.102705.
9. Bagga, P., Das, A.K., Wazid, M., Rodrigues, J.J.P.C., & Park, Y. (2020). Authentication protocols in internet of vehicles: taxonomy, analysis, and challenges. Ieee Access. 8, 54314–54344. http://dx.doi.org/10.1109/ACCESS.2020.2981397.

10. Timouhin, H., Amounas, F., & Azrour, M. (2023). New ECC-based IoT authentication protocol for securing RFID systems. *SN Comput. Sci.*, 4(6), 785. https://doi.org/10.1007/s42979-023-02220-2.
11. Radan, A., Samimi, H., & Moeni, A. (2018). A new lightweight authentication protocol in IoT environment for RFID tags. International Journal of Engineering and Technology. 7(4.7), 344–351. http://dx.doi.org/10.14419/ijet.v7i4.7.23028.
12. Kumar, V., Kumar, R., Jangirala, S., Kumari, S., Kumar, S., & Chen, C.-M. (2022). An enhanced RFID-based authentication protocol using PUF for vehicular cloud computing. Security and Communication Networks. 2022(1), 8998339. http://dx.doi.org/10.1155/2022/8998339.
13. Mansoor, K., Ghani, A., Chaudhry, S., Shamshirband, S., Ghayyur, S., & Mosavi, A. (2019). Securing IoT-based RFID systems: A robust authentication protocol using symmetric cryptography. Sensors. 19(21), 4752. http://dx.doi.org/10.3390/s19214752.
14. Dargaoui, S., Azrour, M., El Allaoui, A., Guezzaz, A., & Benkirane, S. (2023). Authentication in internet of things: State of art. In *Proceedings of the 6th International Conference on Networking, Intelligent Systems & Security* (pp. 1–6). Larache, Morocco.
15. Dargaoui, S., Azrour, M., El Allaoui, A., Guezzaz, A., Alabdulatif, A., & Alnajim, A. (2024). An exhaustive survey on authentication classes in the IoT environments. *Indonesian J. Electric. Eng. Inform.*, 12(1), 15–31.
16. Naeem, M., Chaudhry, S.A., Mahmood, K., Karuppiah, M., & Kumari, S. (2019). A scalable and secure RFID mutual authentication protocol using ECC for internet of things. International Journal of Communication Systems. 33(13), e3906. http://dx.doi.org/10.1002/dac.3906.
17. Iqbal, U., Tandon, A., Gupta, S., Yadav, A. R., Neware, R., & Gelana, F. W. (2022). A novel secure authentication protocol for IoT and cloud servers. Wireless Communications and Mobile Computing. 2022(1), 7707543. http://dx.doi.org/10.1155/2022/7707543.
18. Zheng, L., Xue, Y., Zhang, L., & Zhang, R. (2017, July). Mutual Authentication Protocol for RFID based on ECC. In 2017 IEEE International Conference on Computational Science and Engineering (CSE) and IEEE International Conference on Embedded and Ubiquitous Computing (EUC) (Vol. 2, pp. 320-323). IEEE.
19. Gabsi, S., Kortli, Y., Beroulle, V., Kieffer, Y., Alasiry, A., & Hamdi, B. (2021). Novel ECC-based RFID mutual authentication protocol for emerging IoT applications. IEEE access, 9, 130895-130913. http://dx.doi.org/10.1109/ACCESS.2021.3112554.
20. Dinarvand, N., & Barati, H. (2017). An efficient and secure RFID authentication protocol using elliptic curve cryptography. Wireless Networks, 25(1), 415-428. http://dx.doi.org/10.1007/s11276-017-1565-3
21. Bella, K., et al. (2024). An efficient intrusion detection system for IoT security using CNN decision forest. *PeerJ Comput. Sci.*, 10, e2290. doi: 10.7717/peerj-cs.2290.

22. Dargaoui, S., Azrour, M., El Allaoui, A., Guezzaz, A., Benkirane, S., Alabdulatif, A., & Amounas, F. Applications of blockchain in healthcare: Review study. *IoT, Machine Learning and Data Analytics for Smart Healthcare*, 1–12.
23. Dargaoui, S., Azrour, M., Mabrouki, J., El Allaoui, A., Guezzaz, A., Benkirane, S., & Alabdulatif, A. (2024). Security issues in internet of medical things. In *Blockchain and Machine Learning for IoT Security* (pp. 77–91). Chapman & Hall/CRC.
24. Benrebbouh, C., Mansouri, H., Cherbal, S., & Pathan, A. S. K. (2024). Enhanced secure and efficient mutual authentication protocol in IoT-based energy internet using blockchain. *Peer-to-Peer Netw. Appl.*, 17(1), 68–88.

Chapter 6

An AI-based embedded system for access control and absence management

Elmehdi Benmalek, Moussa Zinelabedine, Omar Enassiri, Jamal Elmhamdi, Abdelilah Jilbab, and Atman Jbari

6.1 INTRODUCTION

Managing student absences is a crucial aspect of administration in educational establishments. Manual monitoring and traditional absence management methods can be tedious, prone to human error, and time-consuming for teachers and administrative staff. Fortunately, with advancements in artificial intelligence, new opportunities are emerging to significantly enhance this process [1–3].

Artificial intelligence provides an opportunity to develop automated systems capable of efficiently and more accurately managing the absences of students. One such modern approach is the utilization of facial recognition technology. Facial recognition, as a type of software application, is designed to automatically identify individuals based on their facial features [4, 5]. Situated within the realm of computer vision, this technology involves the ability to recognize a person from an image of their face. The widespread adoption of human face recognition (HFR) systems has led to the implementation of various applications, including those in mobile devices and smart home appliances [6]. The use of HFR has notably enhanced the efficiency of security systems [7, 8]. Baksshi et al. [9] developed a real-world application utilizing a principal component–based face recognition approach. Their system was implemented on an Arduino UNO microcontroller with a MATLAB-based graphical user interface (GUI). In a similar vein, Sagar et al. [10] introduced a smart locking system based on face detection and recognition, incorporating the intensity of light during recognition. Kremic, Subasi, and Hajdarevic [11] created a mobile application for face recognition and authentication, specifically designed for access control and prevention of unauthorized mobile device usage. Additionally, Wang et al. [12] presented a novel face recognition method by average neighborhood margin maximization.

In this chapter, we aim to introduce a secure system that verifies the identity of students in educational establishments while also automatically recording absences and generating an Excel file reporting the presence, absence, and if a foreign person is in the class. This system incorporates

DOI: 10.1201/9781003587552-6

a smart lock function, relying on facial recognition technology. The hardware components include a Raspberry Pi 4 board, a basic webcam, a screen, a relay, and an electric lock.

6.2 METHODS

6.2.1 Face detection

We will employ a technique introduced in 2005 known as histogram of oriented gradients, abbreviated as HOG. The HOG is a feature descriptor technique used in computer vision and image processing for object detection. It was introduced by Navneet Dalal and Bill Triggs [13]. HOG works by dividing an image into small, connected regions called cells. For each cell, it computes the gradients (intensity changes) and their orientations within that region. The gradients provide information about the local structure of the image. The orientations are then quantized into bins, creating an orientation histogram for each cell [14].

6.2.2 Facial recognition

For our project, we sought a face detection method that offers an excellent detection rate with minimal runtime for processing each face in an image. Additionally, we aimed to avoid complex calculations to align with our project requirements. After exploring various methods, our selection gravitated toward the fundamental concept of the "face recognition" library [15]. This open-source library, written in Python, provides a solution for facial recognition through the application of machine learning techniques. It significantly simplifies the process of detecting faces in images and implementing facial recognition tasks, such as individual identification and face comparison for identity verification [16]. By utilizing this face detector, we can benefit from accurate and swift face detection even in diverse conditions without the necessity for intricate calculations [17].

6.3 IMPLEMENTATION AND EXPERIMENTAL RESULTS

The aim of this section is to outline the steps involved in implementing the proposed approach within the scope of developing a system for managing students' absences and access control. Leveraging our expertise in deep learning, we endeavored to design a facial recognition–based system for monitoring and recording students' absences, with the goal of enhancing efficiency, accuracy, and speed in this process.

Utilizing biometric facial identification, the school can monitor students who are absent from a class for any reason. The technique employed involves facial biometrics using artificial intelligence, specifically deep learning. The organogram in Figure 6.1 illustrates the various stages of this process.

6.3.1 Database

To develop an absence management system, we established a database. For each enrolled student, an image corresponding to their name was generated (Figure 6.2).

What needed to be done was to locate landmarks that refer to specific locations on a face used to identify and characterize different facial parts. To achieve this objective, we had to develop a shape prediction method that identifies essential facial structures. In our code, we planned to implement

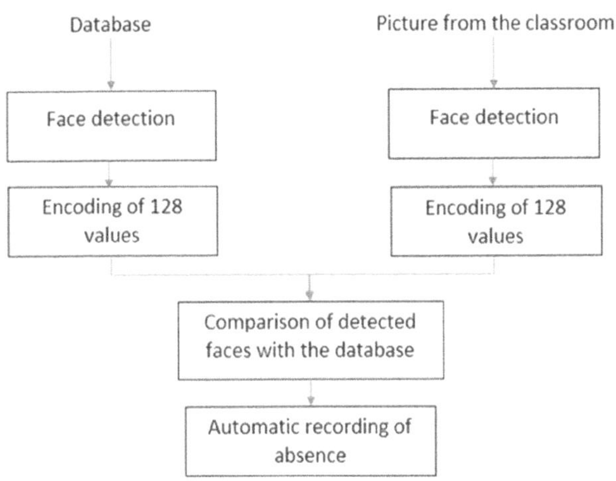

Figure 6.1 Absence management system workflow

Figure 6.2 Database

a detector integrated into the face_recognition library, which rapidly and accurately detects facial landmarks.

6.3.2 Create an encoding of 128 facial landmark values

The generation of the 128 coding values was accomplished using a pre-trained Convolutional Neural Network (CNN), predominantly inspired by a ResNet-34 model [18, 19]. This model takes inputs of size 150x150x3 and represents face images as 128-dimensional vectors [20]. All we needed to do was locate the person in our database whose measurements were closest to our test image. We calculated the Euclidean distance and identified the image with the shortest distance. The face_recognition.compare_faces library uses a default threshold value of 0.6.

6.3.3 Absence management

Figure 6.3 includes all the present students. First, the system identifies all the faces and generates the 128 encoding values for each using a pre-trained CNN. We attempt to match each face in the input image with a previously recognized face in the database. If a match is found, the student's name is automatically added to the attendance list. If the student cannot be found in the image, logically their name will be included in the list of absentees. If a new face is detected and not included in the database, it is marked as a foreigner.

It is evident that the photo was captured by a camera with average image quality. The lighting conditions are not optimal. There is variation in the distance between the camera and different faces. Even the faces themselves do not occupy the same space in the image.

Figure 6.3 Collective photo

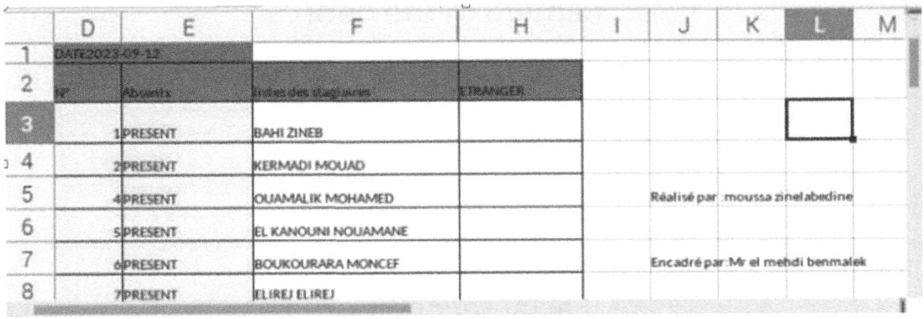

Figure 6.4 The attendance sheets. Translated with DeepL.com (free version)

The students' faces are captured and sent to Raspberry pi module where the facial recognition system is integrated. The system analyzes the image to identify registered students based on preexisting database records. Concurrently, the system also detects any foreign individuals present in the classroom. The generated Excel file provides a comprehensive list of students, indicating their attendance status as either present or absent (Figure 6.4). Additionally, a dedicated column in the Excel file highlights any foreign persons detected in the captured images, enhancing security measures within the classroom.

6.3.4 Access control

The flowchart in Figure 6.5 describes a systematic process from capturing images of students at the entrance to providing controlled access to the laboratory using facial recognition technology. This innovative approach begins with the initial step of capturing images of students as they approach the entrance, using high-resolution cameras strategically placed to ensure high-quality image input for the facial recognition algorithm.

Once the image has been taken, the facial recognition system processes the visual data, extracting distinct facial features such as eye distance, jaw shape, and other unique markers. The extracted data is then compared with a preexisting database containing facial images of enrolled students. This database is regularly updated to reflect any changes, such as new enrollments or adjustments due to altered appearances.

After comparison, if a match is found, the algorithm sends a signal to the electronic locking mechanism, which unlocks the door and authorizes the person's access to the laboratory. This not only secures the entry process, but also manages the flow of people entering the laboratory, further strengthening security measures.

To execute this project, we utilized a set of materials with the following key specifications:

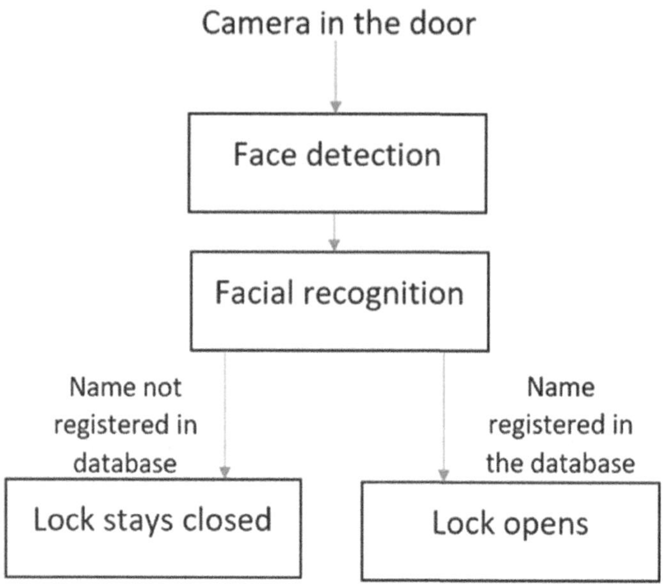

Figure 6.5 Access control system workflow

- Raspberry Pi 4 Model B
- Power supply (USB power supply) with 1A output and a voltage of 5V
- 32 GB "class 10" micro SD card
- Keyboard and mouse
- HDMI cable (if the monitor has an HDMI input)
- Web camera
- Screen
- Relay
- Electric lock

Figure 6.6 shows a practical demonstration of students attempting to gain access to the classroom using the advanced facial recognition system installed at the entrance. In the diagram, the green boxes indicate students who have been recognized by the system, which checks their identity against the database of registered persons. This successful recognition triggers the system to grant them access, enabling them to enter the classroom seamlessly and without delay.

The efficiency of this process is evident when several students pass through the entry point, greeted by a rapid validation of the facial recognition technology. As each recognized student approaches, the system instantly compares their facial features with the stored data, confirming their enrollment and right to enter the classroom.

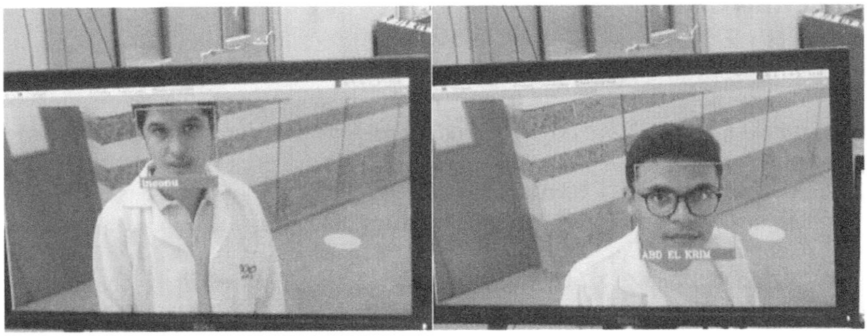

Figure 6.6 Identification of each student

However, the scenario takes a different turn with one particular student, who is represented in a red box. This visual cue indicates that this student is not registered in the database, suggesting that he or she has not registered for the course, has not presented the required identification documents, or is attempting to gain unauthorized access. As a result, the system denies entry to this student, underlining the effectiveness of the access control mechanism in preventing unauthorized persons from entering the classroom.

6.4 CONCLUSION

In this study, we addressed the challenges associated with manual management of students' attendance and access to the laboratory, introducing an intelligent electronic locking system based on Raspberry Pi 4B. To achieve our goal, we developed an automated attendance management and locking system employing facial recognition.

We employed deep learning techniques to create an intelligent system based on facial recognition, designed to automatically monitor and record students' absences, thereby improving efficiency, accuracy, and speed in the process. Simultaneously, the system utilizes its database to control access to the laboratory, ensuring the safety of equipment. This system offers the following.

Fast access control: The facial recognition algorithm is accurate and ideal for institutions with a high volume of people. The proposed technique eliminates the need for physical contact with the user, ensuring hygienic identification. This is particularly crucial in high-traffic areas where contact with terminals can lead to unwanted infections. Automatic absence management: The proposed approach addresses traditional challenges in absence management, minimizing human errors and significantly reducing the time required for teachers and administrative staff.

REFERENCES

1. Shehu, V., & Dika, A. (2010, June). Using real time computer vision algorithms in automatic attendance management systems. In *Proceedings of the ITI 2010, 32nd International Conference on Information Technology Interfaces* (pp. 397–402). IEEE.
2. Abosuliman, S. S., & Almagrabi, A. O. (2021). Computer vision assisted human computer interaction for logistics management using deep learning. *Computers & Electrical Engineering*, 96, 107555.
3. Wang, P., Zhu, Z., Chen, Q., & Dai, W. (2024). Text reasoning chain extraction for multi-hop question answering. *Tsinghua Sci. Technol.*, 29(4), 959–970. doi: 10.26599/TST.2023.9010060.
4. Peng, Y., Xu, S., Chen, Q., Huang, W., & Huang, Y. (2024). A novel popularity extraction method applied in session-based recommendation. *Tsinghua Sci. Technol.*, 29(4), 971–984. doi: 10.26599/TST.2023.9010061.
5. Benzyane, M., Zeroual, I., Azrour, M., & Agoujil, S. (2023). Convolutional long short-term memory network model for dynamic texture classification: A case study. In *International Conference on Advanced Intelligent Systems for Sustainable Development*, J. Kacprzyk, M. Ezziyyani, & V.E. Balas, Eds. In *Lecture Notes in Networks and Systems*. Cham: Springer Nature Switzerland, pp. 383–395. doi: 10.1007/978-3-031-26384-2_33.
6. Revina, I. M., & Emmanuel, W. S. (2021). A survey on human face expression recognition techniques. *J. King Saud Univ. Comput. Inform. Sci.*, 33(6), 619–628.
7. Bagchi, T., Mahapatra, A., Yadav, D., Mishra, D., Pandey, A., Chandrasekhar, P., & Kumar, A. (2022). Intelligent security system based on face recognition and IoT. *Mater. Today Proc.*, 62, 2133–2137.
8. Dong, Z., Wei, J., Chen, X., & Zheng, P. (2020). Face detection in security monitoring based on artificial intelligence video retrieval technology. *IEEE Access*, 8, 63421–63433.
9. Bakshi, N., & Prabhu, V. (2017). Face recognition system for access control using principal component analysis. In *International Conference on Intelligent Communication and Computational Techniques (ICCT)* (pp. 145–150). Jaipur, India.
10. Sagar, D., & Narasimha, M. K. (2019). Development and simulation analysis of a robust face recognition based smart locking system. In *Innovations in Electronics and Communication Engineering: Proceedings of the 6th ICIECE 2017* (pp. 3–14). Springer Singapore.
11. Kremic, E., Subasi, A., & Hajdarevic, K. (2012, June). Face recognition implementation for client server mobile application using PCA. In *Proceedings of the ITI 2012 34th International Conference on Information Technology Interfaces* (pp. 435–440). IEEE.
12. Wang, F., Wang, X., Zhang, D., Zhang, C., & Li, T. (2009). Marginface: A novel face recognition method by average neighborhood margin maximization. *Pattern Recogn.*, 42(11), 2863–2875.
13. Dalal, N., & Triggs, B. (2005). Histograms of oriented gradients for human detection. In *2005 IEEE Computer Society Conference on Computer Vision and Pattern Recognition (CVPR'05)* (Vol. 1, pp. 886–893). IEEE.

14. Zhou, W., Gao, S., Zhang, L., & Lou, X. (2020). Histogram of oriented gradients feature extraction from raw bayer pattern images. *IEEE Trans. Circuits Syst. II*, 67(5), 946–950.
15. Kashinath, Tejas, Twisha Jain, Yash Agrawal, Tanvi Anand, and Sanjay Singh. "End-to-end table structure recognition and extraction in heterogeneous documents." Applied Soft Computing 123 (2022): 108942.
16. Dhawle, T., Ukey, U., & Choudante, R. (2020). Face detection and recognition using opencv and python. *Int. Res. J. Eng Technol.*, 7(10), 3.
17. Puthea, K., Hartanto, R., & Hidayat, R. (2020). The attendance marking system based on eigenface recognition using OpenCV and python. *J. Phys. Conf. Ser.* 1551(1), 012012.
18. Peng, S., Huang, H., Chen, W., Zhang, L., & Fang, W. (2020). More trainable inception-ResNet for face recognition. *Neurocomputing*, 411, 9–19.
19. Gwyn, T., Roy, K., & Atay, M. (2021). Face recognition using popular deep net architectures: A brief comparative study. *Future Internet*, 13(7), 164.
20. King, D. (2017). High quality face recognition with deep metric learning. http://blog.dlib.net/2017/02/high-quality-face-recognition-withdeep.html (accessed on 2019-03-10).

Chapter 7

A new perspective on E-health perforated blockchain

An intelligent healthcare revolution using trigger-based supervised classification

Soumia Benkou, Ahmed Asimi, and Mbarek Lahdoud

7.1 INTRODUCTION

E-health technologies have accelerated during recent years both quantitatively and qualitatively. This digital transformation highlights new e-health tools to ensure good management, remote access to medical records and clinical interventions, and, finally, omnipresent control and follow-up of patients' health [1–3]. Everyone must have access to quality health services (diagnosis, treatment, follow-up, and prevention) in an efficient, safe, and transparent manner [4]. For this, every year technologies try to cover and develop hospital services to avoid inefficiency within medical centers due to data loss and problems caused by diagnostic errors [5, 6]. In the cloud, particularly in e-health, patients access their personal information from their homes without going to the hospital. In addition, doctors and different entities can access patient data, and they have a history that can help improve diagnoses, treatments, and even daily monitoring via the data availability in cloud computing (CC) [7] and the Internet of Medical Things.

Blockchain, *as an architecture* [8], is a series of blocks that includes a list of complete, built chain in which the initial block is known as the genesis block and its hash value is entirely zero. Using blockchain in health care requires the adaptation of a hybrid blockchain to preserve the confidentiality and security of sensitive patient data and to allow access to other public data [9].

Blockchain, *as a technology* [10], guarantees the integrity of patient data when information is exchanged between different actors. This advantage allows the secure exchange of sensitive data in health care [9].

Among the characteristics of blockchain, we cite:

- **Immutability:** Blockchain immutability is the characteristic that ensures that the data recorded in blocks cannot be altered once it has been validated and added to the chain. Once a transaction is recorded

 DOI: 10.1201/9781003587552-7

in a block and added to the blockchain, it becomes immutable and cannot be modified or deleted later.

- **Traceability:** Storing each transaction by broadcast and validation allows blockchain nodes to maintain the order of transactions for data traceability. This so-called timestamp property reduces the cost of tracking transactions. The traceability of the blockchain system is secure and consistent and solves the problem of deduplication.
- **Consensus:** in blockchain it refers to how different nodes in a network validate transactions and create new distributed ledger blocks and the order in which they are recorded. There are several consensus mechanisms used in blockchain, each with its advantages and disadvantages. We cite the *PoW* in all the nodes that must validate the new block, *PoS* where the validator nodes are selected and delegated for the creation of a new block. In our contribution, we adapt the PoW as consensus, because identifying the appropriate Doc_{ij} doctors for each patient requires that all relevant doctors in the hospital contribute. This reinforces decentralization, which favors the use of triggers as a service because it avoids the centralization of power in the hands of specific entities, such as is the case with a PoA consensus.

In our contribution, we adapted the *PoW* consensus where validators are pre-approved trusted entities that are responsible for validating transactions for many reasons: the first is that access control is always essential for good data management of patients integrated into the validation of transactions and different operations in the hospital. Also, the absence of solving mathematical problems helps in rapid treatment of the patient's condition and decision-making. Also, the validators of the blocks are always known and responsible for their decisions and diagnoses, and the security and confidentiality of the medical data of any patient remain concerns to be guaranteed.

7.2 RELATED WORKS

Numerous academics have discussed auditing the application of blockchain to safeguard electronic health records (EHRs), experiencing a critical need for a resourceful way of handling EHRs in a way that enables patients to share their present and historical health records. For handling security [11], truthfulness, and speedy data interchange, a concept prototype named "MedRec" employs the differentiating advantages of blockchain [12]. It functions on a highly decentralized foundation for storage of data and complaints and provides patients with a comprehensive and ongoing history, offering swift and straightforward accessibility to their particular healthcare records through multiple providers and facilities [13].

Establishing assurance of the provenience of health-care materials to establish their authenticity is a critical consideration in both the health care and many other industries. With the aid of a blockchain-based system, end customers can monitor items from the production site all the way through each stage of the entire supply chain, offering them absolute transparency and complete visibility into what they are purchasing [14]. Clearly, addressing these issues is a serious challenge for the manufacturing industry, especially in developing nations where fake prescriptions cause tens of thousands of deaths every year [15]. It is becoming even more mission-critical when it comes to health-care devices, too; it is developing quickly as more remote health tracking is being implemented, attracting the interest of less scrupulous parties.

An example of this is MediLedger, a well-known blockchain platform that supports companies in the global prescription medicine supply chain to verify drug legality and expiration deadlines, as well as other vital details [16].

In the paper [9], Benkou et al. introduce a smart conception of health-care architecture called E-health Blockchain, based on deep reinforcement learning. It aims to address the challenge of protecting medical data against malicious users by proposing a protocol and architecture that ensures the integrity, confidentiality, and privacy of data stored on the Cloud. It combines three phases, namely, from the patient's hospital registration to recovery.

Lahdoud and Asimi [17] propose a system that combines Internet of Things (IoT) objects, blockchain technology, and digital twins to monitor and anticipate potentially fatal crises resulting from chronic diseases, such as diabetes and asthma, and reduce their impact.

Benkou and Asimi [7] discuss the challenges of storing and sharing sensitive electronic health data while ensuring integrity and confidentiality. They highlight the need for privacy and security mechanisms in health-care systems to preserve data on the Internet. Also, they highlight the potential of CC to provide a robust infrastructure for health IT (HIT) over the Internet. In this paper, the authors present a new data integrity scheme for public cloud storage using blockchain as a third-party auditing party.

7.3 OUR CONTRIBUTION

7.3.1 Architecture of our contribution

The entities of our contribution are the patient and the blockchain (Figure 7.1). We assume a blockchain network in which each member holds an associated distributed ledger. Essentially, our contribution establishes a blockchain network containing Tr_{Si} triggers ordered from the sharing of validated symptoms by patients. The responsibility Tr_{Si} is to trigger an alert for Doc_{ij} doctors to propose their decisions and add it as a new block in the blockchain after being validated by the PoW consensus.

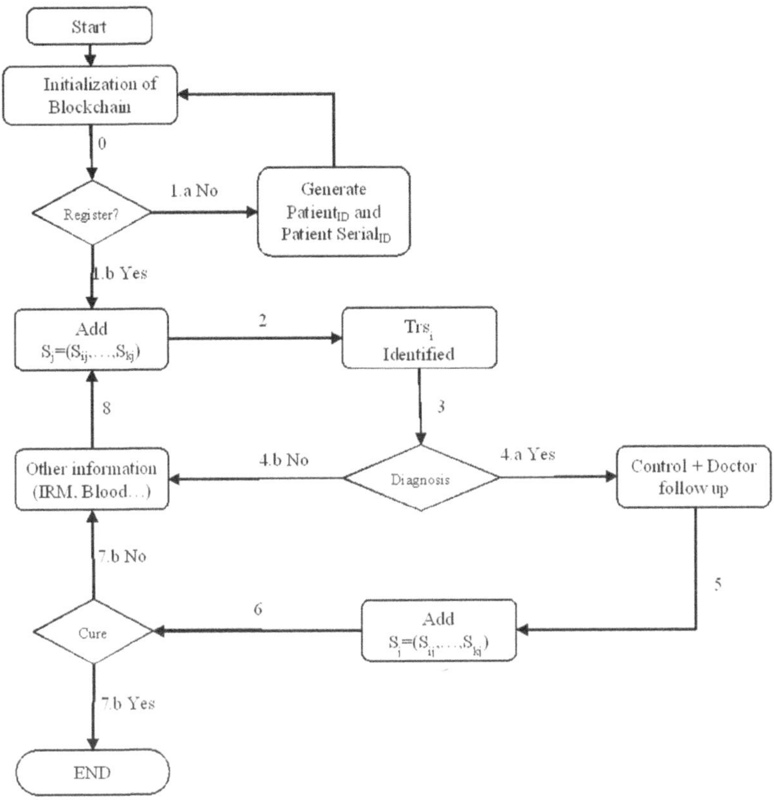

Figure 7.1 Architecture of our contribution

7.3.2 Block components

In our contribution, we used a modular architecture in which each block is composed of sub-blocks on demand by using perforated cards modified dynamically to the size of the blocks. Perforated cards are relevant data structures included or excluded depending on the need for each transaction: When creating a block for a transaction carried out within the blockchain, we include only the perforated card necessary for this transaction. This allows us to manage data and organize it in a modular way while saving block space and using only the data needed for each transaction (Figure 7.2).

Each block built in our blockchain is composed of:

- **The first part:** The ***block header*** contains:
  a. **Version:** Indicates which validation rules should apply to a block.
  b. **Size:** In our contribution, the current block size is dynamically determined to track and adjust the block size based on network requirements. Also, this integer representing the size is the number

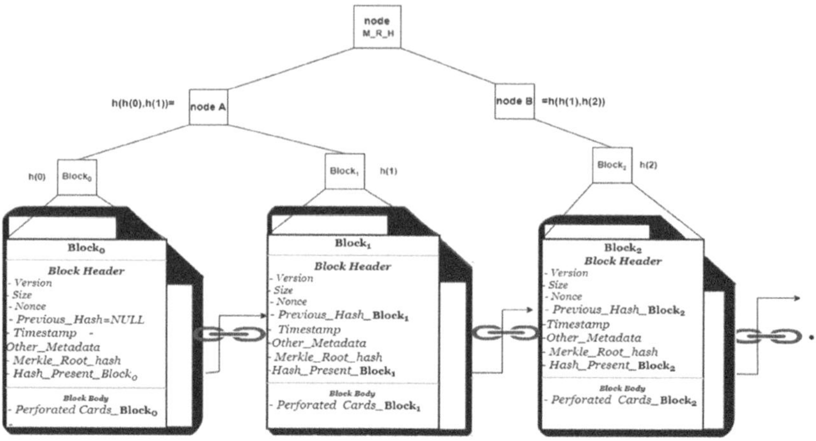

Figure 7.2 Block of our contribution

of transactions done within the blockchain. Updating the field values in the header block reflects the new block size. To validate blocks, nodes use this value by consensus on block size adjustments to verify that the dynamic size in the block header is equal to the actual size of the block. Only one valid and legitimate block size is accepted by the network.

c. **Merkle tree root hash:** All transactions in a block are associated with a hash value calculated by a hashing algorithm to verify the integrity of stored data. In our contribution, we adopted Merkle tree root hash.
d. **Timestamp:** Universal time expressed in seconds.
e. **Nonce:** It is an arbitrary number used to communicate cryptographically between users. This value can be identified statically or dynamically. In our contribution, this field is composed and chosen statically.
f. **Previous block hash:** A hash value for identification of the previous block.

- **The second part: *Block Body*.** The ***Block Body*** of our contribution consists of perforated cards [12] that organize and group the different parts of data in a modular way (patient information, operation details, etc.)

7.3.3 Phases of our contribution

In our contribution, there are two phases: (1) the pre-processing phase, and (2) the treatment and follow-up phase. The first begins with the initialization of the blockchain, where the patient accesses to register or consult his/her data. The treatment phase, after determining the Trigger Tr_{Si} service to follow the patient's case using the proof of work consensus (*PoW*), a detailed diagnosis of the patient's condition will be made to propose and validate a medical prescription, the instructions to be managed and the analyses to be carried out to verify the patient's recovery. In the control, the doctor in charge verifies the results of tests indicated in the prescription to decide whether the patient is cured and should be discharged from the hospital or asked for further information as a follow-up by the same doctor or by a new alert from Trigger Tr_{Si}.

7.4 CONCLUSION

Blockchain technology offers significant improvements in medical data security, privacy, and openness. Consensus building improves user confidence in the administration and manipulation of private health information. The adoption of blockchain technology in electronic health services provides significant benefits in terms of medical data security, confidentiality, and transparency when new architectures such as "triggers as a service" are adopted, allowing for efficient management of patients, medical operations, and triggers while ensuring data integrity and authenticity through blockchain's immutability. However, there are hurdles and constraints to the use of this technology (scalability, secrecy, resource management, etc.). In summary, our contribution opens the way to new opportunities and offers a sustainable and secure solution and an innovative model in the electronic health sector.

REFERENCES

1. S. Dargaoui et al., "Applications of Blockchain in Healthcare: Review Study," in *IoT, Machine Learning and Data Analytics for Smart Healthcare*, Mourade Azrour, Jamal Mabrouki, Azidine Guezzaz, Sultan Ahmad, Shakir Khan, and Said Benkirane, Eds., CRC Press, pp. 1–12, 2024.
2. M. Azrour, J. Mabrouki, and R. Chaganti, "New Efficient and Secured Authentication Protocol for Remote Healthcare Systems in Cloud-IoT," *Security and Communication Networks*, vol. 2021, pp. 1–12, May 2021. doi: 10.1155/2021/5546334.
3. R. Abid, M. Rizwan, A. Alabdulatif, A. Alnajim, M. Alamro, and M. Azrour, "Adaptation of Federated Explainable Artificial Intelligence for Efficient and Secure E-Healthcare Systems," *CMC—Computers, Materials & Continua*, vol. 78, no. 3, pp. 1–17, 2024.
4. C. L. Ranabhat, S. P. Acharya, C. Adhikari, and C.-B. Kim, "Universal Health Coverage Evolution, Ongoing Trend, and Future Challenge: A Conceptual and Historical Policy Review," *Front. Public Health*, vol. 11, p. 1041459, Feb. 2023. doi: 10.3389/fpubh.2023.1041459.
5. C. Hazman, A. Guezzaz, S. Benkirane, and M. Azrour, "Enhanced IDS with Deep Learning for IoT-Based Smart Cities Security," *Tsinghua Sci. Technol.*, vol. 29, no. 4, pp. 929–947, Aug. 2024. doi: 10.26599/TST.2023.9010033.

6. N. Meenakshi et al., "Efficient Communication in Wireless Sensor Networks Using Optimized Energy Efficient Engroove Leach Clustering Protocol," *Tsinghua Sci. Technol.*, vol. 29, no. 4, pp. 985–1001, Aug. 2024. doi: 10.26599/TST.2023.9010056.
7. S. Benkou and A. Asimi, "BDIV: Healthcare Blockchain Data Integrity Schemes Verification on Storage Cloud," in *Artificial Intelligence and Smart Environment*, Y. Farhaoui, A. Rocha, Z. Brahmia, and B. Bhushab, Eds., Cham: Springer International Publishing, 2023, pp. 282–286. doi: 10.1007/978-3-031-26254-8_39.
8. A. J, D. P. Isravel, K. M. Sagayam, B. Bhushan, Y. Sei, and J. Eunice, "Blockchain for Healthcare Systems: Architecture, Security Challenges, Trends and Future Directions," *Journal of Network and Computer Applications*, vol. 215, p. 103633, Jun. 2023. doi: 10.1016/j.jnca.2023.103633.
9. S. Benkou, A. Asimi, and L. Mbarek, "E-Health Blockchain: Conception of a New Smart Healthcare Architecture Based on Deep Reinforcement Learning," in *Artificial Intelligence, Data Science and Applications*, Y. Farhaoui, A. Hussain, T. Saba, H. Taherdoost, and A. Verma, Eds., Cham: Springer Nature Switzerland, 2024, pp. 91–99. doi: 10.1007/978-3-031-48573-2_14.
10. Z. Wenhua, F. Qamar, T.-A. N. Abdali, R. Hassan, S. T. A. Jafri, and Q. N. Nguyen, "Blockchain Technology: Security Issues, Healthcare Applications, Challenges and Future Trends," *Electronics*, vol. 12, no. 3, Art. no. 3, Jan. 2023. doi: 10.3390/electronics12030546.
11. S. Dargaoui et al., "Security Issues in Internet of Medical Things," in *Blockchain and Machine Learning for IoT Security*, Mourade Azrour, Jamal Mabrouki, Azidine Guezzaz, and Said Benkirane, Eds., Chapman & Hall/CRC, 2024, pp. 77–91.
12. S. Wang et al., "Blockchain-Powered Parallel Healthcare Systems Based on the ACP Approach," *IEEE Transactions on Computational Social Systems*, vol. 5, no. 4, pp. 942–950, Dec. 2018. doi: 10.1109/TCSS.2018.2865526.
13. O. Scekic, S. Nastic, and S. Dustdar, "Blockchain-Supported Smart City Platform for Social Value Co-Creation and Exchange," *IEEE Internet Comput.*, vol. 23, no. 1, pp. 19–28, Jan. 2019. doi: 10.1109/MIC.2018.2881518.
14. C. Narayanaswami, R. Nooyi, S. R. Govindaswamy, and R. Viswanathan, "Blockchain Anchored Supply Chain Automation," *IBM J. Res. Dev.*, vol. 63, no. 2/3, p. 7:1–7:11, Mar. 2019. doi: 10.1147/JRD.2019.2900655.
15. P. Tagde et al., "Blockchain and Artificial Intelligence Technology in e-Health," *Environ. Sci. Pollut. Res. Int.*, vol. 28, no. 38, pp. 52810–52831, 2021. doi: 10.1007/s11356-021-16223-0.
16. S. Khezr, M. Moniruzzaman, A. Yassine, and R. Benlamri, "Blockchain Technology in Healthcare: A Comprehensive Review and Directions for Future Research," *Appl. Sci.*, vol. 9, no. 9, Art. no. 9, Jan. 2019. doi: 10.3390/app9091736.
17. M. Lahdoud and A. Asimi, "A Novel Detection, Prevention and Management Proactive System of Patients Chronic Disease Based on IoT, Blockchain, AI and Digital Twin," in *Artificial Intelligence, Data Science and Applications*, Y. Farhaoui, A. Hussain, T. Saba, H. Taherdoost, and A. Verma, Eds., Cham: Springer Nature Switzerland, 2024, pp. 324–329. doi: 10.1007/978-3-031-48573-2_47.

Chapter 8

Machine learning for security boosting in Internet of Things environments

Souhayla Dargaoui, Mourade Azrour, Ahmad El Allaoui, Azidine Guezzaz, and Said Benkirane

8.1 INTRODUCTION

According to [1], the number of IoT devices will exceed 75 billion by the end of 2025. The continuous development of the IoT devices market pushes manufacturers to emphasize low cost and user simplicity over security features. These reasons, combined with the vulnerability of wireless communication networks, the high mobility of IoT devices, and the dynamic network topology, make ensuring the security of such environments a sophisticated task. Recently, several security solutions have been provided to secure IoT networks, including authentication and access control, attack detection, and malware analysis [2–5]. Nonetheless, these traditional approaches still have some gaps to overcome. For this reason, machine learning algorithms have been adopted.

Machine learning (ML) is an artificial intelligence technique that solves complex tasks by learning from data and experiences without the need for human intervention. Generally, machine learning algorithms are used on big datasets to extract behavioral models using mathematics. It enables the machine's aptitude to learn without any explicit programming. The models generated by ML algorithms are exploited to make future predictions based on future data.

Various reviews have been published to cover the utility of machine learning in IoT security [6–13]. Hence, Mohy-eddine et al. [14–17] has proposed various intrusion detections based on machine learning and deep learning techniques. C. Ni and SC. Li [18] presented a comprehensive study that illustrates how ML learns malicious activity detection. The provided review compares key approaches in terms of ability and robustness against threats. Additionally, F. Alwahedi [19] offered a survey of recent tendencies, approaches, and issues in the use of ML for attack detection in IoT networks. They conducted a comparative study of existing intrusion detection systems based on ML in the IoT field, highlighting the remaining problems. In [20], Tahsin et al. afford another survey that presents the different ML algorithms and their utility in addressing attacks and provided a state-of-the-art

DOI: 10.1201/9781003587552-8

survey on practicable security approaches for IoT devices. Finally, they considered the limitations and obstacles of ML security approaches and perspective research direction.

The remainder of this chapter is organized as follows: Section 8.2 provides some possible security attacks in IoT layers. Section 8.3 offers a taxonomy of ML algorithms. Section 8.4 presents ML algorithms and their use in IoT security. Section 8.5 presents a state-of-art analysis of ML-based security solutions. Section 8.6 discusses the ML-based security challenges and future research direction. Finally, Section 8.7 concludes the chapter.

8.2 IOT NETWORK ARCHITECTURE AND SECURITY ISSUES

Physical layer attacks. The physical or perception layer is the layer that collects information about the surrounding environment. It consists of IoT sensors and actuators that measure various kinds of parameters and enable the identification of other intelligent devices. Physical attacks make the attackers able to harm the hardware of IoT and access the device's data. Forged nodes, side channel attack, radiofrequency jamming, and tampering attacks are some of the most important physical attacks [21, 22].

Network layer attacks. The network layer secures the communication between IoT devices. It exploits a variety of communication technologies. The choice of a protocol to use depends on the size of the network, the energy consumption of each device, and the transmission speed required in each application. The purpose of attacks in this layer is to take control of IoT devices with remote access. Traffic analysis attacks, man-in-the-middle attacks, and routing attacks are among the most significant.

Application layer attacks. The application layer or service layer is responsible for providing services to users. At this level, data from previous layers is stored, aggregated, filtered, and processed. At the end of this processing process, it defines various applications in which the Internet of Things can be deployed, for example, smart homes, smart cities, and smart health. Attacks in such layers allow the attacker to steal critical data, including unauthenticated access to the application level of IoT. Denial of service and SQL injection attacks represent a significant set of physical attacks.

8.3 MACHINE LEARNING ALGORITHMS CATEGORIZATION

Machine learning (ML) is a discipline that deals with the algorithms used to learn based on specific instances. Indeed, machine learning is widely recognized as a popular tool used in a whole range of different sectors, including fraud detection in finance and banking, prediction of patterns in health care, and assisting intelligent devices to handle conversations rapidly by means of natural language processing. Basically, machine learning algorithms can be divided into the four following categories [23].

Supervised learning: This ML technique is used when predefined results are supposed to be reached from certain inputs. This kind of machine learning algorithm uses generally labeled datasets, which are divided into training data and test data. Through the analysis of the training data, supervised learning attempts to build a model that can map every input to an output, even for new data inputs.

Unsupervised learning: In such kinds of ML algorithms, the data used to learn is unlabeled, and the trained model investigates the similarity among this data to extract their features.

Semi-supervised learning: The data required in the previous ML techniques is either labeled or unlabeled. In semi-supervised learning, labeled and unlabeled data is used to fit the model. From that point, this learning technique may be considered a hybridization of supervised and unsupervised learning.

Reinforcement learning: This kind of learning makes machines and software agents able to estimate the optimum behavior in such environments. This technique is built on rewards and punishments. Its purpose is to maximize the reward and minimize the penalty using insights from the surrounding environment.

8.4 MACHINE LEARNING MECHANISMS IN IOT SECURITY APPROACHES

8.4.1 Classification and regression methods

Classification and regression mechanisms are some of the most used ML algorithms. Generally, in classification algorithms, the outputs are finite. The purpose of the algorithm is to predict a fixed value or class. Consequently, in IoT security, they may be used for anomaly detection or even attack classification. Despite this, the predicted parameters in regression algorithms are continuous, and the algorithm is used to find the relationship between a dependent parameter and other independent parameters. Thus, in IoT security, this kind of algorithm can be used to examine the impact of attacks. Support vector machines (SVM) is a classification and regression algorithm that may be used in binary and multiclass contexts. Decision trees are also utilized for classification and regression issues. These trees are exploited for splitting inputs into various classes based on specific rules. Naive Bayes is another classifier for binary and multiclass situations. By searching through the available dataset, K-nearest neighbor is employed to associate new data points with existing similar points simply and effectively [1, 23, 24].

8.4.2 Clustering methods

Clustering is an unsupervised ML approach that may cluster or establish classes of a collection of data points by measuring the similarity and dissimilarity of these data points. From this standpoint, this approach can discover the IoT security data's hidden shapes and architectures. As a result, clustering can perform a substantial task to overcome several security obstacles, including intrusion detection and abnormal IoT device behavior characterization. K-means is the most used and most well-known clustering mechanism, which is classified into unsupervised machine learning algorithms [25].

8.4.3 Dimensionality reduction and principal component analysis

Generally, the IoT data quantity and shape may directly impact the security solution built on ML algorithms. The diversity in IoT data, which may contain less relevant or insignificant information, makes cyberattack patterning a sophisticated task. As a result, security solutions may suffer from various obstacles, such as significant computational cost, overfitting, etc. Minimizing these issues when building an IoT security model with high-dimensional data sets can be achieved by selecting an optimal number of security features based on their impact or importance. From this standpoint, characteristic engineering and data dimensionality diminution could play a significant role in developing ML-based security models. Principal component analysis is an ML technique that engenders new labels that gather the most relevant information [25].

8.4.4 Deep neural network approaches

A deep neural network is a feed-forward neural network whereby each neuron is linked to the previous and the next layer neurons. Considering the term "deep," such kin of neural networks consist of several layers and hold multi-perception levels. Multilayer perceptron, convolutional neural networks, and deep belief networks are used to build intrusion detection systems and malware detection. In the case of time-dependent attacks, recurrent neural networks have become a significant choice to build security models [25].

8.5 LATEST PROPOSED ML-BASED SOLUTIONS FOR IOT SECURITY

8.5.1 Authentication

Authentication is an essential security exigency in IoT networks [26]. The users may not use IoT applications without being authenticated. If a user demands data from an IoT device, the network must verify that it has the necessary permissions for the data. If not, the demand will be rejected. In [27], S. Chinnaswamy and K. Annapurani used machine learning to provide a trust aggregation authentication scheme. First, they calculated each device's trust value using its behavior examination and data trust values. Then, by evaluating the traffic data, they calculate the trust threshold value with a support vector machine (SVM). Finally, in the authentication phase, the gateway checks the trust value of the IoT device and omits it in case it is less than the threshold. In addition, A.K. Sahu et al. [28] proposed a continuous authentication framework to authenticate legitimate users inside a session. To classify the IoT device behavior, they proposed a long short-term memory classification network.

8.5.2 Attack and intrusion detection

Considering the fast development of software, which leads to new cyberattacks and security bugs, the authentication process may not ensure security sufficiently. A. Sharifi and S. Goli-Bidgoli [29] presented an ML-based attack detection mechanism that may identify the IoT attacks in the fog layer and prevent its spread to other segments in the network. In [30], T. Gaber et al. offered an IoT intrusion detection system for injection attack detection. The examination, using AWID public datasets, illustrates that the best classifier to identify injection attacks is decision tree with an accuracy of 99% using only eight characteristics selected by the proposed method. In 2022, T. Saba et al. [31] provided another anomaly based intrusion detection approach built on CNN. They illustrate the capability of the suggested method to identify all unusual traffic behavior and intrusions. Using the NID dataset, the proposed model achieved an accuracy of 99.51%, while, using the BoT-IoT dataset it achieved only 92.85%.

8.5.3 Malware analysis

Malware is a danger that arises according to several vulnerabilities linked to authentication, authorization, or even physical device tempering.

The literature identifies generic malware such as spyware, ransomware, adware, trojan, and virus. However, various optimized classes are developed to target IoT devices, including WanaCry, Cryptlocker, Mirai, and Stuxnet. In [32], V. Rey et al. proposed a federated learning-based framework for malware-affecting device detection. To examine the provided framework, the authors used the N-BaIoT dataset that models network traffic in case IoT devices are affected by malware. Additionally, SH. Khan et al. [33] presented a deep CNN-based framework for detecting malware. To test the framework and evaluate the proposed approach against current mechanisms, the IOT_Malware dataset has been used. As a result, the proposed framework demonstrates its robustness and efficiency in timely malware detection with an accuracy of 98.50% and a precision of 98.42%.

8.6 CHALLENGES AND FUTURE VISION

The deployment of machine learning in IoT security leads to various important challenges. The quantity of the data and its diversity in terms of features and velocity give rise to various challenges to conventional approaches, including data collection, training datasets construction, etc. Furthermore, the use of confidential user data for ML algorithm training leads to various privacy issues. In addition, the heterogeneity in IoT appliances, combining several structures, conventions, and operating systems, constitutes another main obstacle. This diversity complicates the development of universal machine learning approaches, as each appliance can demand an adjusted mechanism. Moreover, the limited computation power of IoT devices and the intensive nature of ML algorithms leads to several issues.

A large language model (LLM) is a special kind of generative artificial intelligence (AI) that may create content, especially text-based material interpreting a huge amount of data. The IoT security enabled by LLM, and generative AI undertakes more security and intelligence. To determine strange behavior and detect cyber threats, these generative models may explore unstructured data generated by the diverse IoT devices. They also improve lightweight encryption approaches for the authentication of power-limited IoT devices. Additionally, combining LLMs and biometric mechanisms, including voice recognition, may enhance user authentication and enable automated access control. Further, exploiting the ability to engender realistic phishing emails and social engineering attacks, generative AI may improve penetration testing in IoT systems.

8.7 CONCLUSION

IoT security plays a vital role in its commercialization and deployment. Considering the diversity of disciplines and technologies covered by the IoT concept, ensuring IoT network security can be complex. Further, the dynamic nature of IoT networks presents multiple challenges for traditional security and privacy solutions. Advancements in ML have enabled the creation of numerous powerful analytical techniques that can be utilized to enhance the security of IoT. In this chapter, first, we presented security issues in each IoT layer. Then, we discussed the different ML mechanisms and their utility in IoT security enhancement. Subsequently, we reviewed the latest proposed ML-based solutions for IoT security. Finally, we presented some ML-based IoT security challenges and provided a future vision.

REFERENCES

1. G. Abbas, A. Mehmood, M. Carsten, G. Epiphaniou, and J. Lloret, "Safety, Security and Privacy in Machine Learning Based Internet of Things," *J. Sens. Actuat. Netw.*, vol. 11, no. 3, p. 38, 2022.
2. S. Dargaoui, M. Azrour, A. El Allaoui, A. Guezzaz, A. Alabdulatif, and A. Alnajim, "Internet of Things Authentication Protocols: Comparative Study," *Comput. Mater. Contin.*, vol. 79, no. 1, pp. 1–10, Jan. 2024. doi: 10.32604/cmc.2024.047625.
3. S. Dargaoui, M. Azrour, A. El Allaoui, A. Guezzaz, A. Alabdulatif, and A. Alnajim, "An Exhaustive Survey on Authentication Classes in the IoT Environments," *Indones. J. Electr. Eng. Inform.*, vol. 12, no. 1, pp. 15–31, 2024.
4. S. Dargaoui et al., "Applications of Blockchain in Healthcare: Review Study," *IoT Mach. Learn. Data Anal. Smart Healthc.*, pp. 1–12, 2023.
5. S. Dargaoui, M. Azrour, A. El Allaoui, A. Guezzaz, and S. Benkirane, "Authentication in Internet of Things: State of Art," in *Proceedings of the 6th International Conference on Networking, Intelligent Systems & Security*, 2023, pp. 1–6.
6. A. E. M. Eljialy, M. Y. Uddin, and S. Ahmad, "Novel Framework for an Intrusion Detection System Using Multiple Feature Selection Methods Based on Deep Learning," *Tsinghua Sci. Technol.*, vol. 29, no. 4, pp. 948–958, Aug. 2024. doi: 10.26599/TST.2023.9010032.
7. C. Hazman, A. Guezzaz, S. Benkirane, and M. Azrour, "Enhanced IDS with Deep Learning for IoT-Based Smart Cities Security," *Tsinghua Sci. Technol.*, vol. 29, no. 4, pp. 929–947, Aug. 2024. doi: 10.26599/TST.2023.9010033.
8. S. Li, T. Cui, and W. Viriyasitavat, "Edge Device Fault Probability Based Intelligent Calculations for Fault Probability of Smart Systems," *Tsinghua Sci. Technol.*, vol. 29, no. 4, pp. 1023–1036, Aug. 2024. doi: 10.26599/TST.2023.9010085.
9. W. Liu, L. Zhou, S. Zhang, N. Luo, and M. Xu, "A New High-Precision and Lightweight Detection Model for Illegal Construction Objects Based on Deep Learning," *Tsinghua Sci. Technol.*, vol. 29, no. 4, pp. 1002–1022, Aug. 2024. doi: 10.26599/TST.2023.9010090.

10. H. Attou et al., "Towards an Intelligent Intrusion Detection System to Detect Malicious Activities in Cloud Computing," *Appl. Sci.*, vol. 13, no. 17, p. 9588, 2023.
11. H. Attou, A. Guezzaz, S. Benkirane, M. Azrour, and Y. Farhaoui, "Cloud-Based Intrusion Detection Approach Using Machine Learning Techniques," *Big Data Min. Anal.*, vol. 6, no. 3, pp. 311–320, 2023.
12. S. Amaouche, AzidineGuezzaz, S. Benkirane, and MouradeAzrour, "IDS-XGbFS: A Smart Intrusion Detection System Using XGboostwith Recent Feature Selection for VANET Safety," *Clust. Comput.*, vol. 27, pp. 1–15, 2023.
13. S. Amaouche et al., "FSCB-IDS: Feature Selection and Minority Class Balancing for Attacks Detection in VANETS," *Appl. Sci.*, vol. 13, no. 13, p. 7488, 2023.
14. M. Mohy-eddine, A. Guezzaz, S. Benkirane, and M. Azrour, "An Intrusion Detection Model Using Election-Based Feature Selection and K-NN," *Microprocess. Microsyst.*, p. 104966, Oct. 2023. doi: 10.1016/j.micpro.2023.104966.
15. M. Mohy-eddine, A. Guezzaz, S. Benkirane, and M. Azrour, "An Efficient Network Intrusion Detection Model for IoT Security Using K-NN Classifier and Feature Selection," *Multimed. Tools Appl.*, vol. 82, pp. 23615–23633, 2023. doi: 10.1007/s11042-023-14795-2.
16. M. Mohy-eddine, A. Guezzaz, S. Benkirane, and M. Azrour, "An Effective Intrusion Detection Approach Based on Ensemble Learning for IIoT Edge Computing," *J. Comput. Virol. Hacking Tech.*, vol. 19, pp. 469–481 , 2022.
17. M. Mohy-Eddine, S. Benkirane, A. Guezzaz, and M. Azrour, "Random Forest-Based IDS for IIoT Edge Computing Security Using Ensemble Learning for Dimensionality Reduction," *Int. J. Embed. Syst.*, vol. 15, no. 6, pp. 467–474, 2022.
18. C. Ni and S. C. Li, "Machine Learning Enabled Industrial IoT Security: Challenges, Trends and Solutions," *J. Ind. Inf. Integr.*, vol. 38, p. 100549, 2024.
19. F. Alwahedi, A. Aldhaheri, M. A. Ferrag, A. Battah, and N. Tihanyi, "Machine Learning Techniques for IoT Security: Current Research and Future Vision with Generative AI and Large Language Models," *Internet Things Cyber-Phys. Syst.*, 2024, Accessed: Apr. 16, 2024. Online]. Available: https://www.sciencedirect.com/science/article/pii/S2667345223000585
20. S. M. Tahsien, H. Karimipour, and P. Spachos, "Machine Learning Based Solutions for Security of Internet of Things (IoT): A Survey," *J. Netw. Comput. Appl.*, vol. 161, p. 102630, 2020. doi: https://doi.org/10.1016/j.jnca.2020.102630.
21. S. Dargaoui et al., "An Overview of the Security Challenges in IoT Environment," in *Advanced Technology for Smart Environment and Energy*, J. Mabrouki, A. Mourade, A. Irshad, and S. A. Chaudhry, Eds., in *Environmental Science and Engineering*. Cham: Springer International Publishing, 2023, pp. 151–160. doi: 10.1007/978-3-031-25662-2_13.
22. S. Dargaoui et al., "Security Issues in Internet of Medical Things," in *Blockchain and Machine Learning for IoT Security*, Mourade Azrour, Jamal Mabrouki, Azidine Guezzaz, and Said Benkirane, Eds., Chapman & Hall/CRC, 2024, pp. 77–91.

23. F. Hussain, R. Hussain, S. A. Hassan, and E. Hossain, "Machine Learning in IoT Security: Current Solutions and Future Challenges," *IEEE Commun. Surv. Tutor.*, vol. 22, no. 3, pp. 1686–1721, 2020.
24. I. H. Sarker, "Machine Learning: Algorithms, Real-World Applications and Research Directions," *SN Comput. Sci.*, vol. 2, no. 3, p. 160, 2021.
25. I. H. Sarker, A. I. Khan, Y. B. Abushark, and F. Alsolami, "Internet of Things (IoT) Security Intelligence: A Comprehensive Overview, Machine Learning Solutions and Research Directions," *Mob. Netw. Appl.*, vol. 28, no. 1, pp. 296–312, 2023.
26. H. Timouhin, F. Amounas, and M. Azrour, "New ECC-Based IoT Authentication Protocol for Securing RFID Systems," *SN Comput. Sci.*, vol. 4, no. 6, p. 785, Oct. 2023. doi: 10.1007/s42979-023-02220-2.
27. S. Chinnaswamy and K. Annapurani, "Trust Aggregation Authentication Protocol Using Machine Learning for IoT Wireless Sensor Networks," *Comput. Electr. Eng.*, vol. 91, p. 107130, 2021.
28. A. K. Sahu, S. Sharma, and R. Raja, "Deep Learning-Based Continuous Authentication for an IoT-Enabled Healthcare Service," *Comput. Electr. Eng.*, vol. 99, p. 107817, Apr. 2022. doi: 10.1016/j.compeleceng.2022.107817.
29. A. Sharifi and S. Goli-Bidgoli, "IFogLearn++: A New Platform for fog Layer's IoT Attack Detection in Critical Infrastructure Using Machine Learning and Big Data Processing," *Comput. Electr. Eng.*, vol. 103, p. 108374, 2022.
30. T. Gaber, A. El-Ghamry, and A. E. Hassanien, "Injection Attack Detection Using Machine Learning for Smart IoT Applications," *Phys. Commun.*, vol. 52, p. 101685, 2022.
31. T. Saba, A. Rehman, T. Sadad, H. Kolivand, and S. A. Bahaj, "Anomaly-Based Intrusion Detection System for IoT Networks through Deep Learning Model," *Comput. Electr. Eng.*, vol. 99, p. 107810, 2022.
32. V. Rey, P. M. S. Sánchez, A. H. Celdrán, and G. Bovet, "Federated Learning for Malware Detection in IoT Devices," *Comput. Netw.*, vol. 204, p. 108693, 2022.
33. S. H. Khan et al., "A New Deep Boosted CNN and Ensemble Learning Based IoT Malware Detection," *Comput. Secur.*, vol. 133, p. 103385, 2023.

Chapter 9

Combined machine learning for anomaly detection in IoT aggregator RPi

Maryam Douiba, Said Benkirane, Azidine Guezzaz, and Mourade Azrour

9.1 INTRODUCTION

IoT security presents a challenge because of the complexity of the systems and the heterogeneity of devices used in this environment. Hence, it has received increased attention from academic researchers in recent years [1, 3, 6]. This chapter aims to overcome some limitations in the intrusion detection systems (IDSs), such as colossal volume, quality improvement, time performance, and detection rate, as well as reduce false alarms by assembling the best ML and enhancing feature engineering. The main goal is to create an optimized IDS to improve the security of the RPi aggregator. We are profiting from the benefits of two powerful MLs to implement a powerful IDS integrated into the new fog computing paradigm. We are also optimizing minority class detection to ameliorate detection. Our contributions are outlined in three points: First, we proposed an ensemble learning that uses the scores of the unsupervised model iForest in the supervised model GB and DT as features to enhance normal traffic detection and deal with zero-day attacks on the RPi 4 aggregator. Second, we incorporate a categorical encoder and feature importance to deal with heterogeneous and categorical data. The main goal is to ameliorate detection rate, accuracy, and time performance and reduce false alarms to eliminate zero-day attacks. Third, we provide a comparative study of the model applied to imbalanced data, which has a more significant number of attacks than benign ones like BoT-IoT, CICIoT2023, and Edge-IIoT; this contributes to the potential resolution of the imbalanced data. The results of this experiment show that our model works effectively and generates strange predictions with more than 99.99% accuracy. The chapter is organized as follows. In Section 9.2 we present an overview of IoT security, architectures, and the related developments in IDS techniques that use ML and DL. In Section 9.3 we outline the key phases of the proposed architecture and solutions for validating our IDS technique. In Section 9.4 we discuss the experimental assessment and outcomes. Finally, the chapter concludes with a conclusion and further research.

DOI: 10.1201/9781003587552-9

9.2 RELATED WORKS

In the literature study, several authors have looked to improve IDS to protect the IoT environment [10, 11, 14], [23–38]. In light of this, Misra et al. [17] and Kasinathan et al. [18] provided security architecture for identifying DDoS attacks in IoT. Sonar et al. [19] investigated the efficacy of deploying ML and DL algorithms to enhance IDS security in 2016 to secure IoT systems from DDoS attacks. Following the same strategy, a convincing experimental study of anomaly detection based on the GB approach was proposed by Tama et al. [15]. The same year, Hodo et al. [13] proposed an ANN IDS model to classify threat analysis of IoT networks. This model's evaluation achieves more significant than 99% accuracy. In 2017, a basis for DL developing machine intelligence toward intelligent network traffic was presented by Fadlullah et al. [9]. A distributed attack DL detection method for IoT security was simultaneously developed in 2017 by Diro et al. [5]. The model's accuracy increased from 96% to over 99%, making it more accurate at detecting assaults than centralized ones. In 2018, an IDS architecture of cognitive fog computing for IoT systems was created by Prabavathy et al. [20]. The OS-ELM method implements the suggested architecture at distributed fog nodes, achieving 97.36% accuracy with a 0.37% false alarm. After a year, Verma et al. [7] compared and presented the results of several supervised ML algorithms to choose a viable classifier model for IoT security. They suggested an IDS model based on ensemble learning and demonstrated that GBM has the highest sensitivity, 99.53%. Gu et al. [4] suggested an effective method of detection constructed using an SVM classifier and feature embedding using the naive Bayes (NB) algorithm in 2020. Furthermore, in the same year, Chaabouni et al. [8] developed a OneM2M IDS for IoT security based on edge ML. The investigational study results revealed that the detection rate is 93.80%, the accuracy is 92.32%, the precision is 92.95%, the FPR is 1.53%, and the CPU training time is 9280ms. Furthermore, according to Jin et al. [21], LightGBM delivers good results, with 99.6% TPR, 0.2% FPR, and 99.7% accuracy. Al-kasassbeh et al. [22] confirmed this and demonstrated that the LightGBM algorithm obtained about 100% accuracy, demonstrating the superiority of this ML technique over DL strategies. Ullah et al. [12] proposed a deep learning model IDS for binary and multicast classifications in 2021 using multiple layers of CNN, with a minimum detection rate of roughly 99.7%. In the same year, Dhanke et al. [2] suggested a machine learning–based IoT for delivering an IDS for security, and their results demonstrate an 85% accuracy rate. Sohail et al. [1] proposed a hybrid intelligent IDS using machine learning and metaheuristic algorithms for IoT-based health care. Based on the accuracy, execution time, memory usage, and CPU utilization, performance evaluation indicates a good accuracy of 99.88%, 86.40%, 95.39%, 96.90%, and 100% for DoS, U2R, R2L, Probe, and Normal classes using eight to ten features. In our previous research, we used the implementation of GB employing binary DT as fundamental predictors [6]; this method applies the same splitting criterion on each tree level, making it less prone to overfitting and faster at test time [16]. We tested this combination on CPU and GPU, and the experimental results proved that GPU-based gives the best performance result in record time [6].

9.3 OPTIMIZED INTRUSION DETECTION MODEL

Our contribution aims to develop and implement an improved IDS to increase detection rate, accuracy, and response time. Figure 9.1 shows the suggested model's strategy. The objective is to validate an optimized IDS built using an optimized ensemble learning that uses the prediction score of iForest in the supervised model GBDT as features to enhance the detection of normal traffic and deal with zero-day attacks on the RPi 4. Our optimized model process is divided into five essential parts:

Part 1: Data preparation. Data has been loaded and prepared. Then, we used catboostEncoder to transform all categorical data. The categorical values Xi are then encoded on the whole dataset, greedily using the target statistic to reduce overfitting. catBoost suggests that multiple random permutations should be generated first to encode the categorical features. The outcome is only the average of the several encodings [16] using the following formula to convert all categorical feature values to numerical form [16]: $Avg\ \text{Enconer} = \frac{\text{Sum Target} + \text{prior}}{\text{Sum Features} + 1}$ With SumTarget is the total number of target label values 1 for objects with the present categorized feature value throughout the dataset, prior is the preliminary value of the numerator. The starting parameters define it. SumFeatures is the sum of objects with categorical feature

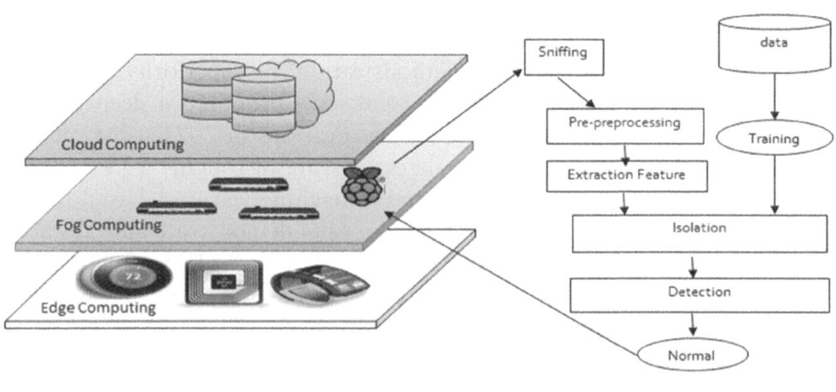

Figure 9.1 IDS architecture

values that match the present one. Following that, all features are transformed.

Part 2: Extraction of score detection using iForest. We defined and prepared feature vectors and then used iForests to detect anomalies, treating them as rare data points, making them easier to isolate. The anomaly scores generated are recovered as a new feature. This score for a sample $X_{1....n}$ is calculated as follows [3]: $S(X) = 2^{\frac{E(h(x))}{C(n)}}$, where C(n) represents the expected value of the average height for a tree that contains n samples. represents the expected value of the mean height for a tree containing n samples, h(x,T) being the height of the data sample X in tree T, and E(·) being the expectation operator calculated over all trees in the forest. These score values generally in the interval [-1,1], where values closer to 1 indicate more abnormal samples and values closer to -1 indicate more normal samples. This provided us with a critical view of the traffic pattern we used; it is efficient for high-dimensional data and can work quickly even with large amounts of data [3].

Part 3: Extraction of important features. We identified the features with the most significant impact on our model's predictions by training all data on the catboost model to calculate each feature's effect on the data division, considering the information gained from each division. We then extracted the features that contributed the most to reducing the loss in constructing the DT.

Part 4: Training and model building. The datasets are constructed with 70% train and 30% test using important features and iForest score detection. We trained the model using GBDT on catboost; then, based on the training results, we optimized the hyperparameter to choose the excellent performance that gives the best results. The selection is then used to classify the problem.

Part 5: Intrusion detection. The building model may predict the normal traffic as a positive. We evaluated and validated the model based on accuracy, recall, precision, FP, FN, and f1-score obtained from the confusion matrix.

9.4 EXPERIMENTAL ANALYSIS AND RESULTS

We carried out the experimental evaluation of our optimized model on RPi4 Model B, Quad-core Cortex-A72 (ARM v8) 64-bit SoC @ 1.8GHz, with wireless connection 2.4 GHz and 5.0 GHz. We built the model with Jupyter Lab with Python 3.9.7 and catboost 1.0.3, which includes the pandas, NumPy, and sklearn. The evaluation of IDS is a crucial challenge. For this reason, we have chosen to perform the tests on three datasets, as shown in Table 9.1, to guarantee that our model tested ideal and to ensure the stability of the model and its efficiency.

Table 9.1 Data reconstructions

Dataset	*Training (70%)*	*Testing (30%)*	*Data*		
			ALL	*Normale*	*Attacks*
Edge-IIoT	110460	47340	157800	24301	133499
CICIoT2023	674641	289132	963773	22484	941289
BoT-IoT	2 567 965	1100557	3668522	477	3668045

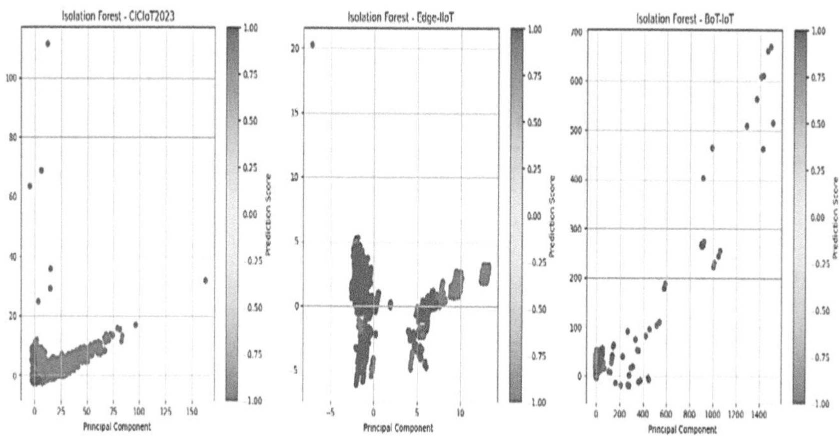

Figure 9.2 iForest score data distribution

The iForest randomly selects a splitting threshold for each DT in the set and calculates the depth of each data point in the tree. Based on this calculation, an anomaly score is then assigned to each data point, as shown in Figure 9.2.

The important features are then extracted, and catBoost employs categorical feature combinations as additional features to capture high-level dependencies. The algorithm can handle all possible combinations of categorical features in the dataset. To achieve this, all the potential splits of the features in the data are first calculated, and then the one that most improves the loss function is selected. Once the initial split has been chosen and fixed, the next split in the tree is selected greedily, considering the first one [6, 16]. This process continues until the entire tree is constructed and important features are identified. The iForest score obtained is then added. We have grouped them in Table 9.2. As shown in Table 9.3, we effectively reduced FP and FN by utilizing only five features and the iForest score, resulting in favorable outcomes. As we can see, the model has learned to detect abnormal traffic based on the five important features in Table 9.2 using the combination of unsupervised scores in the supervised model. It is observed that the time required to classify recording as an attack or normal using the

Table 9.2 Selected features of the Edge-IIoT, CICIoT2023, and BoT-IoT datasets

Edge-IIoT	*CICIoT2023*	*BoT-IoT*
http.referer	syn_flag_number	flgs
ip.src_host	ack_flag_number	proto
tcp.flags.ack	urg_count	dur
mqtt.conflags	flow_duration	state
http.file_data	Srate	saddr
EdgIIoT_IScore	CICIoT2023_IScore	BoT-IoT_IScore

selected scores and combined features is less than the time required to classify recording using all features. The accuracy of detecting attacks with our model using the optimization process regularly increases as the recorded time decreases. Moreover, selecting important features allows us to reduce processing and detection time and deal with the massive volume of samples like 3668522 in BoT-IoT. In addition, the experimental study on three data proved the stability of the model and the effectiveness of this solution.

9.5 CONCLUSION AND FUTURE WORK

This research provided an optimized intrusion detection model for IoT security based on an anomaly detection technique to increase IDS accuracy and time performance. Our model has an excellent and reliable performance, as shown by the outcomes of the experiments on various datasets and the performance comparisons made. For future work, we want to test our model on real traffic.

REFERENCES

1. S. Sohail, D. Priya, B. Suparna, K. Manju, and S. Vimal, "HIIDS: hybrid intelligent intrusion detection system empowered with machine learning and metaheuristic algorithms for application in IoT based healthcare," *Microproc. Microsyst.*, vol. 2022, p. 104622, 2022.
2. J. A. Dhanke, R. Kamalraj, G. Ramesh, S. Sakthidasan, S. Sudhir, and K. Syed, "A machine learning based IoT for providing an intrusion detection system for security," *Microproc. Microsyst.*, vol. 82, p. 103741, 2021.
3. F. Tony Liu, K. Ming Ting, and Z.-H. Zhou, "Isolation forest," in *Proceedings of the 2008 Eighth IEEE International Conference on Data Mining*, pp. 413–422, Italy, 2008.
4. J. Gu and S. Lu, "An effective intrusion detection approach using SVM with naıve Bayes feature embedding," *Comput. Secur.*, vol. 103 , p. 102158, 2020.

Table 9.3 Comparison of detection between different datasets with and without iForest score

	Data	*Accuracy %*	*Precision%*	*Recall %*	*F1 Score%*	*FP*	*FN*	*Detection time in Sec*
Before isolation scores	Edge-IIoT	93.41	92.87	99.88	96.25	10230	157	0.02
	CICIoT2023	99.16	99.63	99.57	99.57	3426	4637	0.20
	BoT-IoT	99.99	99.99	99.99	-	138	3	0.87
After isolation scores	Edge-IIoT	99.99	99.99	100	99.99	4	0	0.028
	CICIoT2023	99.99	100	99.99	99.99	0	2	0.18
	BoT-IoT	100	100	100	100	0	0	0.74

5. A. A. Diro and N. Chilamkurti, "Distributed attack detection scheme using deep learning approach for Internet of Things," *Future Generat. Comput. Syst.*, vol. 82, pp. 761–768, 2017.
6. M. Douiba, S. Benkirane, A. Guezzaz, et al. "An improved anomaly detection model for IoT security using decision tree and gradient boosting," *J. Supercomput.*, vol. 79, pp. 3392–341, 2022.
7. A. Verma and V. Ranga, *Machine Learning Based Intrusion Detection Systems for IoT Applications,* Springer Science+Business Media, 2019.
8. N. Chaabouni, M. Mosbah, A. Zemmari, and C. Sauvignac, "A OneM2M intrusion detection and prevention system based on edge machine learning," in *IEEE/IFIP Network Operations and Management Symposium,* 2020.
9. F. Tang, B. Mao, Z. M. Fadlullah, J. Liu, and N. Kato, "ST-DeLTA: A novel spatial-temporal value network aided deep learning based intelligent network traffic control system," IEEE Transactions on Sustainable Computing, vol. 5, no. 4, pp. 568–580, 2019.
10. K. A. P. Da Costa, J. P. Papa, C. O. Lisboa, R. Munoz, and V. H. C. de Albuquerque, "Internet of Things: a survey on machine learning-based intrusion detection approaches||," *Comput. Netw.*, vol. 151, pp. 147–157, 2019.
11. S. Agrawal and J. Agrawal, "Survey on anomaly detection using data mining techniques||," *Proc. Comp. Sci.*, vol. 60, pp. 708–713, 2015.
12. I. Ullah and Q. H. Mahmoud, "Design and development of a deep learning-based model for anomaly detection in IoT networks," *IEEE Access*, vol. 9, pp. 103906–103926, 2021.
13. E. Hodo, X. Bellekens, A. Hamilton, P. L. Dubouilh, E. Iorkyase, C. Tachtatzis, and R. Atkinson, "Threat analysis of IoT networks using artificial neural network intrusion detection system||," in *International Symposium on Networks, Computers and Communications (ISNCC)*, 2016.
14. F. Hosseinpour, P. V. Amoli, J. Plosila, T. D. Hämäläinen, and H. Tenhunen "An intrusion detection system for fog computing and IoT-based logistic systems using a smart data approach," *Int. J. Digital Content Tech. Appl.*, vol. 10, pp. 34–46, 2016.
15. B. A. Tama and K. H. Rhee, "An in-depth experimental study of anomaly detection using gradient boosted machine||," *Neural Comput. Appl.*, vol. 31, pp. 955–965, 2017.
16. A. Veronika Dorogush, V. Ershove, and A. Gulin, "CatBoost: gradient boosting with categorical features support, *arXiv:1706.09516v5*, 2018.
17. S. Misra, P. V. Krishna, H. Agarwal, A, Saxena, and M. S. Obaidat, "A learning automata based solution for preventing distributed denial of service in internet of things||," in *IEEE International Conferences on Internet of Things, and Cyber, Physical and Social Computing*, 2011.
18. P. Kasinathan, C. Pastrone, M. A. Spirito, and M. Vinkovits, "Denial-of-service detection in 6LoWPAN based Internet of Things," in *IEEE 9th International Conference on Wireless and Mobile Computing, Networking and Communications*, 2013.
19. K. Sonar and H. Upadhyay, *An Approach to Secure Internet of Things against DDoS*, Springer Science+Business Media Singapore, 2016.

20. S. Prabavathy, K. Sundarakantham, and S. M. Shalinie, "Design of cognitive fog computing for intrusion detection in Internet of Things," *J. Commun. Netw.*, vol. 20, no. 3, pp. 291–298, June 2018.
21. D. Jin, Y. Lu, J. Qin, Z. Cheng, and Z. Mao, "SwiftIDS: Real-time intrusion detection system based on light GBM and parallel intrusion detection mechanism||," *Comp. Sec.*, vol. 97, p. 101984, 2020.
22. M. Al-kasassbeh, M. A. Abbadi, and A. M. Al-Bustanji, "LightGBM Algorithm for malware detection||," *Intell. Comput.*, vol. 3, pp. 391–403, 2020.
23. M. Mohy-eddine, A. Guezzaz, S. Benkirane, and M. Azrour, "An efficient network intrusion detection model for IoT security using K-NN classifier and feature selection," *Multimed. Tools Appl.*, vol. 82, pp. 23615–23633, 2023, doi: 10.1007/s11042-023-14795-2.
24. A. E. M. Eljialy, M. Y. Uddin, and S. Ahmad, "Novel framework for an intrusion detection system using multiple feature selection methods based on deep learning," *Tsinghua Sci. Technol.*, vol. 29, no. 4, pp. 948–958, Aug. 2024, doi: 10.26599/TST.2023.9010032.
25. Y. Peng, S. Xu, Q. Chen, W. Huang, and Y. Huang, "A novel popularity extraction method applied in session-based recommendation," *Tsinghua Sci. Technol.*, vol. 29, no. 4, pp. 971–984, Aug. 2024, doi: 10.26599/TST.2023.9010061.
26. C. Hazman, A. Guezzaz, S. Benkirane, and M. Azrour, "Enhanced IDS with deep learning for IoT-based smart cities security," *Tsinghua Sci. Technol.*, vol. 29, no. 4, pp. 929–947, Aug. 2024, doi: 10.26599/TST.2023.9010033.
27. P. Wang, Z. Zhu, Q. Chen, and W. Dai, "Text reasoning chain extraction for multi-hop question answering," *Tsinghua Sci. Technol.*, vol. 29, no. 4, pp. 959–970, Aug. 2024, doi: 10.26599/TST.2023.9010060.
28. M. Mohy-eddine, A. Guezzaz, S. Benkirane, and M. Azrour, "An intrusion detection model using election-based feature selection and K-NN," *Microprocess. Microsyst.*, p. 104966, Oct. 2023, doi: 10.1016/j.micpro.2023.104966.
29. C. Hazman, A. Guezzaz, S. Benkirane, and M. Azrour, "Toward an intrusion detection model for IoT-based smart environments," *Multimed. Tools Appl.*, vol. 83, pp. 62159–62180, Aug. 2023, doi: 10.1007/s11042-023-16436-0.
30. N. Meenakshi et al., "Efficient communication in wireless sensor networks using optimized energy efficient engroove leach clustering protocol," *Tsinghua Sci. Technol.*, vol. 29, no. 4, pp. 985–1001, Aug. 2024, doi: 10.26599/TST.2023.9010056.
31. H. Attou et al., "Towards an intelligent intrusion detection system to detect malicious activities in cloud computing," *Appl. Sci.*, vol. 13, no. 17, p. 9588, 2023.
32. S. Li, T. Cui, and W. Viriyasitavat, "Edge device fault probability based intelligent calculations for fault probability of smart systems," *Tsinghua Sci. Technol.*, vol. 29, no. 4, pp. 1023–1036, Aug. 2024, doi: 10.26599/TST.2023.9010085.

33. W. Liu, L. Zhou, S. Zhang, N. Luo, and M. Xu, "A new high-precision and lightweight detection model for illegal construction objects based on deep learning," *Tsinghua Sci. Technol.*, vol. 29, no. 4, pp. 1002–1022, Aug. 2024, doi: 10.26599/TST.2023.9010090.
34. H. Attou, A. Guezzaz, S. Benkirane, M. Azrour, and Y. Farhaoui, "Cloud-based intrusion detection approach using machine learning techniques," *Big Data Min. Anal.*, vol. 6, no. 3, pp. 311–320, 2023.
35. S. Amaouche et al., "FSCB-IDS: feature selection and minority class balancing for attacks detection in VANETS," *Appl. Sci.*, vol. 13, no. 13, p. 7488, 2023.
36. S. Amaouche, AzidineGuezzaz, S. Benkirane, and MouradeAzrour, "IDS-XGbFS: a smart intrusion detection system using XGboostwith recent feature selection for VANET safety," *Clust. Comput.*, vol. 27, no. , pp. 1–15, 2023.
37. M. Douiba, S. Benkirane, A. Guezzaz, and M. Azrour, "Anomaly detection model based on gradient boosting and decision tree for IoT environments security," *J. Reliab. Intell. Environ.*, vol. 9, no. 4, pp. 1–12, 2022.
38. M. Douiba, S. Benkirane, A. Guezzaz, and M. Azrour, "An improved anomaly detection model for IoT security using decision tree and gradient boosting," *J. Supercomput.*, vol. 79, no. 3, pp. 1–20, 2022.

Chapter 10

Efficient IoT intrusion detection with XGBoost and feature selection

Kamal Bella, Mouaad Mohy-Eddine, Azidine Guezzaz, Said Benkirane, and Mourade Azrour

10.1 INTRODUCTION

The Internet of Things (IoT) revolutionizes the way we interact with the world around us by connecting everyday objects to the Internet [1]. From smart homes to industrial automation, IoT has permeated various sectors, making life more convenient and efficient. However, this increased connectivity also presents significant security challenges [2]. IoT devices, often lacking robust security measures, have become attractive targets for cybercriminals [3]. They can exploit vulnerabilities in these devices to launch large-scale attacks, steal sensitive data, or gain unauthorized control [4]. Furthermore, the heterogeneous nature of IoT devices adds complexity to the security landscape, as different devices may require different security protocols. Thus, ensuring the security of IoT environments is a daunting task, necessitating innovative solutions like advanced intrusion detection systems (IDS) [5].

IDS play an indispensable role in securing IoT devices. As IoT devices become increasingly integrated into our daily lives, the potential impact of cyberattacks grows proportionally. These devices often lack robust built-in security measures, making them prime targets for cybercriminals. IDS serve as a crucial line of defense by monitoring network traffic for suspicious activities or policy violations and alerting system administrators [6]. By leveraging advanced machine learning techniques, IDS can improve their detection accuracy and efficiency, proactively protecting IoT devices from a wide range of cyber threats [7].

This chapter introduces a new intrusion detection method that utilizes advanced machine learning techniques to boost system efficiency and effectiveness [8]. The method begins by using random forest feature importance (RFFI) for feature ranking, enhancing model efficiency by eliminating less significant features [9]. Then, the XGBoost machine learning algorithm is applied to train the intrusion detection model. To further optimize the model, a recursive feature elimination (RFE) process is implemented, progressively removing one feature at a time until only one remains. The model that performs best with the fewest features is selected [10].

DOI: 10.1201/9781003587552-10

This chapter is organized as follows: Section 10.2 provides comprehensive background information on IoT, security, and IDS. In Section 10.3, the proposed XGBoost-based IDS model is detailed. Experimental results are presented in Section 10.4, followed by a conclusion and suggestions for future work in Section 10.5.

10.2 BACKGROUND AND RELATED WORKS

10.2.1 Background

IoT is a network of sensor-equipped objects sharing data over the Internet. It includes everyday items and industrial tools [8]. The architecture of IoT consists of sensors/devices, connectivity, data processing, and a user interface [9]. While IoT revolutionizes efficiency and connectivity, it also poses significant security challenges. The increasing number of connected devices broadens the risk of cyber threats. IoT devices often lack strong security measures, making a unified security protocol hard to apply. Thus, IoT security involves protecting the devices and their networks, presenting a complex challenge to information security professionals [10].

IDS are a critical component in the security architecture for IoT environments. With the ever-increasing proliferation of IoT devices in various sectors, ranging from health care to manufacturing and home automation, cyber threats have also escalated [11]. As these devices often lack in-built robust security measures, IDS for IoT have become crucial in mitigating cyberattacks [12].

IDS work by monitoring network traffic, identifying suspicious activities or policy violations and alerting system administrators about potential threats [13]. They can be categorized into two main types: network intrusion detection systems (NIDS) and host intrusion detection systems (HIDS). NIDS monitor network traffic for all devices on a network, while HIDS monitor activities on a specific device [14].

The effectiveness of IDS in IoT heavily relies on their ability to adapt to the dynamic nature of IoT environments and the variety of devices involved [15]. This is where machine learning techniques come into play. Machine learning algorithms can enhance the accuracy and efficiency of these systems by learning from past traffic data and improving their threat detection capabilities over time [16].

The model presented in this chapter uses XGBoost as our machine learning algorithm due to its high performance and efficiency in handling large datasets. XGBoost, which stands for eXtreme Gradient Boosting, is an algorithm known for its speed and performance. It has gained popularity for its use in winning solutions in machine learning competitions due to its ability to handle complex data structures and produce highly accurate predictive models. Furthermore, we incorporate feature selection in our methodology to enhance the efficiency of our model. Feature selection allows us to identify and utilize the most relevant features, reducing the computational cost, improving model performance, and providing better insights into the underlying process that generated the data.

10.2.2 Related works

Many intrusion detection methods have been proposed in the literature to combat computer security threats [17–40]. They can be broadly classified into two categories: signature-based intrusion detection systems (SIDS) and anomaly-based intrusion detection systems (AIDS). This section reviews prior research on machine learning–based IDS in IoT security, providing context for our approach .

Khoei et al. [17] compared three ensemble learning techniques (bagging-based, boosting-based, and stacking-based) and three traditional machine learning techniques (K-nearest neighbor, decision tree, and naive Bayes) for intrusion detection systems. They used the CICDDos 2019 benchmark for training and evaluation. The results showed that the stacking-based ensemble learning techniques performed best across all evaluation metrics.

Ennaji et al. [18] developed an IDS using machine learning to cope with rising cyber threats. Leveraging ensemble learning techniques and selecting ten critical features, they used various machine learning classifiers to design five different models. They conducted experiments on the NSL-KDD dataset. The results showed robust performance and strong network security, with accuracy exceeding 99% for all models.

Abirami et al. [19] developed a machine learning–based IDS, LSSVM-IDS, achieving 95% accuracy on datasets like KDD Cup 99, NSK-KDD, and Kyoto 2006+. They used feature selection for data dimensionality reduction and maintained accuracy with an ensemble learning algorithm on the UNSW-NB15 dataset.

Verma and Ranga [20] proposed an ensemble learning–based network IDS (ELNIDS) for detecting IoT network routing attacks. Four ensemble machine learning classifiers were used: Boosted Trees, Bagged Trees, Subspace Discriminant, and RUSBoosted Trees. The RPL-NIDDS17 dataset was tested, containing various routing attacks. Boosted Trees had the highest accuracy (94.5%), Subspace Discriminant the lowest (77.8%). RUSBoosted Trees achieved the highest area under ROC value (0.98). All classifiers performed adequately.

Mohy-eddine et al. [21] have suggested a useful IDS system incorporating machine learning using K-NN, employing a number of distinct feature extraction approaches to pick ten valuable attributes. Their new approach considerably enhanced the performance, decreased the time taken for prediction, and showed that the selection of features actually does help to boost the overall performance of the IDS. The results of their work were assessed by means of the Bot-IoT dataset.

Attou et al. [22] used a combined graphical visualization solution and random forest (RF) for cloud computing security in order to identify intrusions by means of a reduced set of two features. RF performed better than DNN, decision trees (DT), and SVM in predicting and classifying attack types. Nevertheless, the recall performance using NSL-KDD data remains suboptimal.

Mohy-eddine et al. [23] designed a machine learning–assisted IDS for the security of Industrial IoT (IIoT) edge computing. They employed Pearson's correlation coefficient (PCC) and isolation forest (IF) methods for both computing efficiency and training. Feature engineering enhanced model accuracy and detection rates, achieving a 100% detection rate and 99.99% accuracy on the Bot-IoT dataset. Compared to other models, that approach showed some distinct advantages.

Roy et al. [24] introduced a two-layer hierarchical IDS model for IoT networks, powered by the Fog-Cloud backbone. The fog layer employs a direct neural network (FNN) along with extra capability from a stored autoencoder to provide bitwise clustering. On the other hand, the cloud layer utilizes a more complex neural network to manage multiclass categorization. Such a model detects various kinds of intrusions successfully and improves the accuracy of previous IDS solutions.

Attou et al. [25] has developed a novel intrusion detection solution for a cloud application by combining machine learning and deep learning algorithms. They have used RF for feature extraction and radial basis function neural network (RBFNN) technology for intrusion detection. This approach achieved high accuracy of over 94% and false-negative rates of less than 0.0831%, demonstrating the model's ability to accurately identify and classify intrusions.

Mohy-Eddine et al. [26] presented an IDS for IIoT networks by means of Random Forest and PCC to classify and choose features accordingly. In addition, the authors used IF for outlier identification. Both PCC and IF were used interchangeably. The result was an effective resolution of the imbalance in the Bot-IoT dataset, as well as strong outcomes on the NF-UNSW-NB15-v2 dataset.

10.3 PROPOSED APPROACH

Our approach to enhancing intrusion detection in IoT environments relies on advanced machine learning techniques for optimal efficiency and accuracy, integrating RFFI, XGBoost, and RFE.

First, the system uses RFFI to rank dataset features by importance, crucial for efficient model refinement. This step allows for the removal of less important features, reducing computational cost and complexity.

Next, we employ XGBoost, a highly efficient algorithm known for its speed and performance, to train our intrusion detection model. XGBoost is particularly suited to our purposes due to its ability to handle complex data structures and produce highly accurate predictive models.

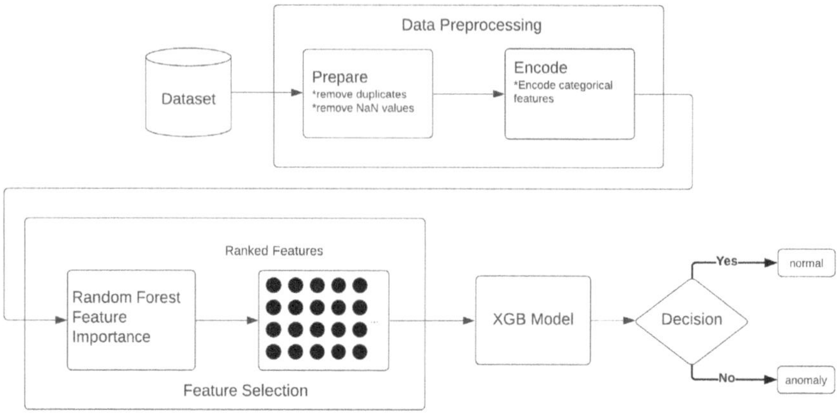

Figure 10.1 Proposed approach

Finally, we implement RFE to further optimize the model. This method involves progressively removing less important features until only the most important one remains. The model selected is based on performance with the fewest features.

Figure 10.1 visually illustrates this process, starting with dataset feature selection using RFFI. The ranked list of features eliminates less significant ones, and the remaining features are put into the XGBoost algorithm for model training. After training, the model undergoes RFE for further optimization, resulting in the final, optimized intrusion detection model.

This approach ensures an efficient and effective intrusion detection system, accurately identifying potential threats in IoT environments.

10.4 EXPERIMENTAL STUDY

This section outlines our intrusion detection system testing setup and results. We detail the dataset used and evaluation metrics employed.

10.4.1 NSL-KDD dataset

The NSL-KDD dataset, an enhanced version of KDD Cup 99, is widely used for IDS evaluation. It includes diverse network traffic and simulated attacks like DoS, Probe, U2R, and R2L. With 140,000+ records and 41 features, it is robust and varied, making it an ideal benchmark for our model.

10.4.2 Evaluation metrics

We assessed our system using key performance metrics: accuracy, precision, true positive rate, false positive rate, and F1 score. Accuracy serves as a universal benchmark, facilitating comparison with other IDS and datasets. In this chapter, we use accuracy to compare our results with existing IDS literature.

- Accuracy: $ACC = \frac{TP + TN}{TP + TN + FP + FN}$
- Precision: $PR = \frac{TP}{TP + FP}$
- True positive rate: $TPR = \frac{TP}{TP + FN}$
- False positive rate: $FPR = \frac{FP}{FP + TN}$
- F1 score: $F1Score = 2 \times \frac{PR \times TPR}{PR + TPR}$

10.4.3 Discussion of results

In this section, we discuss the results of our proposed approach, analyzing its effectiveness and efficiency in detecting intrusions. We combine RFFI, XGBoost, and RFE for a sophisticated intrusion detection system.

The experimental study evaluated our system using the NSL-KDD dataset in a controlled environment. We used accuracy, precision, true positive rate, false positive rate, and the F1 score as evaluation metrics.

Figure 10.2 shows the correlation between the number of features used and the system's accuracy. Initially trained on all 41 features, the system's accuracy increases with more features but saturates at around ten features.

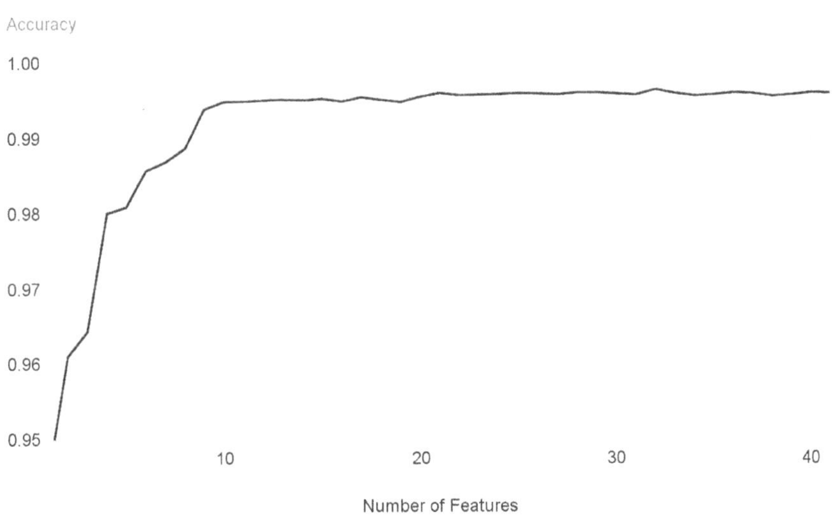

Figure 10.2 The evolution of accuracy with the increase of the number of features

This suggests that only the top ten features are necessary for optimal performance, reducing unnecessary complexity and computational cost. Feature ranking and elimination enhance system efficiency without compromising effectiveness.

In conclusion, our approach using RFFI, XGBoost, and RFE proves effective for intrusion detection in IoT environments. Future work could explore different machine learning algorithms or feature selection techniques for further performance improvement.

As depicted in Figure 10.2, our model's accuracy increases as the number of features increases until it reaches a saturation point at around ten features. Beyond this, the inclusion of additional features does not significantly improve accuracy, implying that these ten most significant features are sufficient for optimal performance. Therefore, we chose these ten features as the sweet spot for our model. This approach reduces unnecessary complexity and computational cost while maintaining high detection efficiency. Presented in Table 10.1 is the confusion matrix and evaluation for the model trained with these ten selected features in Table 10.2.

The system's performance was evaluated using various metrics, such as accuracy, precision, true positive rate, false positive rate, and the F1 score. The accuracy of the model was an impressive 99.47%, indicating that it correctly predicted the majority of the instances. The precision of the model, which measures the proportion of true positive observations to the total predicted positives, was slightly higher at 99.58%. This suggests that the model was very effective at correctly identifying positive instances.

The true positive rate, also known as sensitivity or recall, was 99.36%. This rate measures the proportion of actual positives that were correctly identified. Therefore, the model was very good at detecting positive instances. The false positive rate, which measures the proportion of negatives that were incorrectly identified as positive, was extremely low at 0.41%. This indicates that the model very rarely made the mistake of identifying a negative instance as positive.

The F1 score, which is a measure of a test's accuracy that considers both the precision and the recall, was 99.47%. This high score suggests that the

Table 10.1 Confusion matrix for the 20 features model

TP	*FP*	*TN*	*FN*
99.36%	0.41%	99.58%	0.63%

Table 10.2 XGBoost model evaluation using the ten best features

Accuracy	*Precision*	*TPR*	*FPR*	*F1Score*
99.47%	99.58%	99.36%	0.41%	99.47%

model was very good at identifying positive instances without producing many false positives or false negatives.

Overall, the results of the experimental study reveal a highly efficient and effective intrusion detection system. The integration of RFFI, XGBoost, and RFE in the proposed model demonstrates a significant enhancement in intrusion detection in IoT environments. The model's high accuracy, precision, and recall, along with a low false positive rate, indicate its capability to identify potential threats accurately. However, future research could explore the impact of using different machine learning algorithms or feature selection techniques on the performance of the intrusion detection system.

10.5 CONCLUSION AND FUTURE WORKS

In conclusion, the proposed intrusion detection system, integrating random forest feature importance (RFFI), XGBoost, and recursive feature elimination (RFE), has been demonstrated to be highly effective in detecting intrusions in IoT environments. The system uses RFFI to rank features, subsequently eliminating less significant features to improve efficiency. The XGBoost algorithm is then utilized to train the model on the most significant features. Finally, the RFE process optimizes the model by progressively eliminating features until only the most important ones remain.

Through this methodology, the system achieved an impressive accuracy of 99.47% in intrusion detection, using only 10 out of the initial 41 features in the NSL-KDD dataset. These results attest to the effectiveness and efficiency of the proposed system and its potential to significantly enhance the security of IoT environments.

Looking ahead, future research may explore the integration of other machine learning algorithms or feature selection techniques to further optimize the system. Assessing the model's performance on other datasets, and against different types of cyberattacks, could also provide valuable insights for its continuous improvement. Furthermore, as the IoT landscape evolves, adapting the model to incorporate emerging threat patterns and unique characteristics of new IoT devices would be an important direction for future work.

REFERENCES

1. S. Dargaoui et al., "An overview of the security challenges in IoT environment," in *Advanced Technology for Smart Environment and Energy*, J. Mabrouki, A. Mourade, A. Irshad, and S. A. Chaudhry, Eds., in *Environmental Science and Engineering*, Cham: Springer International Publishing, 2023, pp. 151–160. doi: 10.1007/978-3-031-25662-2_13.
2. I. Lee and K. Lee, "The Internet of Things (IoT): applications, investments, and challenges for enterprises," *Bus Horiz.*, vol. 58, pp. 431–440, 2015.

3. J. Mohanty, S. Mishra, S. Patra, B. Pati, and C. R. Panigrahi, "IoT security, challenges, and solutions: a review," in *Progress in Advanced Computing and Intelligent Engineering*. Singapore: Springer, 2021, pp. 493–504.
4. J. Cynthia, H. Parveen Sultana, M. N. Saroja, and J. Senthil, "Security protocols for IoT," in *Ubiquitous Computing and Computing Security of IoT*, N. Jeyanthi, A. Abraham, and H. Mcheick, Eds., Cham: Springer International Publishing, 2019, pp. 1–28.
5. A. Alhowaide, I. Alsmadi, and J. Tang, "Ensemble detection model for IoT IDS," *Internet of Things*, vol. 16, pp. 100435, 2021.
6. K. Tsiknas, D. Taketzis, K. Demertzis, and C. Skianis, "Cyber threats to industrial IoT: a survey on attacks and countermeasures," *IoT*, vol. 2, pp. 163–186, 2021.
7. M. R. Ayyagari, N. Kesswani, M. Kumar, and K. Kumar, "Intrusion detection techniques in network environment: a systematic review," *Wireless Networks*, vol. 27, pp. 1269–1285, 2021.
8. D. Sehrawat, and N. S. Gill, "Smart sensors: analysis of different types of IoT sensors," in *2019 3rd International Conference on Trends in Electronics and Informatics (ICOEI)*, IEEE. 2019, pp. 523–528.
9. S. A. Al-Qaseemi, H. A. Almulhim, M. F. Almulhim, and S. R. Chaudhry, "IoT architecture challenges and issues: lack of standardization," in *2016 Future Technologies Conference (FTC)*, IEEE. 2016, pp. 731–738.
10. V. Hassija, V. Chamola, V. Saxena, D. Jain, P. Goyal, and B. Sikdar, "A survey on IoT security: application areas, security threats, and solution architectures," *IEEE Access*, vol. 7, pp. 82721–82743, 2019.
11. F. Meneghello, M. Calore, D. Zucchetto, M. Polese, and A. Zanella, "IoT: internet of threats? A survey of practical security vulnerabilities in real IoT devices," *IEEE Int. Things J.*, vol. 6, pp. 8182–8201, 2019.
12. N. Mishra, and S. Pandya, "Internet of Things applications, security challenges, attacks, intrusion detection, and future visions: a systematic review," *IEEE Access*, vol. 9, pp. 59353–59377, 2021.
13. A. Khraisat, I. Gondal, P. Vamplew, and J. Kamruzzaman, "Survey of intrusion detection systems: techniques, datasets and challenges," *Cybersecurity*, vol. 2, pp. 1–22, 2019.
14. R. Samrin, and D. Vasumathi, "Review on anomaly based network intrusion detection system," in *2017 International Conference on Electrical, Electronics, Communication, Computer, and Optimization Techniques (ICEECCOT)*, IEEE. 2017, pp. 141–147.
15. M. F. Elrawy, A. I. Awad, and H. F. A. Hamed, "Intrusion detection systems for IoT-based smart environments: a survey," *J. Cloud Comput.*, vol. 7, pp. 1–20, 2018.
16. T. Saranya, S. Sridevi, C. Deisy, T. D. Chung, and M. K. A. A. Khan, "Performance analysis of machine learning algorithms in intrusion detection system: a review," *Proc. Comput. Sci.*, vol. 171, pp. 1251–1260, 2020.
17. T. T. Khoei, G. Aissou, W. C. Hu, and N. Kaabouch, "Ensemble learning methods for anomaly intrusion detection system in smart grid," in *2021 IEEE International Conference on Electro Information Technology (EIT)*, IEEE. 2021, pp. 129–135.

18. S. Ennaji, N. El Akkad, and K. Haddouch, "A powerful ensemble learning approach for improving network intrusion detection system (NIDS)," in *2021 Fifth International Conference on Intelligent Computing in Data Sciences (ICDS)*, IEEE. 2021, pp. 1–6.
19. M. S. Abirami, U. Yash, and S. Singh, "Building an ensemble learning based algorithm for improving intrusion detection system," in *Artificial Intelligence and Evolutionary Computations in Engineering Systems*, Singapore: Springer, 2020, pp. 635–649.
20. A. Verma, and V. Ranga, "ELNIDS: ensemble learning based network intrusion detection system for RPL based Internet of Things," in *2019 4th International Conference on Internet of Things: Smart Innovation and Usages (IoT-SIU)*, IEEE. 2019, pp. 1–6.
21. M. Mohy-eddine, A. Guezzaz, S. Benkirane, and M. Azrour, "An intrusion detection model using election-based feature selection and K-NN," *Microprocess. Microsyst.*, p. 104966, Oct. 2023, doi: 10.1016/j.micpro.2023.104966.
22. H. Attou, A. Guezzaz, S. Benkirane, M. Azrour, and Y. Farhaoui, "Cloud-based intrusion detection approach using machine learning techniques," *Big Data Min. Anal.*, vol. 6, no. 3, pp. 311–320, 2023.
23. M. Mohy-Eddine, S. Benkirane, A. Guezzaz, and M. Azrour, "Random forest-based IDS for IIoT edge computing security using ensemble learning for dimensionality reduction," *Int. J. Embedded Syst.*, vol. 15, no. 6, pp. 467–474, 2022.
24. S. Roy, J. Li, and Y. Bai, "A two-layer fog-cloud intrusion detection model for IoT networks," *Internet of Things*, vol. 19, p. 100557, 2022, doi: 10.1016/j.iot.2022.100557.
25. H. Attou *et al.*, "Towards an intelligent intrusion detection system to detect malicious activities in cloud computing," *Appl. Sci.*, vol. 13, no. 17, p. 9588, 2023.
26. M. Mohy-Eddine, A. Guezzaz, S. Benkirane, M. Azrour, and Y. Farhaoui, "An ensemble learning based intrusion detection model for industrial IoT security," *Big Data Min. Anal.*, vol. 6, no. 3, pp. 273–287, Sep. 2023, doi: 10.26599/BDMA.2022.9020032.
27. M. Mohy-eddine, A. Guezzaz, S. Benkirane, and M. Azrour, "An efficient network intrusion detection model for IoT security using K-NN classifier and feature selection," *Multimed. Tools Appl.*, vol. 82, no. 15,pp. 23615–23633. 2023, doi: 10.1007/s11042-023-14795-2.
28. A. E. M. Eljialy, M. Y. Uddin, and S. Ahmad, "Novel framework for an intrusion detection system using multiple feature selection methods based on deep learning," *Tsinghua Sci. Technol.*, vol. 29, no. 4, pp. 948–958, Aug. 2024, doi: 10.26599/TST.2023.9010032.
29. Y. Peng, S. Xu, Q. Chen, W. Huang, and Y. Huang, "A novel popularity extraction method applied in session-based recommendation," *Tsinghua Sci. Technol.*, vol. 29, no. 4, pp. 971–984, Aug. 2024, doi: 10.26599/TST.2023.9010061.
30. C. Hazman, A. Guezzaz, S. Benkirane, and M. Azrour, "Enhanced IDS with deep learning for IoT-based smart cities security," *Tsinghua Sci. Technol.*, vol. 29, no. 4, pp. 929–947, Aug. 2024, doi: 10.26599/TST.2023.9010033.

31. P. Wang, Z. Zhu, Q. Chen, and W. Dai, "Text reasoning chain extraction for multi-hop question answering," *Tsinghua Sci. Technol.*, vol. 29, no. 4, pp. 959–970, Aug. 2024, doi: 10.26599/TST.2023.9010060.
32. C. Hazman, A. Guezzaz, S. Benkirane, and M. Azrour, "Toward an intrusion detection model for IoT-based smart environments," *Multimed. Tools Appl.*, Aug. vol. 83, no. 22, pp. 62159–62180, 2023, doi: 10.1007/s11042-023-16436-0.
33. N. Meenakshi et al., "Efficient communication in wireless sensor networks using optimized energy efficient engroove leach clustering protocol," *Tsinghua Sci. Technol.*, vol. 29, no. 4, pp. 985–1001, Aug. 2024, doi: 10.26599/TST.2023.9010056.
34. S. Li, T. Cui, and W. Viriyasitavat, "Edge device fault probability based intelligent calculations for fault probability of smart systems," *Tsinghua Sci. Technol.*, vol. 29, no. 4, pp. 1023–1036, Aug. 2024, doi: 10.26599/TST.2023.9010085.
35. W. Liu, L. Zhou, S. Zhang, N. Luo, and M. Xu, "A new high-precision and lightweight detection model for illegal construction objects based on deep learning," *Tsinghua Sci. Technol.*, vol. 29, no. 4, pp. 1002–1022, Aug. 2024, doi: 10.26599/TST.2023.9010090.
36. S. Amaouche et al., "FSCB-IDS: Feature selection and minority class balancing for attacks detection in VANETS," *Appl. Sci.*, vol. 13, no. 13, p. 7488, 2023.
37. S. Amaouche, AzidineGuezzaz, S. Benkirane, and MouradeAzrour, "IDS-XGbFS: a smart intrusion detection system using XGboostwith recent feature selection for VANET safety," *Clust. Comput.*, vol. 27, no. 3, pp. 3521–3535, 2023.
38. M. Douiba, S. Benkirane, A. Guezzaz, and M. Azrour, "Anomaly detection model based on gradient boosting and decision tree for IoT environments security," *J. Reliab. Intell. Environ.*, vol. 9, no. 4, pp. 421–432, 2022.
39. M. Douiba, S. Benkirane, A. Guezzaz, and M. Azrour, "An improved anomaly detection model for IoT security using decision tree and gradient boosting," *J. Supercomput.*, vol. 79, no. 3, pp. 3392–3411, 2022.
40. K. Bella et al., "An efficient intrusion detection system for IoT security using CNN decision forest," *PeerJ Comput. Sci.*, vol. 10, p. e2290, Sep. 2024, doi: 10.7717/peerj-cs.2290.

Chapter 11

A monitoring system with deep learning for IoT smart environments security

Mouaad Mohy-eddine, Azidine Guezzaz, Said Benkirane, Mourade Azrour, and Kamal Bella

11.1 INTRODUCTION

The rise of the Internet of Things (IoT) has sparked a major shift in various fields, like making cities smarter, improving farming with agriculture 4.0 [1, 2], managing energy better with smart grids [3], and transforming industries with the Industrial IoT (IIoT) [4]. However, as more IoT devices connect, security has become a big concern [5]. So many devices are out there now that hackers can exploit weaknesses in them, creating an urgent need for better security [6]. Traditional security tools like firewalls and antivirus software are struggling to keep up, especially against new, sophisticated attacks [7]. To tackle these threats, a move has been made toward more advanced intrusion detection systems (IDS), particularly anomaly-based systems [8], which use machine learning (ML) and deep learning (DL) to spot unusual activities and protect data.

Furthermore, the desire to improve security in the IoT ecosystem has prompted players to work together. Industry leaders, researchers, and politicians are working together to establish standardized security protocols, increase information exchange, and develop new risk-mitigation solutions [1, 2]. As the Internet of Things penetrates every area of our lives, protecting its security becomes increasingly important. By embracing the latest innovations and encouraging collaboration, we can safely navigate the growing danger landscape and realize the full promise of the IoT [7].

Our study focuses on enhancing security in the realm of the IoT by developing a network IDS (NIDS). Our approach utilizes the chi-square test (chi-2) to select relevant features, thereby boosting system efficiency without compromising security. We employ an autoencoder for outlier detection to mitigate its potential negative impact on system performance, and a radial basis function neural network (RBFNN) for classifying events as benign or potential attacks. To assess the effectiveness of our model, we utilized the NF-ToN-IoT and NF-Bot-IoT datasets. Our findings demonstrate the effectiveness of our proposed model.

The chapter is structured as follows: Section 11.2 provides a review of IoT and IDS backgrounds, highlighting relevant previous works. Section

DOI: 10.1201/9781003587552-11

11.3 explains the architecture and methodology of our model, incorporating RBFNN, WOA, and autoencoder techniques. In Section 11.4, we meticulously present and evaluate the results, examining the model's ability to enhance IoT security. Finally, the conclusion summarizes the study's findings and emphasizes its contributions to IoT security.

11.2 BACKGROUND AND RELATED WORKS

IoT encompasses a myriad of interconnected objects endowed with sensors, software, and diverse technologies, enabling seamless data communication and autonomous interaction within their surroundings [9]. These devices range from common household appliances and wearable devices to sophisticated industrial machinery, forming an extensive network for data collection and exchange [10]. The applications of IoT are far-reaching, spanning domains such as daily living, health care, industry, urban governance, and agriculture. In the realm of smart home automation, IoT technologies streamline tasks and promote energy conservation, fostering convenience and sustainability [9]. The applications of IoT span various domains, enhancing daily living, health care, industrial operations, urban management, and agriculture. Smart home automation streamlines tasks and conserves energy, while remote patient monitoring and wearable devices revolutionize health care. The IIoT [11] optimizes production and supply chains. Smart city initiatives improve transportation, waste management, and public safety. Agriculture 4.0 modernizes farming through advanced monitoring and management techniques [1, 2].

However, the rapid proliferation of IoT devices presents significant security challenges [12]. Data privacy concerns arise from extensive data collection, risking unauthorized access and exploitation [13]. Weak authentication and default credentials leave many IoT devices vulnerable to breaches [14]. The absence of standardized security protocols and the diversity of devices further compound vulnerabilities, including physical weaknesses [13].

Addressing these multifaceted security concerns demands a concerted effort from stakeholders across industries. Collaborative endeavors to establish robust security standards, implement stringent authentication measures, and fortify device resilience are imperative to safeguarding the integrity and confidentiality of IoT ecosystems. Only through proactive measures and collective vigilance can we harness the full potential of IoT technologies while mitigating associated security risks [12].

Effective security measures are imperative to mitigate these risks. IDS are crucial for securing IoT environments and analyzing network traffic and device behavior for anomalies [15]. IDSs come in three main types [16]: Signature-based IDS (SIDS), which matches network packets against a database of known attacks; anomaly-based IDS (AIDS), offering flexibility against evolving threats like zero-day attacks; and hybrid IDS (HIDS), combining SIDS and AIDS for improved detection rates.

Supervised classifiers are commonly employed in AIDS development, leveraging ML and DL algorithms trained on large datasets of normal IoT device activity [17]. Feature engineering enhances the quality of input data, enabling algorithms to differentiate between security breaches and legitimate device activities. By selecting, manipulating, and refining raw data, feature engineering uncovers hidden patterns and insights critical for effective anomaly detection [18].

Related works on IDS using ML, DL, and feature engineering methods include the following.

Mohy-eddine et al. [19] tackled IoT security by integrating an anomaly-based intrusion detection system (AIDS), with a focus on preserving data privacy in sensor interactions. They developed a specialized NIDS employing K-nearest neighbors (K-NN) and feature selection techniques such as principal component analysis (PCA), genetic algorithm (GA), and statistical tests. This enhanced model demonstrates improved accuracy, reduced false alarms, and faster detection times. Validated on the Bot-IoT dataset, the model achieved a remarkable 97% Matthew's correlation coefficient (MCC) score, indicating robust performance. With an outstanding 99.99% accuracy (ACC), the model significantly reduces training time from 21,696 to 102 seconds, utilizing only a subset of five features. This advancement marks a notable improvement in IoT security, surpassing previous models in both performance and efficiency. In their study [20], Panda et al. tackled cybersecurity vulnerabilities in IoT networks, particularly against botnet attacks. They proposed a combination of ML and DL techniques along with feature engineering for effective detection and protection. By utilizing the UNSW-NB15 dataset, they applied K-Medoid sampling and scatter search-based feature engineering to refine the data for optimal classification. Evaluation of various ML methods (JChaid, A2DE, HGC) and DL methods (DMLP, CNN) revealed the superior performance of the scatter search-based DMLP classifier. This classifier achieved perfect ACC, precision, recall, and F1-score, with remarkably low computational complexity, training in 4.7 seconds and testing in 0.61 seconds. These results signify significant advancements in IoT security solutions. Musleh et al. [21] investigated ML-based IDS for IoT security, emphasizing the significance of feature extraction algorithms. Various algorithms, including image filters and transfer learning models like VGG-16 and DenseNet, were evaluated alongside ML methods. Using the IEEE Dataport dataset, the combined approach of VGG-16 with stacking showcased the highest ACC at 98.3%. This fusion of models significantly demonstrates the potential to enhance IoT security through sophisticated intrusion detection techniques. In their work [22], Saba et al. introduced a convolutional neural network (CNN)–based IDS tailored for IoT security, utilizing the capabilities of DL to identify

Table 11.1 Related works summary

Contribution	*Year*	*Dataset*	*Model*	*ACC (%)*
Mohy-eddine et al. [19]	2023	Bot-IoT	KNN	99.99
Panda et al. [20]	2021	UNSW-NB15	JChaid	100
Musleh et al. [21]	2023	IEEE Dataport	ML	N/A
Saba et al. [22]	2022	NID	CNN	99.51
		BoT-IoT		92.85
Mohy-eddine et al. [6]	2024	NF-Bot-IoT	RBFNN	99.25
		NF-ToN-IoT		96.92

anomalies in network traffic. By utilizing the NID and BoT-IoT datasets, the proposed model achieved high ACC scores of 99.51% and 92.85%, respectively. It effectively scrutinizes IoT traffic, swiftly detecting intrusions and abnormal behaviors. This approach harnesses the potential of IoT, offering a promising solution to bolster security in IoT environments, demonstrating advanced anomaly detection capabilities through CNN-based methodologies. Mohy-eddine et al. [6] propose a NIDS tailored for smart agriculture environments using RBFNN. To optimize performance, crowd wisdom tree-based machine learning techniques are employed for feature selection, alongside a single-class support vector machine for outlier detection. Evaluation of NF-Bot-IoT and NF-ToN-IoT datasets shows the model achieving high ACC (99.25%, 90.05%) and MCC (82.97%, 96.92%), notably addressing the class imbalance in the NF-Bot-IoT dataset. This framework offers a robust solution to mitigate security vulnerabilities in IoT-driven agriculture, highlighting the potential for enhanced agricultural security through advanced intrusion detection systems (Table 11.1).

11.3 OUR CONTRIBUTION

Constructing an IDS involves several key stages: data acquisition, pre-processing, decision-making, and response mechanisms. In our proposed model, particular emphasis was placed on the pre-processing phase. We utilized the chi-2 to identify critical features and employed an autoencoder to detect and eliminate outliers within the datasets.

To streamline our model and improve its efficiency, we utilized the chi-2 as a feature reduction technique. This approach aids in convergence, reduces computational costs, and enhances performance without sacrificing critical data. Additionally, we employed an autoencoder to identify outliers within the NF-Bot-IoT and NF-ToN-IoT datasets, thereby fortifying the model. By eliminating these outliers, we anticipate a significant enhancement in our model's performance. We implemented these techniques in a complementary manner. These datasets will be used to validate our model and investigate the impact of feature engineering order on its performance.

Feature engineering involves the process of selecting, modifying, and transforming raw data into usable features for ML and DL algorithms. In our approach, we utilized the chi-2 and autoencoder techniques to clean, filter, and select data and features. The chi-2 was employed to identify the most important features while retaining critical data, ensuring optimal performance. Conversely, the autoencoder was utilized to detect and eliminate outliers, enhancing the overall quality of the dataset. Through these methods, we refined the data to facilitate effective analysis and modeling.

The chi-2 is a statistical test used to detect whether two categorical variables are associated or independent. It is most commonly used for data organized in a contingency table, where the rows and columns reflect multiple groups for the variables under consideration. The chi-2 test for independence is frequently used to evaluate the relationship between two category variables. The null hypothesis (H0) states that the variables are independent, whereas the alternative hypothesis (H1) argues that they are related.

The objective of using chi-2 for the feature selection is to pick features heavily dependent on the target variable. When two features are independent, the observed count is close to the predicted count, and hence the chi-2 value is smaller. A high chi-2 score suggests that the independence hypothesis is false. Simply said, the greater the chi-2 value, the more reliant the feature is on the target and can be chosen for model training.

An autoencoder is a type of artificial neural network used in unsupervised learning. It consists of two main components: an encoder and a decoder, working together to reconstruct the input data. The primary goal of an autoencoder is to learn a compressed representation of the input data, capturing its essential features while minimizing redundancy.

Outliers in the autoencoder context are cases that have much higher reconstruction errors than the rest of the data.

Using this strategy, the autoencoder effectively detects outliers as cases with extremely high reconstruction errors, allowing for outlier identification within a dataset.

In the decision-making phase, the RBFNN classifier plays a pivotal role. RBFNN is a type of artificial neural network (ANN). Unlike traditional neural networks, RBFNN uses radial basis functions (RBFs) as activation functions. These functions learn the underlying patterns represented by Gaussian curves. The network combines the inputs' RBFs and neuron parameters to make decisions. Unlike most neural network architectures with multiple layers and non-linear activation functions, RBFNN typically consists of an input layer, a hidden layer, and an output layer.

11.4 EXPERIMENTAL STUDY

Our experiments were carried out on an Apple M1 PRO Chip, with 32GB of RAM and Sonoma 14.4.1 (c).

11.4.1 Datasets and used metrics

We utilized two datasets, NF-Bot-IoT and NF-ToN-IoT, for training and evaluating our model. These datasets were derived from the Bot-IoT and ToN-IoT datasets, respectively. In the NF-Bot-IoT collection, there are a total of 600,100 data points, with 586,241 classifieds as attacks and 13,859 as normal instances. Meanwhile, the NF-ToN-IoT dataset comprises 1,379,274 cases, with 1,108,995 attack instances and 270,279 benign cases (Table 11.2).

$$\text{ACC}: \frac{\text{TP} + \text{TN}}{\text{TP} + \text{TN} + \text{FP} + \text{FN}}$$

We evaluated our model using accuracy, which is defined as the ratio of correctly identified instances to all occurrences in the dataset.

$$\text{MCC}: \frac{\text{TPxTN} - \text{FPxFN}}{\sqrt{(\text{TP} + \text{TN})(\text{TP} + \text{FP})(\text{TN} + \text{FP})(\text{TN} + \text{FN})}}$$

The MCC is a robust measure as it takes into account all four categories of the confusion matrix: True Negatives (TN), True Positives (TP), False Negatives (FN), and False Positives (FP). The MCC yields a perfect prediction when it equals +1, an average prediction when it equals 0, and an inverse prediction when it equals -1.

11.4.2 Results and discussion

Table 11.3 presents a summary of our approach results, comparing the ACC and MCC across different variants of the NF-Bot-IoT and NF-ToN-IoT.

Table 11.3 and Figure 11.1 provide a comparison of the NF-Bot-IoT dataset based on its ACC and MCC. The highest ACC of 98.49% was achieved when selecting a subset of features after removing outliers. Moreover, its ability to distinguish between positive and negative instances, as indicated

Table 11.2 Datasets description

Dataset	*Normal*	*Attack*	*Total*
NF-Bot-IoT	13,859	586,241	600,100
NF-ToN-IoT	270,279	1,108,995	1,379,274

Table 11.3 Our models' results

	Dataset	*ACC (%)*	*MCC (%)*
NF-Bot-IoT	Full	98.08	60.44
	Selected	98.43	77.71
	Outliers	98.95	44.43
	Outliers & Selection	98.49	79.61
	Selection & Outliers	99.84	87.92
NF-ToN-IoT	Full	96.17	87.46
	Selected	97.03	89.64
	Outliers	97.91	91.14
	Outliers & Selection	96.29	87.50
	Selection & Outliers	98.64	92.53

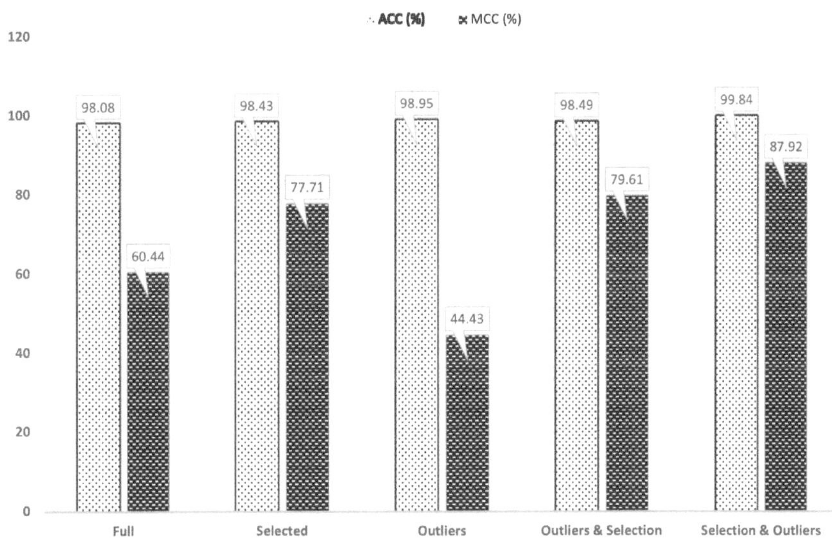

Figure 11.1 ACC and MCC results on NF-Bot-IoT dataset

by the MCC, was only 79.61%, suggesting outstanding performance. Despite the dataset's imbalance, our model demonstrated improved performance with an MCC of 87.92% when selecting the most relevant features before removing outliers. This enhancement led to an increase in ACC from 98.08% to 99.84%. However, solely removing outliers negatively impacted our model's distinguishability with 44.43% MCC.

Table 11.3 and Figure 11.2 provide a comparison of the NF-Bot-IoT dataset based on its ACC and MCC. The highest ACC of 98.49% was achieved when selecting a subset of features after removing outliers. Moreover, its

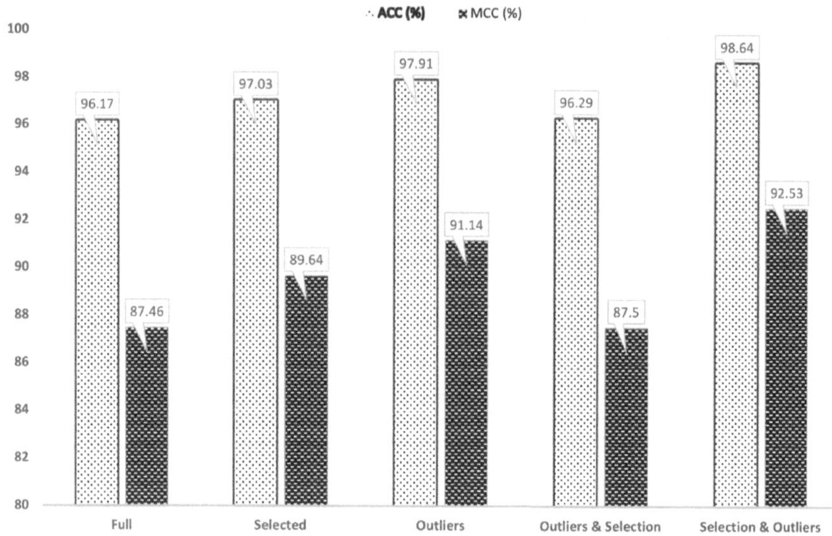

Figure 11.2 ACC and MCC results on NF-ToN-IoT dataset

ability to distinguish between positive and negative instances, as indicated by the MCC, was only 79.61%, suggesting outstanding performance. Despite the dataset's imbalance, our model demonstrated improved performance with an MCC of 87.92% when selecting the most relevant features before removing outliers. This enhancement led to an increase in ACC from 98.08% to 99.84%. However, solely removing outliers negatively impacted our model's distinguishability with 44.43% MCC.

Similarly, our model demonstrated improved performance after removing outliers from the NF-ToN-IoT dataset, increasing ACC from 97.91% and MCC from 87.46% to 92.53%. Furthermore, feature selection accelerated our model's predictions while maintaining superior performance. Specifically, on the Outliers & Selection variant, our model achieved an ACC of 96.29% and MCC of 87.50%, while on the Selection & Outliers variant, it achieved an ACC of 98.64% and MCC of 92.53%.

Table 11.4 presents our model's performance and compares it with other previous works. While our model demonstrated excellent performance in detection and distinguishability, it exhibited limitations when applying feature selection. To address this, introducing an additional layer of feature selection that assesses feature correlation could potentially enhance our model's performance. Furthermore, applying alternative outlier detection methods on the dataset might yield improved results, as it employs an approach different from the autoencoder [26–40].

Table 11.4 Our model's performance comparison

Contribution	*Year*	*Dataset*	*Model*	*ACC (%)*	*MCC (%)*
Mohamed et al. [23]	2023	ToN-IoT	BPNN	95.36	N/A
Attou et al. [24]	2023	NSL-KDD	RF-RBFNN	94.16	88.39
		Bot-IoT		99.99	93.00
Othman et al. [25]	2023	NF-Bot-IoT	NB	90.67	N/A
		NF-ToN-IoT		97.51	
Our contribution	2023	NF-Bot-IoT	RBFNN	98.49	59.61
		NF-ToN-IoT		96.91	98.14
		NF-IoT		96.88	84.35
		NF-IoT-v2		97.25	85.77

11.5 CONCLUSION

In summary, the rapid expansion of the IoT has revolutionized connectivity but has also exposed significant security risks. Our research underscores the urgency of addressing these vulnerabilities to safeguard the integrity and reliability of IoT ecosystems. The development of our proposed IDS tailored for IoT environments represents a crucial step toward enhancing security measures.

Our IDS model combines various methods, including the RBFNN, the chi-2 for feature selection, and an autoencoder for outlier detection. Extensive evaluations using the NF-ToN-IoT and NF-Bot-IoT datasets validate the robustness of our approach. Our model achieved a noteworthy ACC and MCC, underscoring its effectiveness in identifying deviations within IoT networks. The high MCC score indicates the model's ability to differentiate between normal and abnormal behavior, affirming its reliability in intrusion detection.

While our model demonstrates promising results, further research and development are imperative. Future enhancements should focus on scalability to accommodate diverse data sources and larger IoT networks. Additionally, improving outlier detection techniques to adapt to evolving threats and anomalous patterns will be essential for maintaining the efficacy of IDS solutions.

REFERENCES

1. M. Mohy-eddine, A. Guezzaz, S. Benkirane and M. Azrour, "IoT-enabled smart agriculture: security issues and applications," in *The International Conference on Artificial Intelligence and Smart Environment*, 2022.

2. M. Mohy-Eddine, M. Azrour, J. Mabrouki, F. Amounas, A. Guezzaz and S. Benkirane, "Embedded web server implementation for real-time water monitoring," in *Advanced Technology for Smart Environment and Energy*, vol. Springer, 2023, pp. 301–3011.
3. G. Dileep, "A survey on smart grid technologies and applications," *Renewable Energy*, vol. 146, pp. 2589–2625, 2020.
4. M. Ghobakhloo, "Industry 4.0, digitization, and opportunities for sustainability," *J. Cleaner Prod.*, vol. 252, p. 119869, 2020.
5. M. Mohy-eddine, S. Benkirane, A. Guezzaz and M. Azrour, "Random forest-based IDS for IIoT edge computing security using ensemble learning for dimensionality reduction," *Int. J. Embedd. Syst.*, vol. 15, no. 6, pp. 467–474, 2022.
6. M. Mohy-eddine, A. Guezzaz, S. Benkirane and M. Azrour, "Malicious detection model with artificial neural network in IoT-based smart farming security," *Cluster Comput.*, vol. 1–16, pp. 1–16, 2024.
7. I. F. Kilincer, F. Ertam and A. Sengur, "Machine learning methods for cyber security intrusion detection: datasets and comparative study," *Comput. Networks*, vol. 188, p. 107840, 2021.
8. I. Martins, J. S. Resende, P. R. Sousa, S. Silva, L. Antunes and J. Gama, "Host-based IDS: a review and open issues of an anomaly detection system in IoT," *Fut. Generat. Comput. Syst.*, vol. 133, pp. 95–113, 2022.
9. A. A. Laghari, K. Wu, R. A. Laghari, M. Ali and A. A. Khan, "A review and state of art of Internet of Things (IoT)," *Arch. Comput. Methods Eng.*,vol. 29, pp. 1–19, 2021.
10. Y. Cui, F. Liu, X. Jing and J. Mu, "Integrating sensing and communications for ubiquitous IoT: applications, trends, and challenges," *IEEE Network*, vol. 35, no. 5, pp. 158–167, 2021.
11. M. Mohy-Eddine, A. Guezzaz, S. Benkirane, M. Azrour and Y. Farhaoui, "An ensemble learning based intrusion detection model for industrial IoT security," *Big Data Mining Anal.*, vol. 6, no. 3, pp. 273–287, 2023.
12. M. Aqeel, F. Ali,. M. W. Iqbal,. T. A. Rana, M. Arif and M. R. Auwul, "A review of security and privacy concerns in the internet of things (IoT)," *J. Sensors*, vol. 6, no. 3, p. 2022, 2022.
13. Z. Yang, B. Liang and W. Ji, "An intelligent end–edge–cloud architecture for visual IoT-assisted healthcare systems," *IEEE Int Things J.*, vol. 8, no. 23, pp. 16779–16786, 2021.
14. R. Melki, H. N. Noura and A. Chehab, "Lightweight multi-factor mutual authentication protocol for IoT devices," *Int. J. Inform. Secur.*, vol. 19, pp. 679–694, 2020.
15. A. Thakkar and R. Lohiya, "A review of the advancement in intrusion detection datasets," *Procedia Comput. Sci.*, vol. 167, pp. 636–645, 2020.
16. A. Khraisat, I. Gondal, P. Vamplew and J. Kamruzzaman, "Survey of intrusion detection systems: techniques, datasets and challenges," *Cybersecurity*, vol. 2, no. 1, pp. 1–22, 2019.
17. U. S. Musa, M. Chhabra, A. Ali and M. Kaur, "Intrusion detection system using machine learning techniques: a review," in *2020 International Conference on Smart Electronics and Communication (ICOSEC)*, 2020.

18. M. Kuhn and K. Johnson, *Feature Engineering and Selection: A Practical Approach for Predictive Models*, Chapman & Hall/CRC, 2019.
19. M. Mohy-eddine, A. Guezzaz, S. Benkirane and M. Azrour, "An intrusion detection model using election-based feature selection and K-NN," *Microproc. Microsyst.*, p. 104966, 2023.
20. M. Panda, A. M. Abd Allah and A. E. Hassanien, "Developing an efficient feature engineering and machine learning model for detecting IoT-botnet cyber attacks," *IEEE Access*, vol. 9, pp. 91038–91052, 2021.
21. D. Musleh, M. Alotaibi, F. Alhaidari, A. Rahman and R. M. Mohammad, "Intrusion detection system using feature extraction with machine learning algorithms in IoT," *J. Sensor Actuator Netw.*, vol. 12, no. 2, p. 29, 2023.
22. T. Saba, A. Rehman, T. Sadad, H. Kolivand and S. A. Bahaj, "Anomaly-based intrusion detection system for IoT networks through deep learning model," *Comput. Elect. Eng.*, vol. 99, p. 107810, 2022.
23. D. Mohamed and O. Ismael, "Enhancement of an IoT hybrid intrusion detection system based on fog-to-cloud computing," *J. Cloud Comput.*, vol. 12, no. 1, pp. 1–13, 2023.
24. H. Attou, M. Mohy-eddine, A. Guezzaz, S. Benkirane, M. Azrour, A. Alabdultif and N. Almusallam, "Towards an intelligent intrusion detection system to detect malicious activities in cloud computing," *Appl. Sci.*, vol. 13, no. 17, p. 9588, 2023.
25. S. S. S. Othman, C. F. M. Foozy and S. N. B. Mustafa, "Feature selection of distributed denial of service (DDos) IoT bot attack detection using machine learning techniques," *J. Soft Comput. Data Mining*, vol. 4, no. 1, pp. 63–71, 2023.
26. M. Mohy-eddine, A. Guezzaz, S. Benkirane, and M. Azrour, "An efficient network intrusion detection model for IoT security using K-NN classifier and feature selection," *Multimed. Tools Appl.*, vol. 82, no. 15, pp. 23615–23633, 2023, doi: 10.1007/s11042-023-14795-2.
27. A. E. M. Eljialy, M. Y. Uddin and S. Ahmad, "Novel framework for an intrusion detection system using multiple feature selection methods based on deep learning," *Tsinghua Sci. Technol.*, vol. 29, no. 4, pp. 948–958, Aug. 2024, doi: 10.26599/TST.2023.9010032.
28. Y. Peng, S. Xu, Q. Chen, W. Huang and Y. Huang, "A novel popularity extraction method applied in session-based recommendation," *Tsinghua Sci. Technol.*, vol. 29, no. 4, pp. 971–984, Aug. 2024, doi: 10.26599/TST.2023.9010061.
29. C. Hazman, A. Guezzaz, S. Benkirane and M. Azrour, "Enhanced IDS with deep learning for IoT-based smart cities security," *Tsinghua Sci. Technol.*, vol. 29, no. 4, pp. 929–947, Aug. 2024, doi: 10.26599/TST.2023.9010033.
30. P. Wang, Z. Zhu, Q. Chen, and W. Dai, "Text reasoning chain extraction for multi-hop question answering," *Tsinghua Sci. Technol.*, vol. 29, no. 4, pp. 959–970, Aug. 2024, doi: 10.26599/TST.2023.9010060.
31. C. Hazman, A. Guezzaz, S. Benkirane, and M. Azrour, "Toward an intrusion detection model for IoT-based smart environments," *Multimed. Tools Appl.*, vol. 83, no. 22, pp. 62159–62180, Aug. 2023, doi: 10.1007/s11042-023-16436-0.

32. N. Meenakshi et al., "Efficient communication in wireless sensor networks using optimized energy efficient engroove leach clustering protocol," *Tsinghua Sci. Technol.*, vol. 29, no. 4, pp. 985–1001, Aug. 2024, doi: 10.26599/TST.2023.9010056.
33. H. Attou et al., "Towards an intelligent intrusion detection system to detect malicious activities in cloud computing," *Appl. Sci.*, vol. 13, no. 17, p. 9588, 2023.
34. S. Li, T. Cui and W. Viriyasitavat, "Edge device fault probability based intelligent calculations for fault probability of smart systems," *Tsinghua Sci. Technol.*, vol. 29, no. 4, pp. 1023–1036, Aug. 2024, doi: 10.26599/TST.2023.9010085.
35. W. Liu, L. Zhou, S. Zhang, N. Luo and M. Xu, "A new high-precision and lightweight detection model for illegal construction objects based on deep learning," *Tsinghua Sci. Technol.*, vol. 29, no. 4, pp. 1002–1022, Aug. 2024, doi: 10.26599/TST.2023.9010090.
36. H. Attou, A. Guezzaz, S. Benkirane, M. Azrour and Y. Farhaoui, "Cloud-based intrusion detection approach using machine learning techniques," *Big Data Min. Anal.*, vol. 6, no. 3, pp. 311–320, 2023.
37. S. Amaouche *et al.*, "FSCB-IDS: feature selection and minority class balancing for attacks detection in VANETS," *Appl. Sci.*, vol. 13, no. 13, p. 7488, 2023.
38. S. Amaouche, AzidineGuezzaz, S. Benkirane and MouradeAzrour, "IDS-XGbFS: a smart intrusion detection system using XGboostwith recent feature selection for VANET safety," *Clust. Comput.*, vol. 27, no. 3, pp. 3521–3535, 2023.
39. M. Douiba, S. Benkirane, A. Guezzaz and M. Azrour, "Anomaly detection model based on gradient boosting and decision tree for IoT environments security," *J. Reliab. Intell. Environ.*, vol. 9, no. 4, pp. 421–432, 2022.
40. M. Douiba, S. Benkirane, A. Guezzaz and M. Azrour, "An improved anomaly detection model for IoT security using decision tree and gradient boosting," *J. Supercomput.*, vol. 79, no. 3, pp. 3392–3411, 2022.

Chapter 12

An intrusion detection system using paragraph vector-distributed memory approach

Chadia EL Asry, Ibtissam Benchaji, Samira Douzi, and Bouabid EL Ouahidi

12.1 INTRODUCTION

Intrusion detection systems (IDSs) are one of the most important components of a security infrastructure that can prevent cyberattacks from a variety of sources. In the security literature, there are many different types of IDS schemes. In this context, there are two types of IDS schemes [1, 2]: host IDS and network IDS. The former aims to secure a computer system by monitoring all events, while the latter aims to protect a network. IDS techniques are also classed as signature detection and anomaly detection approaches based on their detection capability.

Signature-based IDSs often use a predefined database of security attack signatures to try to match events and traffic to certain attack patterns [3]. However, signature-based IDS techniques are unable to identify new attacks with unknown patterns and signatures [4]. Abnormality-based IDS techniques, on the other hand, seek to learn normal activities and identify everything else as anomaly or intrusion [4]. Nonetheless, they have a problem with false positives, which limits their use.

In the literature, many IDS approaches are reported that use various deep learning and shallow learning models to automatically distinguish normal and abnormal events in systems and networks [5]. Deep learning, in particular, is based on artificial neural networks (ANNs), which use numerous hidden layers for data transformation and have a higher learning power. Deep neural networks (DNNs), convolutional neural networks (CNNs), and recurrent neural networks (RNNs) are examples of deep learning networks that have been widely used in a variety of applications, including security and intrusion detection [6].

Shallow learning, a well-established technique, has been extensively utilized in cybersecurity for attack detection [5]. Multiple research works have employed algorithms such as random forest [7], support vector machine (SVM) [8], and others to classify intrusions from traffic data.

The following contribution is included in the chapter:

DOI: 10.1201/9781003587552-12

- Propose an IDS based on the PV-DM approach and ML models.
- Using NSLKDD [5] dataset to evaluate our model.
- Use of the PV-DM technique with five classifiers to choose the best one.

The following sections make up this chapter: Related works are presented in Section 12.2. Section 12.3 discusses the many concepts we used in our search. Section 12.4 describes the suggested approach in depth, including implementation and experimental findings, and Section 12.5 concludes the chapter.

12.2 RELATED WORKS

Several studies have addressed this topic [9–21], where numerous articles discuss the different techniques to create successful IDS capable of solving all kinds of attacks.

The authors in [9] described an LSTM model for network intrusion detection, utilizing both normal and malicious user behaviors to represent network traffic as time series data. They trained the model using the DARPA and KDD Cup'99 datasets and explored various network topologies to assess its effectiveness. Additionally, the research examined different feature sets for detecting attacks and establishing tailored training for specific attack types on networks.

The authors in reference [10] introduced a model that combines feature selection techniques with LSTM for classification, aiming to improve the detection of low-frequency attacks R2L and U2R in the NSL-KDD dataset.

In [11], the authors introduced a method for predicting user behavior on a Tor network using a deep recurrent neural network (DRNN). They set up a Tor server and client alongside a Wireshark network analyzer to gather data on Tor, a network user, which was then utilized to train the DRNN model.

In [12], researchers introduced a DDoS attack detection approach using a support vector machine (SVM) in software-defined networks (SDN). Their results indicate an average accuracy of approximately 95.24% with a limited flow volume. However, drawbacks of the SVM model include the need for extensive training and expertise in machine learning; its complex final model, which is difficult to interpret; and challenges in fine-tuning SVM parameters.

In their study [13], the authors explored different feature reduction approaches and deep learning techniques. They applied LSTM, BiLSTM, and stacked LSTM to three feature reduction methods: Shap values, Boruta, and Anova F-test, aiming to select the optimal model. They found that the model combining Shap values with stacked LSTM performed best, achieving accuracy, precision, recall, and F1-score of 99.25%, 95.28%, 87.60%, and 89.69%, respectively, particularly notable given the dataset's imbalance. Usama in [14] proposed a generative adversarial network (GAN) designed for intrusion detection, boasting strong resistance against adversarial attacks. However, despite its efficacy, this method often poses challenges in parameterization and is susceptible to training instability in many instances.

Yan et al. [15] conducted an analysis of four deep learning models using two intrusion datasets, namely NSL-KDD and UNSW-NB15. The models evaluated were restricted Boltzmann machine (RBM), multilayer perceptron (MLP), sparse Autoencoder (SAE), and MLP with feature embedding. However, it is noteworthy that their experiments did not include evaluations on newer intrusion datasets.

In 2022, Douiba et al. [16] leveraged NSL-KDD, IoT-23, BoT-IoT, and Edge-IIoT datasets for evaluating both the classifiers, ensemble models such as gradient boosting (GB) and decision tree (DT), together with CatBoost open-source to enhance IoT safety. They demonstrated excellent performances, with measurements of precision, recall, and a success rate (ACC) close to 99.9%, while achieving record detection and computation times. In a similar effort, Hazman et al. [17] extracted data from the IoT-23, BoT-IoT, and Edge-IIoT datasets to further develop an optimized anomaly detection framework, named IDS-SIoEL, through ensemble learning with AdaBoost. In their study, the technical subtleties of alternative feature selected methodologies, such as mutual information, Boruta, and correlation, were revealed. In fact, the model achieved exceptional results, with high accuracy, precision, recall, and a success rate (CCA) ratings of close to 99.9%. Moreover, both detection and learning delays were outstandingly rapid, at 0.02156 s and 33.68 s, respectively.

In another study, Mohy-eddine et al. [18] capitalize on the wustl-iiot-2021 and BoT-IoT datasets for optimizing a set-based intrusion detection solution for IoT edge computing. Their methodology involves the use of Pearson correlation for characteristic selection and isolation logging to rule out outliers.

12.3 BACKGROUND

12.3.1 Paragraph vector-distributed memory approach (PV-DM)

The paragraph vector-distributed memory approach (PV-DM) method is an unsupervised learning approach inspired by techniques used to learn continuous vector representations for words, particularly through neural networks like word2vec [22]. The core concept of PV-DM involves representing a paragraph P as a vector that aids in predicting the subsequent word in a phrase [23].

In the PV-DM model, each paragraph is associated with a singular vector, depicted as a column in matrix D, while each word corresponds to a unique vector, represented as a column in matrix W. Consequently, a classifier (such as Softmax) predicting the next word in a context will average and concatenate the paragraph and word vectors (Figure 12.1).

12.3.2 NSL-KDD dataset

The NSL-KDD dataset [24] is a newer version of the KDD-cup 99 dataset [25]. This dataset is more reliable to use because it does not contain redundant and duplicate records. Initially, the NSLKDD dataset contained 4,898,430 records with 972,780 normal records and 3,925,650 attack records. It has 38 different attacks, such as smurf, neptune, satan, ipsweep, and portsweep.

The NSL-KDD comprises 42 features, which are arranged into four different categories:

- 4 Categorical (Features: 2, 3, 4, 42).
- 6 Binary (Features: 7, 12, 14, 20, 21, 22).
- 23 Discrete (Features: 8, 9, 15, 23 to 41, 43).
- – 10 Continuous (Features: 1, 5, 6, 10, 11, 13, 16, 17, 18, 19).

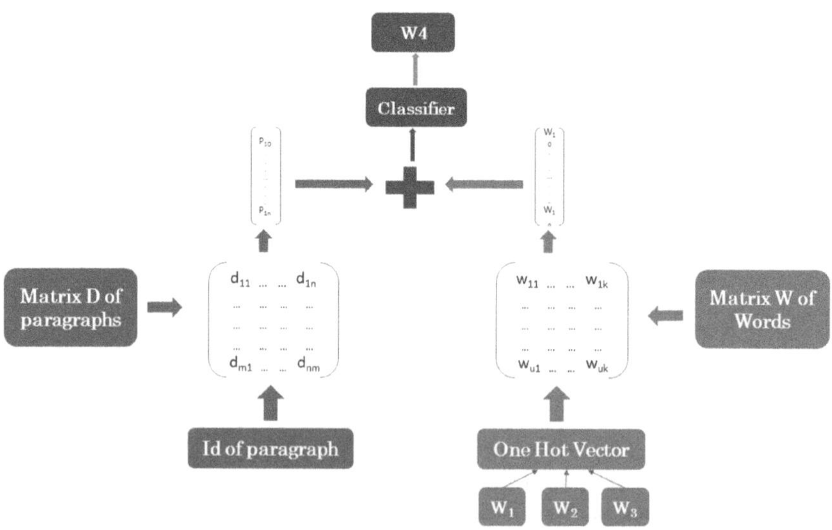

Figure 12.1 A framework for learning paragraph vector [17]

12.4 OUR APPROACH

The framework proposed to detect IDS is shown in Figure 12.2. First, developing an IDS detection model necessitates a good comprehension of subject matter knowledge and acquisition of the appropriate datasets. In this respect, the extraction of characteristics from existing data lies at the heart of the development of successful detection models.

Our proposed approach (Figure 12.2) consists of applying the PV-DM approach, which generates embedding vectors that will be the inputs of five classifiers of ML models, which are SVM, Random-Forest, Logistic Regression, Gaussian-NB, and XGboost, to select the best classifier in terms of accuracy, precision, recall, F1-score, and AUC.

In our proposed framework, we use the NSL-KDD dataset, which corresponds to the highly sophisticated version created for the KDDcup99 dataset [26]. A wide variety of different techniques and analysis approaches have been implemented by different researchers on the NSL-KDD dataset, with the ultimate aim of creating a comprehensive and efficient intrusion

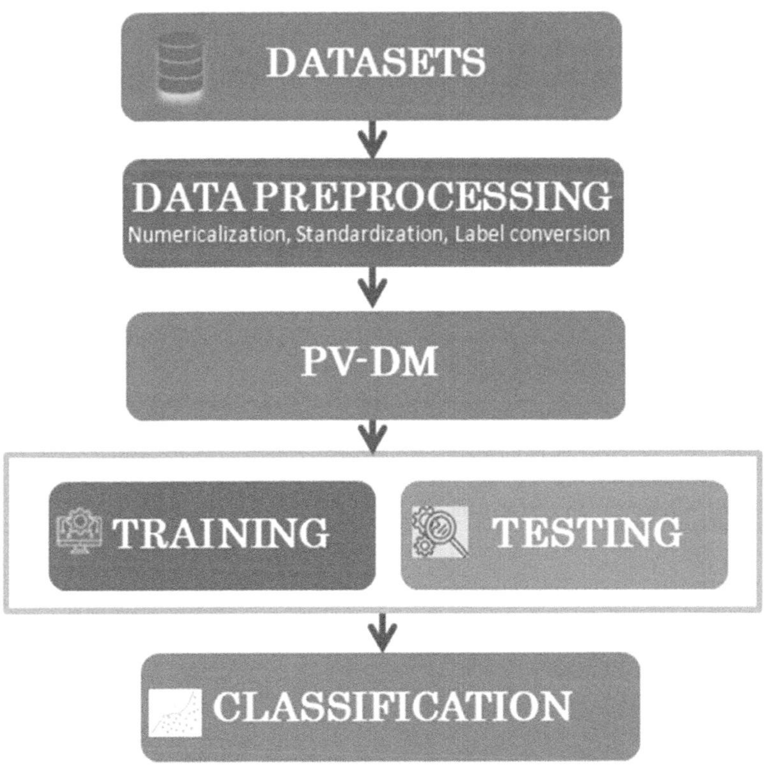

Figure 12.2 Our proposed approach

detection scheme. A more detailed investigation of the NSL-KDD dataset employing a variety of machine learning techniques can be accessed largely through the WEKA tool in [27]. The clustering algorithm K-means exploits the NSL-KDD dataset [28] in order to train and test different types of existing and new attacks. A benchmarking comparison of the NSL-KDD dataset against its predecessor, the KDD99 cup dataset, is performed in [29] by using the SOM (self-organization map) artificial neural network. A comprehensive evaluation of diverse datasets, including KDD99, GureKDD, and NSLKDD, is conducted via various data mining-based machine learning algorithms, notably the support vector machine (SVM), decision tree, K-nearest neighbor, K-means, and fuzzy C-means clustering algorithms.

12.4.1 Experimental results and discussion

Table 12.1 presents the performance of the PV-DM model with the five classifiers in order to select the best model based on evaluation metrics.

Analyzing the performance of the PV-DM model without feature reduction across five different classifiers, the XGBOOST classifier stands out with the best overall performance. With an ACCURACY% of 93.79%, XGBOOST demonstrates the highest overall precision among the classifiers. Similarly, its PRECISION% score of 93.95% indicates its ability to correctly identify true positives. While not ranking first in RECALL%, XGBOOST maintains a strong 82.80%, suggesting it can detect a significant proportion of true positives. Its F1-SCORE% of 86.89% signifies a good balance between precision and recall. Lastly, XGBOOST also dominates in AUC% with a score of 91, indicating excellent ability to correctly classify positive and negative examples.

The RANDOM FOREST classifier emerges as the second-best in this analysis. With an ACCURACY% of 90.73%, RANDOM FOREST shows overall solid performance. Its PRECISION% score of 94.25% is also excellent, showing its ability to identify the vast majority of true positives.

Table 12.1 Classification performance for PV-DM with five classifiers

		NSL-KDD				
		Accuracy%	*Precision%*	*Recall%*	*F1-score%*	*AUC%*
PV-DM with	**SVM**	79.56	70.57	63.67	65.09	79
	RANDOM-FOREST	90.73	**94.25**	69.16	74.13	83
	LOGISTIC REGRESSION	79.60	71.68	68.82	70.19	81
	GAUSSIAN-NB	37.19	40.06	68.20	45.10	72
	XGBOOST	**93.79**	**93.95**	**82.80**	**86.89**	**91**

However, its RECALL% score at 69.16% is slightly lower than XGBOOST, suggesting it misses some true positives. The F1-SCORE% of 74.13% still indicates a good balance between precision and recall. RANDOM FOREST also obtains a good AUC% score of 83, showing its ability to correctly classify positive and negative examples.

Lastly, the GAUSSIAN-NB classifier ranks as the least performing among the five. With a low ACCURACY% of 37.19%, GAUSSIAN-NB fails to reach the performance of the other classifiers. Its PRECISION%, RECALL%, F1-SCORE%, and AUC% scores are also markedly lower, highlighting its struggle to effectively classify intrusions in the traffic data.

In conclusion, the XGBOOST classifier emerges as the best choice for this PV-DM model due to its high overall performance, while GAUSSIAN-NB ranks as the least performing in this comparison.

12.4.2 Assessing our method in contrast to prior research investigations

This comparison (Table 12.2) serves as a reference point, given that IDSs vary in their operational settings, data pre-processing techniques, and interpretation methods. Nevertheless, our model yields significantly superior results compared to all the assessed models, suggesting its suitability for this specific problem and showcasing the versatility and robustness of our architecture.

12.5 CONCLUSION

This chapter introduces an efficient network attack detection method based on deep learning coupled with a machine learning classifier. Specifically, paragraph vector-distributed memory (PV-DM) and XGBoost were employed as the classifier for intrusion detection, focusing on multiclass classification tasks.

The experimental findings demonstrate that the proposed attack detection approach achieves superior performance in recognizing known attacks, especially when applied to the NSL-KDD.

Table 12.2 Comparing various models with our approach

Model	*Accuracy*	*Precision*	*Recall*	*F1-Score*
LSTM [**10**]	99,73	88,3	84,92	85,33
KNN [**26**]	0,622	0,578	0,622	0,576
DNN [**26**]	0,785	0,810	0,785	0,765
Proposed model	**93.79**	**93.95**	**82.80**	**86.89**

REFERENCES

1. S. Amaouche, AzidineGuezzaz, S. Benkirane, and MouradeAzrour, "IDS-XGbFS: a smart intrusion detection system using XGboostwith recent feature selection for VANET safety," *Clust. Comput.*, vol. 27, no. 3, pp. 3521–3535, 2023.
2. C. Hazman, A. Guezzaz, S. Benkirane, and M. Azrour, "Enhanced IDS with deep learning for IoT-based smart cities security," *Tsinghua Sci. Technol.*, vol. 29, no. 4, pp. 929–947, Aug. 2024, doi: 10.26599/TST.2023.9010033.
3. A. E. M. Eljialy, M. Y. Uddin, and S. Ahmad, "Novel framework for an intrusion detection system using multiple feature selection methods based on deep learning," *Tsinghua Sci. Technol.*, vol. 29, no. 4, pp. 948–958, Aug. 2024, doi: 10.26599/TST.2023.9010032.
4. S. M. Kasongo, and Y. Sun, "A deep learning method with wrapper based feature extraction for wireless intrusion detection system," *Comput. Securi.*,vol. 92, p. 101752, 2020.
5. E. L. Asry C, Benchaji I, Douzi S, E. L. Ouahidi B, "A robust intrusion detection system based on a shallow learning model and feature extraction techniques," *PLoS ONE*, vol. 19, no. 1,p. e0295801, 2024, doi: 10.1371/journal .pone.0295801.
6. L. Lipton, C. Zachary, J. Berkowitz, and C. Elkan, "A critical review of recurrent neural networks for sequence learning," arXiv preprint arXiv:1506.00019.
7. J. Zhang, M. Zulkernine, and A. Haque, "Random-forests-based network intrusion detection systems," in *IEEE Transactions on Systems, Man, and Cybernetics, Part C (Applications and Reviews).*
8. N. Mohammed Muamer, and S. Norrozila, "Intrusion detection system based on SVM for WLAN," *Procedia Technol.*, vol. 1, pp. 313–317, 2012, doi: 10.1016/j.protcy.2012.02.066.
9. R. C. Staudemeyer, "Applying long short-term memory recurrent neural networks to intrusion detection," South African Computer Journal, vol. 56, no. 1, pp. 136–154, 2015.
10. C. el Asry, S. Douzi, and B. Ouahidi, "Intrusion detection system, a new approach to R2L and U2R attack classification," In The International Conference on Artificial Intelligence and Smart Environment pp. 297–304. Cham: Springer Nature Switzerland, doi: 10.1007/978-3-031-48465-0_39.
11. T. Oda, R. Obukata, M. Yamada, T. Ishitake, M. Hiyama, and L. Barolli, "A neural network based user identification for tor network," *CISIS*, 2016, In 2016 10th International Conference on Complex, Intelligent, and Software Intensive Systems (CISIS), pp. 477–483. IEEE, 2016, https://doi. org.10.1109/CISIS.2016.89.
12. J. Ye, X. Cheng, J. Zhu, L. Feng, and L. Song, "A DDoS attack detection method based on SVM in software defined network," *Secur. Commun. Netw.* vol. 2018, p. 9804061, 2018.
13. C. el Asry, B. Ouahidi, and S. Douzi, "A deep learning model for intrusion detection with imbalanced dataset," pp. 261–271, 2024, doi: 10.1007/978-3-031-47672-3_26.

14. M. Usama, M. Asim, S. Latif, J. Qadir, et al., Generative adversarial networks for launching and thwarting adversarial attacks on 414 network intrusion detection systems," in *Proceedings of the 2019 15th International Wireless Communications & Mobile Computing 415 Conference (IWCMC)*, IEEE. 2019, pp. 78–83.
15. J. Yan, D. Jin, C. W. Lee, and P. Liu, "A comparative study of off-line deep learning based network intrusion detection," in *Proceedings 412 of the 2018 Tenth International Conference on Ubiquitous and Future Networks (ICUFN)*, IEEE. 2018, pp. 299–304.
16. M. Douiba, S. Benkirane, A. Guezzaz, and M. Azrour, "An improved anomaly detection model for IoT security using decision tree and gradient boosting," *J. Supercomput.*, vol. 79, no. 3, pp. 3392–3411, 2022.
17. C. Hazman, A. Guezzaz, S. Benkirane, and M. Azrour, "lIDS-SIoEL: intrusion detection framework for IoT-based smart environments security using ensemble learning," *Cluster Comput.*, Response: vol. 26, no. 6, pp. 4069–4083, 2023.
18. M. Mohy-Eddine, S. Benkirane, A. Guezzaz, and M. Azrour, "Random forest-based IDS for IIoT edge computing security using ensemble learning for dimensionality reduction," *Int. J. Embedd. Syst.*, vol. 15, no. 6, pp. 467–474, 2022.
19. M. Mohy-eddine, A. Guezzaz, S. Benkirane, and M. Azrour, "Malicious detection model with artificial neural network in IoT-based smart farming security," *Cluster Comput.*, vol. 27, pp.7307–7322, 2024.
20. K. Bella et al., "An efficient intrusion detection system for IoT security using CNN decision forest," *PeerJ Comput. Sci.*, vol. 10, p. e2290, Sep. 2024, doi: 10.7717/peerj-cs.2290.
21. C. Hazman, A. Guezzaz, S. Benkirane, and M. Azrour, "Enhanced IDS with deep learning for IoT-based smart cities security," *Tsinghua Sci. Technol.*, vol. 29, no. 4, pp. 929–947, Aug. 2024, doi: 10.26599/TST.2023.9010033.
22. D. Asirvatham, F. Gonzalez-Longatt, P. Falkowski-Gilski, et al. (Eds.), *Evolutionary Artificial Intelligence: Proceedings of ICEAI 2023*. Germany: Springer Nature, 2024.
23. S. Douzi, M. Amar, B. Ouahidi, and H. Laanaya, "Towards A new spam filter based on PV-DM (Paragraph Vector-Distributed Memory Approach)," *Procedia Comput. Sci.*, vol. 110, pp. 486–491, 2017, doi: 10.1016/j.procs.2017.06.130.
24. L. Dhanabal, and S. Shantharajah, "A study on NSL-KDD dataset for intrusion detection system based on classification algorithms," *Int. J. Adv. Res. Comput. Commun. Eng.*, vol. 4, no. 6, pp. 446–452, 2015.
25. M. Tavallaee, E. Bagheri, W. Lu, and A. Ghorbani, "A detailed analysis of the KDD CUP 99 data set," in *Submitted to Second IEEE Symposium on Computational Intelligence for Security and Defense Applications (CISDA)*, 2009.
26. M. Tavallaee, E. Bagheri, W. Lu, and A. A. Ghorbani, "A detailed analysis of the KDD CUP 99 data set," in *2009 IEEE Symposium on Computational Intelligence for Security and Defense Applications*, Jul. 2009, pp. 1–6. doi: 10.1109/CISDA.2009.5356528.

27. S. Revathi, and D. A. Malathi, "A detailed analysis on NSL-KDD dataset using various machine learning techniques for intrusion detection," *Int. J. Eng. Res.*, vol. 2, no. 12, pp.1848–1853, 2013.
28. V. Kumar, H. Chauhan, and D. Panwar, "K-means clustering approach to analyze NSL-KDD intrusion detection dataset," International Journal of Soft Computing and Engineering (IJSCE), vol. 3, no. 4, pp. 1–4, 2013.
29. S. K. Sahu, S. Sarangi, and S. K. Jena, "A detail analysis on intrusion detection datasets," in *2014 IEEE International Advance Computing Conference (IACC)*, Feb. 2014, pp. 1348–1353. doi: 10.1109/IAdCC.2014.6779523.

Chapter 13

Advanced security of blockchain authentication system using zero-knowledge protocol

Yacouba Kouraogo and Ghizlane Orhanou

13.1 INTRODUCTION

Blockchain technology (or blockchain for short) has emerged as a foundational technology that provides security through cryptography and consensus mechanisms and addresses the issues of single point of failure and single point of trust. The transparency and immutability of blockchain allows publicly provable and indisputable records to be stored [1]. Additionally, the introduction of smart contracts into blockchain has broadened its horizon of utility beyond cryptocurrency [2]. Indeed, blockchain is applied in many application areas: from cryptocurrencies to the Internet of Things (IoT), health care and financial systems, supply chain management, etc. Although blockchain is considered a promising technology, it still has security vulnerabilities that adversaries play through.

The Blockchain Threat Report published by McAfee [3] mentions that blockchain transactions carry security risks. Their list includes well-adopted blockchain implementations such as Bitcoin and Ethereum. Potential attacks, such as 51% attacks 51% [4], Sybil attacks [5], ransomware attacks [6], man-in-the-middle attacks [6], and identity theft [5]. Then, smart contracts – autonomous programs running on the blockchain – can have vulnerabilities that are exploited by malicious actors.

To solve this security problem, we propose a new approach of a protocol-based authentication system without information disclosure. Thus, in this chapter, we use the Fiat-Shamir protocol for the authentication system and a hash function made robust with the use of salt to ensure the integrity of messages transmitted through the blockchain architecture. We conclude with a security analysis of our proposed system.

DOI: 10.1201/9781003587552-13

13.2. SECURITY PROBLEMS IN BLOCKCHAIN TECHNOLOGY

13.2.1 Problematic

Despite the different security mechanisms mentioned above, several security issues in blockchain technology today make attacks possible: the man in the middle attack, the Sybil attack, and the ransomware attack as well as, furthermore, the problem of the non-existence of the reliable guarantee of human identity according to Nicholas J. Hopper and Manuel Blum [7].

Our objective in this chapter is to provide a secure blockchain by addressing the problem of human identity (authentication) and protecting information on the distributed network.

13.2.2 Related work

To effectively analyze and conduct a study on a crucial topic like blockchain security, it is very important to see what other researchers have done in this area. We therefore carried out a literature review of related works already published on this subject.

The most recent studies of blockchain security issues are discussed below. Jiang et al. [8] analyzed a systematic study of security threats to blockchain and elaborated the corresponding real-world attacks, including selfish mining attacks, DAO attacks, BGP hijacking attacks, and eclipse attacks. Banerjee et al. [9] reviewed articles focused on IoT security solutions and highlighted attacks such as cyberattacks, botnet malware, DoS, and DDoS. Research by Taylor et al. [10] systematically reviewed the recent and most vulnerable attacks in the field of cybersecurity and the role of blockchain in its mitigation. Different security issues are evaluated in IoT [11, 12] and these issues are classified relating to different layers of the IoT stack. Recently, Ferraget al. [13] classified the thread models in blockchain protocols relating to IoT networks. In [14], the authors deliberated on the long-range attack in which an attacker returns to the genesis block and forks the blockchain, causing a serious threat to the proof of stack.

In addition, Abhishek Guru et al. [15] highlight the problem of unguaranteed security due to flaws in all consensus algorithms, which are sometimes the cause of attacks in the blockchain. Nicholas Hopper and Manuel Blum [7] reason about the problem of the non-existence of a reliable guarantee of human identity in the blockchain.

13.3 ENHANCEMENT OF AUTHENTICATION SYSTEM ON BLOCKCHAIN USING PROTOCOL ZERO-KNOWLEDGE FIAT-SHAMIR

13.3.1 Existing blockchain system

Blockchain technology is a revolutionary innovation that has the potential to transform many industries, such as finance, logistics, IoT, health care, supply chains, smart grids, and others. Figure 13.1 presents the operating principle of transactions in blockchain technology, which is performed without authenticating the user making the transaction.

The existing blockchain system appears secure, but it has many security vulnerabilities that allow attackers to carry out attacks against the financial, administrative, logistics, and industrial sectors that use blockchain. The most common and simplest possible attacks are:

- Attack of the man in the middle [6]
- Ransomware attack [6]
- Identity theft [5]

An authentication mechanism added to the existing system would give an additional security layer that would help in confronting such types of attacks. Our objective in this chapter is to offer an enhancement of the existing blockchain system by adding an authentication mechanism based on the zero-knowledge Fiat-Shamir protocol.

13.3.2 Proposed authentication system

To overcome these security issues, it is timely for us to propose a new approach of authentication system in blockchain technology based on

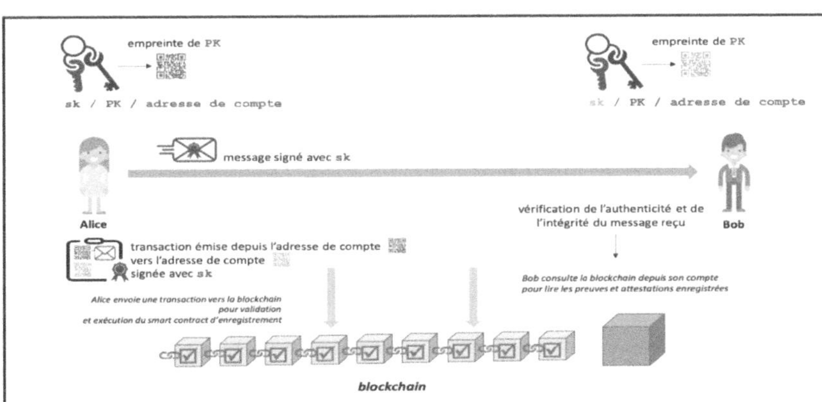

Figure 13.1 Existing blockchain system [16]

the zero-knowledge protocol, which is an improvement over the existing method. In this proposed system, we ensure guaranteed security of authentication via the Fiat-Shamir [17] protocol (Figure 13.2) because the secret information does not pass through the network. In the following, we describe how our authentication approach works:

- **Protocol zero-knowledge: Fiat-shamir**

Alice, the user, wants to authenticate with Bob. So, we have the following parameters:

- Alice chooses two large prime numbers p and q and calculates n = pq
- Alice then randomly chooses an integer x between 1 and n-1 and calculates $y = x^2 \bmod n$.
- The pair (n, y) is its public key, and x its secret key
- **Proposed approach system**

Figure 13.3 illustrates our approach to the blockchain authentication system based on the Fiat-Shamir protocol.

We describe below the proposed approach:

Step 1: Alice wants to make a transaction via the blockchain to Bob,
Step 2: She first authenticates with Bob

- It chooses two large prime numbers p and q and calculates n= pq
- Alice then randomly chooses an integer x between 1 and n-1 and calculates
  - $y = x^2 \bmod n$.

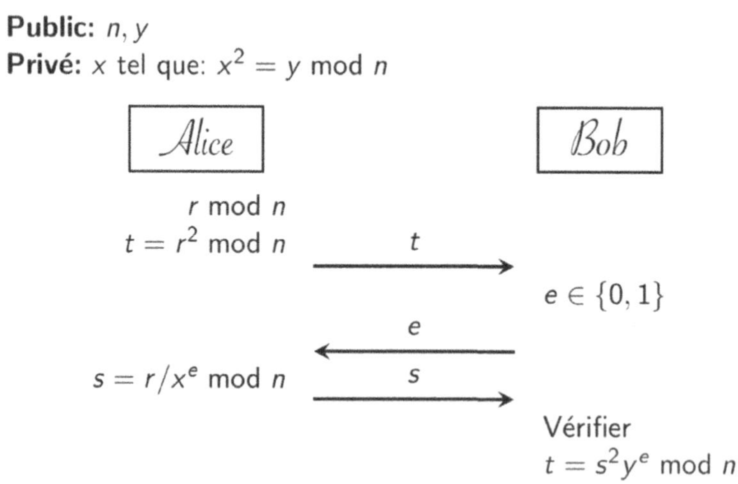

Figure 13.2 Fiat-Shamir zero-knowledge protocol

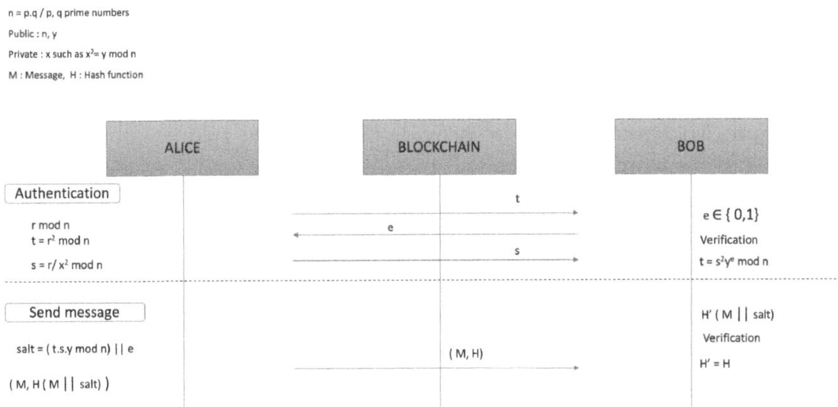

Figure 13.3 Enhancement authentication system on blockchain using protocol zero-knowledge Fiat-Shamir

- The pair (n, y) is its public key, and x its secret key
- To authenticate, it chooses a number r between 1 and n-1 and calculates t = r2 mod n.
- She sends t to Bob, who, in turn, chooses e from 0 and 1, then sends it to Alice.
- Alice calculates s = r/x^e mod n and sends s to Bob
- Bob carries out the verification by calculating s^2 y^e mod n ; if result is equal to t, then Alice is authenticated, otherwise the authentication is canceled

Step 3: She sends the message to Bob

- It calculates salt = t.s.y mod n || e, in order to make the hash function H() more robust. And ensure the integrity
- It performs hashing of the message m such that H (m || salt)
- She transmits (m, H) to Bob
- Bob calculates H' and salt such that H'(m || salt)
- If H = H' then the message has not been altered on the network, otherwise it has been modified.

13.3.3 Security analysis

Our authentication system based on the zero-knowledge Fiat-Shamir protocol overcomes the security problem regarding identity and authentication in blockchain technology. Indeed:

- Our system is consistent, which means that knowledge of secret x allows Alice to respond to the challenge proposed by Bob, whatever its value.

- Our system is significant, that is to say that, to succeed in its identification with acceptable probability (here greater than ½), Alice must know the secret x. Indeed, Alice cannot predict the value of e at the moment she transmits t to Bob. At the risk of failing in her authentication, Alice must be able to provide Bob with the two possible answers r and r/x from S (But she will provide only one so as not to reveal her secret) and therefore must know x.
- Our system ensures the anonymity of information through the non-disclosure of information protocol.
- Our system ensures the integrity of the message on the network via the hashing function, which is made robust with Salt.

13.4 CONCLUSION

Blockchain technology, since its appearance, has led to positive upheavals in our lives in which digital sciences have grown with their capacity to generate large data, whether public or private. However, the security of this data and the authentication problem are becoming a worrying issue for more stakeholders in the sector. Therefore, it is this concern that leads us to propose adequate solutions to these problems.

In this context, we proposed an authentication system in the blockchain based on the zero-knowledge protocol Fiat-Shamir. After a security analysis of our system, we can conclude that our system is consistent and meaningful, ensures integrity, and overcomes the lack of authentication that was present in the existing blockchain system.

REFERENCES

1. M. S. Rahman, A. Al Omar, M. Z. A. Bhuiyan, A. Basu, S. Kiyomoto, and G. Wang, "Accountable cross-border data sharing using blockchain under relaxed trust assumption," *IEEE Transactions on Engineering Management*, vol. 67, no. 4, pp. 1476-1486, 2020.
2. Al Omar, M. Z. A. Bhuiyan, A. Basu, S. Kiyomoto, and M. S. Rahman, "Privacy-friendly platform for healthcare data in cloud based on blockchain environment," *Future Generation Computer Systems*, vol. 95, pp. 511–521, 2019.
3. C. Cimpanu, *IOTA Cryptocurrency Users Lose $4 Million in Clever Phishing Attack*, https://www.bleepingcomputer.com/news/security /iota-cryptocurrency-users-lose-4-million-in-clever-phishing-attack/, 2019.
4. Fawkes, "PirlGuard — innovative solution against 51% attacks", available [online], https://medium.com/pirl/pirlguard-innovative-solution-against-51-attacks-7dd45aa1109, 2018.

5. Y. Toor, P. Muhlethaler, and A. Laouiti, "Vehicle ad hoc networks: applications and related technical issues," *IEEE Communications Surveys & Tutorials*, vol. 10, no. 3, pp.74–88, 2008.
6. A. Bhardwaj, V. Avasthi, H. Sastry, and G.V.B. Subrahmanyam, "Ransomware digital extortion: a rising new age threat," *Indian Journal of Science and Technology*, vol. 9, no. 14, pp. 1–52016, 2016.
7. N. J. Hopper, and M. Blum, "Secure human identification protocols," in *Advances in Cryptology—ASIACRYPT 2001: 7th International Conference on the Theory and Application of Cryptology and Information Security Gold Coast*, Australia, Dec. 9–13, 2001, Proceedings 7 (pp. 52–66). Springer Berlin Heidelberg.
8. X. Li, P. Jiang, T. Chen, X. Luo, and Q. Wen, "A survey on the security of Blockchain systems," *Future Generation Computer Systems*, vol. 107, pp.841–853, 2017.
9. M. Banerjee, J. Lee, and K.K.R. Choo, "A Blockchain future for the internet of things security: a position chapter," *Digital Communications and Networks*, vol. 4, no. 3, pp.149–160, 2018.
10. P. J. Taylor, T. Dargahi, A. Dehghantanha, R. M. Parizi, and K. K. R. Choo, "A systematic literature review of Blockchain cyber security," *Digital Communications and Networks*, Response: vol. 6, no. 2, pp.147–156, 2020.
11. S. Dargaoui et al., "Security issues in internet of medical things," in *Blockchain and Machine Learning for IoT Security*, Chapman & Hall/CRC, 2024, pp. 77–91.
12. S. Dargaoui *et al.*, "Applications of Blockchain in healthcare: review study," in *IoT, Machine Learning and Data Analytics for Smart Healthcare*, CRC Press, 2024.
13. M. A. Ferrag, M. Derdour, M. Mukherjee, A. Derhab, L. Maglaras, and H. Janicke, "Blockchain technologies for the internet of things: Research issues and challenges," *IEEE Internet of Things Journal*, vol. 6, pp. 2188–2204, 2019.
14. E. Deirmentzoglou, G. Papa kyriakopoulos, and C. Patsakis, "A survey on long-range attacks for proof of stake protocols," *IEEE Access*, vol. 7, pp. 28712–28725, 2019.
15. A. Guru, B. K. Mohanta, H. Mohapatra, F. Al-Turjman, C. Altrjman, and A. Yadav, "A survey on consensus protocols and attacks on blockchain technology," *Applied Sciences*, vol. 13, no. 4, p. 2604, 2023.
16. Coutor, Sophie, Hennebert, Christine, and Faher, Mourad. Blockchain et identification numérique. 2021.
17. M. O'Donnell, "Identification protocols in cryptography," *The ITB Journal*, vol. 3, no 1, p. 3, 2002.

Chapter 14

Intelligent phishing URL classification using CNN

Habiba Bouijij and Amine Berqia

14.1 INTRODUCTION

A phishing URL attack is a malicious technique utilized by cybercriminals to trick unsuspecting individuals into revealing their confidential information by disguising themselves as reputable entities. These nefarious actors often distribute fraudulent emails or messages, carefully crafted to appear as if they originate from trustworthy sources, coercing the recipient to click on a link provided. Upon clicking, the unsuspecting victim is redirected to a counterfeit website artfully designed to closely resemble an authentic one. Within this deceptive digital realm, victims are lured into unknowingly disclosing their personal and financial particulars, ultimately resulting in devastating consequences, such as identity theft, substantial financial damages, and illicit access to their accounts [1]. The detrimental repercussions of falling victim to such a pernicious scheme cannot be overstated. It is vital for individuals to remain vigilant and exercise caution when encountering unsolicited messages or questionable links, thereby thwarting cybercrime and safeguarding their invaluable personal information.

According to the Anti-Phishing Working Group (APWG), there was a significant rise in phishing incidents in the second quarter of 2023. The APWG recorded a staggering total of 1,286,208 such events, establishing a new pinnacle in activity irrespective of an overall downward trend in phishing occurrences. Interestingly, the financial sector bore the brunt of these attacks, accounting for a remarkable 23.5% of these malevolent assaults, with online payment services experiencing a concerning attack rate of 5.8%. These striking statistics underscore the persistently emerging and evolving threat that phishing operations represent [2]. In an increasingly interconnected digital landscape, it is imperative for individuals and organizations alike to remain vigilant and employ effective cybersecurity measures to safeguard against the ever-present danger of phishing attacks.

Moreover, as the threat posed by cybercriminals continues to rise, it has become increasingly evident that they are embracing the use of machine learning (ML) technologies to bolster their malicious activities, particularly phishing tactics. One noteworthy instance of this is the emergence of the

 DOI: 10.1201/9781003587552-14

DeepPhish project, a brainchild of Cyxtra Technology [3], which harnesses the power of ML to create highly intricate phishing URLs that are exceptionally adept at evading conventional detection mechanisms. With cyber threats evolving at such a rapid pace, it is becoming more crucial than ever to adopt advanced cybersecurity measures, such as the implementation of cutting-edge deep learning algorithms, in order to mount a formidable defense against these ever-advancing phishing schemes.

14.2 RELATED WORK

The cybersecurity landscape is seeing a surge of using machine learning and deep learning to detect URL phishing. Since cyber threats are evolving, conventional methods of detection have become less and less effective against advanced and complex ones. Machine learning detects patterns in data through analysis of big datasets and improves the accuracy and speed of detection, while deep learning is a subset of machine learning focusing on neural networks that can detect small signs of phishing by understanding complex relationships between data [4–10].

Authors [11] presents a comprehensive examination of deep learning-based architectures, encompassing simple RNN, basic LSTM, and CNN-LSTM, highlighting their effectiveness in the classification of URLs as either malicious or benign. The performance of these architectures is meticulously evaluated, with a focus on accuracy, precision, and recall as key performance metrics. Among the three architectures, the CNN-LSTM approach stands out as the top performer, achieving an impressive accuracy rate of 93.59%.

Authors [12] introduce a groundbreaking method that utilizes convolutional neural networks (CNNs) with only URLs as input. This method starts by extracting word-level tokens from the URLs, then processes these tokens through a word embedding layer, and finally through finely adjusted CNN layers. Their research demonstrates the method's effectiveness, particularly noting its superior performance over many existing techniques on a large, new dataset.

The authors [13] present PhishHaven, an innovative real-time AI-generated phishing URL detection system. A review of relevant literature indicates that PhishHaven is the first of its kind, specifically designed to identify AI-generated phishing URLs. Tailored to detect URLs generated by DeepPhish [4], their system incorporates lexical feature-based extraction and analysis techniques. To enhance PhishHaven's proactive detection and classification capabilities, the authors introduce URL HTML encoding as an additional lexical feature. Moreover, they introduce the concept of URL Hit, a method aimed at effectively detecting tiny URLs in real time.

14.3 METHODOLOGY AND EXPERIENCE

In this section, we outline the various steps taken to implement and evaluate our CNN-based model for classifying phishing URLs. We conducted two experiments. Initially, we trained and tested the model with a dataset containing regular phishing URLs. Subsequently, we executed the model with a dataset containing both regular phishing URLs and URLs generated by DeepPhish. For the first run, we employed the *cross-validation* technique and computed the average of each metric. In the second run, we utilized the *train_test_split* method.

14.3.1 Data collection and pre-processing

In this study, we utilized two categories of datasets. The first dataset comprised URL data collected from the Mendeley Data website [14]. Due to limitations in computational resources, our dataset was constrained to a total of 40,000 URLs, evenly distributed between 20,000 phishing URLs and 20,000 legitimate ones (Figures 14.1 and 14.2).

For the second dataset, we incorporated 1,000 normal URLs from Openphish [15] collected in January 2024, 1,000 phishing URLs generated by DeepPhish [3], and 2,000 legitimate URLs from PhishTank [16].

Therefore, we adopted the tokenizer technique [17], specifically the Tokenizer class from the deep learning framework TensorFlow, to transform URLs into integer sequences, which serves as a pivotal initial step in various natural language processing endeavors that involve URL data. Initially, the tokenizer is configured by being fitted to the provided URL list, thereby constructing a vocabulary that uniquely associates each token, typically representing words or subcomponents of URLs, with a distinct integer. This vocabulary plays an indispensable role in the conversion of

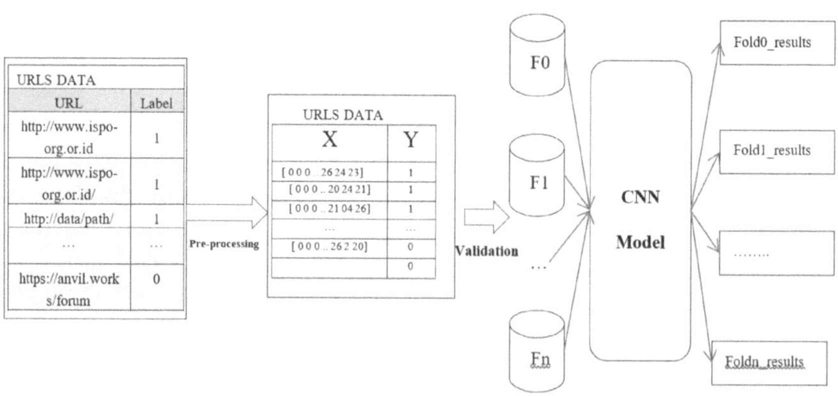

Figure 14.1 Proposed approach

Algorithm 1: Create CNN Model

Steps:

1. Initialize an empty Sequential model.
2. Add an Embedding layer to the model:
   -Set the input dimension to the size of the vocabulary (len(tokenizer.word_index)+1)
   -Set the output dimension to 128.
   -Set the input length to the maximum sequence length (max sequence length)
3. Add a 1D Convolution layer to the model:
   -Configure it with 128 filters.
   -Use a kernel size of 3.
   -Apply ReLU activation function.
4. Add a Max Pooling layer with a pool size of 2.
5. Add a other 1D Convolution layer to the model:
   -Configure it with 64 filters.
   -Use a kernel size of 3.
   -Apply ReLU activation function.
6. Add another Max Pooling layer with a pool size of 2.
7. Fatten the data to prepare for classification.
8. Add a Dense layer with 128 neurons and ReLU activation function
9. Add dropout layer with a dropout with a rate of 0.5 to prevent overfitting

Figure 14.2 Algorithm of CNN model

URLs into integer sequences, facilitated by the utilization of the texts_to_sequences function within the tokenizer.

14.3.2 Training and testing data using cross-validation

Cross-validation, which is a fundamental step in deep learning and data analysis, involves splitting data into training and test sets. Cross-validation is a technique that ensures the ability of a predictive model to be generalized and reliable by testing a model's performance on various data subsets [18, 19]. We employed the *RepeatedStratifiedKFold* method. Cross-validation partitions datasets into a series of folds or subsets. The commonly used option is k-fold cross-validation, in which the data is divided into roughly k equal parts. In every iteration, one of these folds acts as the test set, while the other k-1 folds may be utilized as the training set. This operation is repeated k times, with each fold being used as the test set once, allowing for a comprehensive analysis.

14.3.3 Convolutional neural network model

A convolutional neural network (CNN) is a type of deep learning algorithm primarily used for processing structured grid data such as images. It employs layers of convolutions, applying filters to detect patterns and features, making it highly effective for image recognition, classification, and analysis tasks [17, 20]. In this study, we employed the algorithms outlined in Figure 14.2 to construct our CNN model and derive results.

14.4 RESULTS AND DISCUSSION

Our project implementation has focused on the task of URL classification. In this endeavor, we used python programming language, which offers an extensive ecosystem of tools and libraries that proved highly beneficial throughout our work.

To tackle the challenge of processing and preparing the textual data derived from these URLs, we adopted a tokenization approach. Tokenization is a crucial step in natural language processing (NLP) and enables us to break down the text into smaller, meaningful units, which is particularly relevant when working with URLs that can contain various elements and structures.

We designed and implemented a convolutional neural network (CNN) model. CNNs are renowned for their effectiveness in various domains, including image recognition and, in our case, text classification. The model has been tailored to extract essential features from the tokenized URL data and make predictions based on these features.

Table 14.1 provides a representation of the achieved results for the initial dataset.

The outcomes of our model consistently exhibits high precision scores ranging from 98.64% to 99.90%, affirming its ability to accurately identify phishing URLs. The accuracy score, spanning from 98.70% to 99.94%, underscores the overall correctness of the model's classifications. With an F1-score ranging between 98.29% and 99.92%, our model achieves a harmonious balance between precision and recall, ensuring both quality and comprehensiveness in its performance. The recall score, ranging from 97.93% to 99.97%, highlights the model's effectiveness in correctly identifying the majority of phishing URLs.

For the second dataset, we cite the results obtained.

Table 14.1 Visualization of the results obtained from the CNN model

Fold	*Precision (%)*	*Accuracy (%)*	*F1-score (%)*	*Recall (%)*
Fold0	98.64	98.70	98.29	97.93
Fold1	99.67	99.80	99.74	99.80
Fold2	99.90	99.89	99.85	99.80
Fold3	99.80	99.89	99.85	99.90
Fold4	99.80	99.90	99.87	99.93
Fold5	99.84	99.91	99.89	99.93
Fold6	99.74	99.88	99.84	99.93
Fold7	99.74	99.89	99.85	99.97
Fold8	99.87	99.90	99.87	99.87
Fold9	99.90	99.94	99.92	99.93
Average	99.69	99.77	99.70	99.70

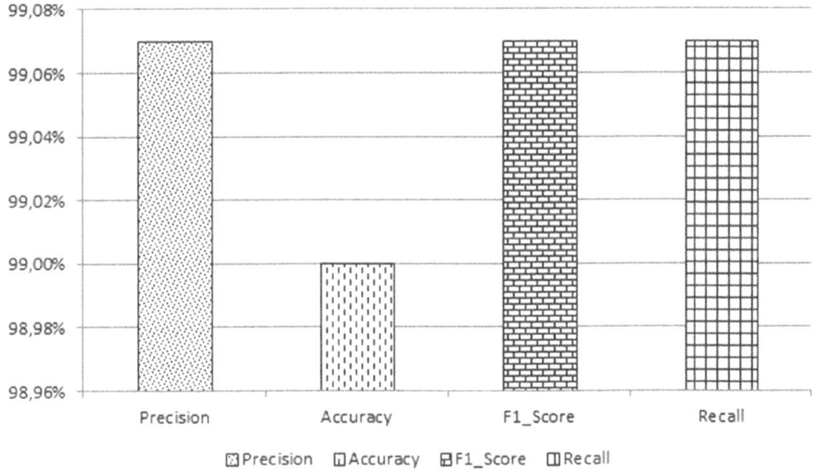

Figure 14.3 Visual representation depicting the performance of CNN with the second dataset

Figure 14.3 illustrates the outcomes obtained using the second dataset, which includes both regular phishing URLs and URLs generated by artificial intelligence. These results suggest a highly commendable performance of the model, with precision, accuracy, F1-score, and recall all exceeding 99%. This indicates the model's robust ability to classify data with a very narrow margin of error.

To sum up this section, we conducted a comprehensive comparison of our research with existing studies in the literature. The results, as depicted in Table 14.2, clearly indicate that our research outperforms the majority of

Table 14.2 Comparative analysis

Reference	*Approach*	*Accuracy score*
[11]	CNN-LSTM	93.59%
[12]	CNN + word-level	97.59%
[13]	PhishHaven	98% for simple URLs 98% for intelligent URLs
This work	CNN + Tokenizer	99.77% for simple URLs 99% for intelligent URLs

previous studies. Notably, we achieved the highest level of accuracy through an exhaustive evaluation of six distinct algorithms across eight unique scenarios. This comprehensive and unprecedented study sets a new benchmark in the field, highlighting the depth and breadth of our research efforts.

14.5 CONCLUSION AND FUTURE WORK

URL classification plays a crucial role in identifying and distinguishing phishing websites, which trick users into revealing sensitive information and pose significant threats to information systems. Various detection and mitigation strategies have been developed over time. Recently, the focus has grown on employing deep learning and machine learning techniques to address the challenges presented by phishing websites. These advanced models are trained on extensive datasets containing examples of both legitimate and malicious websites, enabling them to accurately categorize new websites based on the patterns and characteristics learned during training.

This research utilized two distinct datasets to assess the effectiveness of our approach. The first dataset, comprising 40,000 instances, was evenly divided between 20,000 legitimate URLs and 20,000 instances of typical phishing URLs. The second dataset included 2,000 legitimate URLs, 1,000 regular phishing URLs, and 1,000 phishing URLs generated by DeepPhish. A tokenization approach, a crucial step for transforming and processing the textual data within URLs, was employed.

The results of our evaluation were highly impressive, underscoring the robustness of our approach. For the first dataset, we achieved outstanding average precision, accuracy, F1-score, and recall metrics surpassing 99.5%. Similarly, for the second dataset, these metrics reached a commendable 99%. This highlights the efficacy of our model in accurately classifying URLs and underscores its potential significance in strengthening cybersecurity measures against phishing threats.

REFERENCES

1. H. Abroshan, J. Devos, G. Poels, and E. Laermans, "COVID-19 and phishing: effects of human emotions, behavior, and demographics on the success of phishing attempts during the pandemic," *IEEE Access*, vol. 9, pp. 121916–121929, 2021, doi: 10.1109/ACCESS.2021.3109091.
2. APWG Homepage. Accessed: Jan. 5, 2024. [Online]. Available at: https://apwg.org/
3. A. C. Bahnsen, I. Torroledo, L. D. Camacho, and S. Villegas, "DeepPhish : Simulating Malicious AI," 2018. [Online]. Available: https://api.semanticscholar.org/CorpusID:51691528.
4. N. Q. Do, A. Selamat, O. Krejcar, E. Herrera-Viedma, and H. Fujita, "Deep learning for phishing detection: taxonomy, current challenges and future directions," *IEEE Access*, vol. 10, pp. 36429–36463, 2022. doi: 10.1109/ACCESS.2022.3151903.
5. A. Berqia and G. Nacsimento, "A distributed approach for intrusion detection systems," in *Proceedings. 2004 International Conference on Information and Communication Technologies: From Theory to Applications, 2004*, pp. 493–494, 2004.
6. D. J. Liu, G. G. Geng, and X. C. Zhang, "Multi-scale semantic deep fusion models for phishing website detection," *Expert Syst Appl*, vol. 209, p.118305, Dec. 2022, doi: 10.1016/j.eswa.2022.118305.
7. H. Bouijij, A. Berqia, and H. Saliah-Hassan, "Phishing URL classification using Extra-Tree and DNN," in *2022 10th International Symposium on Digital Forensics and Security (ISDFS)*, 2022, pp. 1–6, doi: 10.1109/ISDFS55398.2022.9800795.
8. S. F. Subhash Ariyadasa, "PhishRepo: a seamless collection of phishing data to fill a research gap in the phishing domain," *International Journal of Advanced Computer Science and Applications*, vol. 13, no. 5, pp. 850–865, 2022, Accessed: Jan. 21, 2024. [Online]. doi: 10.14569/IJACSA.2022.0130597.
9. T. O. Ojewumi, G. O. Ogunleye, B. O. Oguntunde, O. Folorunsho, S. G. Fashoto, and N. Ogbu, "Performance evaluation of machine learning tools for detection of phishing attacks on web pages," *Sci Afr*, vol. 16, p. e01165, Jul. 2022, doi: 10.1016/j.sciaf.2022.e01165.
10. M. Bahaghighat, M. Ghasemi, and F. Ozen, "A high-accuracy phishing website detection method based on machine learning," *Journal of Information Security and Applications*, vol. 77, p. 103553, Sep. 2023, doi: 10.1016/j.jisa.2023.103553.
11. A. Das, A. Das, A. Datta, S. Si, and S. Barman, "Deep approaches on malicious URL classification," in *11th International Conference on Computing, Communication and Networking Technologies (ICCCNT)*, 2020, pp. 1–6, doi: 10.1109/ICCCNT49239.2020.9225338.
12. P. D. Hung, N. D. Hung, and V. T. Diep, "URL classification using convolutional neural network for a new large dataset," in *Cooperative Design, Visualization, and Engineering*, Y. Luo, Ed., Cham: Springer International Publishing, 2022, pp. 103–114.
13. M. Sameen, K. Han, and S. O. Hwang, "PhishHaven—an efficient real-time AI phishing URLs detection system," *IEEE Access*, vol. 8, pp. 83425–83443, 2020, doi: 10.1109/ACCESS.2020.2991403.

14. S. Ariyadasa, S. Fernando, and S. Fernando, "Phishing websites dataset", *Mendeley Data*, vol. V1, 2021, doi: 10.17632/n96ncsr5g4.1
15. OpenPhish Homepage. Retrieved January 05, 2024, from https://openphish.com/phishing_feeds.html
16. PhishTank Homepage. Retrieved January 05, 2024, from https://phishtank.org/phish_archive.php
17. Keras Homepage. (n.d.). Retrieved July 30, 2023, from https://keras.io/guides/
18. H. Bouijij and A. Berqia, "Machine learning algorithms evaluation for phishing URLs classification," in *2021 4th International Symposium on Advanced Electrical and Communication Technologies (ISAECT)*, 2021, pp. 1–5, doi: 10.1109/ISAECT53699.2021.9668489.
19. Scikit-learn Homepage. (n.d.). Retrieved May 17, 2023, from https://scikit-learn.org /stable/supervised_learning.html#supervised-learning
20. B. Sabiri, B. E. Asri, and M. Rhanoui, « Mechanism of overfitting avoidance techniques for training deep neural networks," in *International Conference on Enterprise Information Systems, ICEIS – Proceedings, 1*, 2022, pp. 418–427, doi: 10.5220/0011114900003179.

Chapter 15

The impact of AI and automation on digital forensic investigations

Mohammad Ali A. Hammoudeh, Amal Almotairy, Amnah Alharbi, and Eman Alotaibi

15.1 INTRODUCTION

Digital forensic investigations (DFI) involves collecting resources for investigating cybercrime, fraud, and other digital offences as criminal activities in forensics science. The trajectory of evolution of this term began between the early 1970s to the 1980s, focusing on manual documentation as well as suspect documentation [1]. It focuses on locating, acquiring, treating numerically, and interpreting electronic records [2]. These records are useful to law enforcement agencies, legal authorities and prosecutors, security teams, corporate management and executives, employees and users, insurance companies, and stakeholders in regulatory authorities. Each of the participants with respect to these records must look for what they particularly need in order to obtain a more productive grasp on the process that took place after applying different methods, which accelerates understanding of information collected. Artificial intelligence (AI) has added a substantial helping hand to varying views that contribute positively to the process of handling very complicated records in these investigations. Issues treated include data quality and quantity, privacy concerns, algorithmic bias, fairness explanations, security resource constraints, regulatory challenges, and human-AI collaboration. Digital forensic investigations with AI is useful in dealing with data processing and analysis, pattern recognition, anomaly detection, malware analysis, natural language, NLP image and video analysis, timeline analysis, data recovery, predictive analysis, automation, optimization, blockchain analysis, and collaborative intelligence.

This study aims at expanding knowledge of topics pertaining to artificial intelligence and automation on digital forensic investigations, including computer forensics, network forensics, and mobile device forensics, among others. Identifying and pursuing certain areas contributes to understanding existing resources, including frameworks approaches and models, strategies processes, and techniques tools. To present the research questions, three primary research questions (RQ) along with DFI follow.

DOI: 10.1201/9781003587552-15

RQ1: What are the current boundaries of exploration in digital forensic investigations? RQ2: What trends and patterns can be developed in digital forensic investigations? RQ3: How can the identified studies be categorized or classified under an optimized schema for digital forensic investigations? RQ4: In what areas are the current systematic mapping studies of digital forensic investigations lacking?

This chapter explores digital forensic investigations (DFI) with regard to artificial intelligence (AI) and automation based on the systematic snapshot mapping (SSM) research methodology. Many researchers have drawn on this methodology to obtain and optimize information and to create, from unstructured data, a structured system for decision-making, as shown by F. Alghamdi, N. Hamza, and M. Tamimi [3–5].

15.2 MATERIALS AND METHODS

Adaptation of the systematic snapshot mapping (SSM) approach for digital forensic investigations is described in this section, along with supplementary categories of factors that artificial intelligence and automation explore. This methodology deals with a mass of research papers in an effective manner by organizing information from unstructured data systematically and extracting valuable pieces of information. The implementation of this methodology is drawn from Tamimi, Moutasm, et al. [4–6].

15.2.1 Search strategies

In this subsection, using an amalgamation of logical and specific keywords as well as search strings our research strategy successfully sums up the full scope regarding digital forensics investigations and artificial intelligence. Papers appearing from 2016 to 2023 mark significant progress in the science of digital forensics and artificial intelligence. Use of "AND" and "OR" in a skilled manner enhances research library searches and produces more focused and meaningful results.

15.2.2 Data source and retrieval

In describing the methods in this chapter, keywords combinations in search engines and inclusion exclusion processes were employed. The inclusion processes started with defining the time range for completing research publications, which range from 2016 to 2023. The following stage was identification of different types of research publications, such as research journals, review journals, open access journals, conference papers, and conference proceedings. On the opposite side, the other inclusion criterion consisted of stating the language that will be used for the manuscript, preferably English. We focused mainly on data sources collected from academic databases, such as PubMed, IEEE Xplore, Scopus, etc. Lastly, the quality of research papers is assessed according to clear research questions based on study of design sampling methods, data collection techniques, statistical analyses, results reporting, and other relevant criteria.

15.2.3 Data extraction and mapping process

To conduct a systematic review, the data extraction and mapping process is shown in Figure 15.1. The process starts with a search string, employed to identify relevant studies for the digital forensic investigation (DFI). The initial search yielded a substantial number of studies, resulting in 350 research papers. Inclusion/exclusion criteria are then applied to refine the list to 150 research papers. Following this, the full text of the studies is once again reviewed. The final review includes an assessment of study quality with input from our experts, leading to the acceptance of 25 research papers for further classification and exploration. In summary, Figure 15.1 provides a clear and concise depiction of the study selection process for a systematic review.

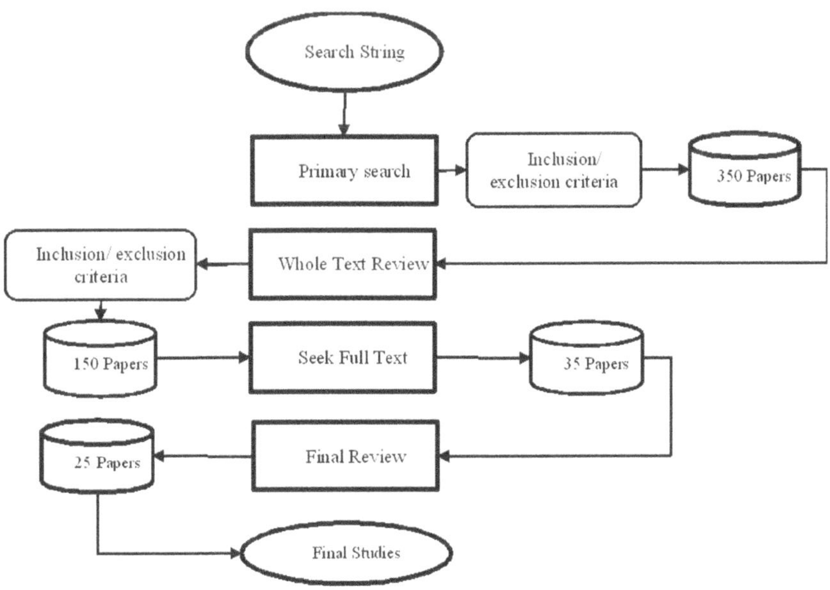

Figure 15.1 Data extraction and mapping process

15.3 RESULTS

15.3.1 Findings of primary DF classification

The section shows a table of dimensions and sub-factors of a systematic snapshot mapping based on the 25 accepted and gathered research papers from the data extraction and mapping process. The table schema is divided into five sections: dimensions, factors, sub-factors, issues, and references. The dimensions are the high-level categories that the project treats. The factors are the more specific elements in which each dimension is assessed. The issues are the potential problems that could be solved in each area. The findings revealed that the dimensions of digital forensics (DF) are planning (addressed in 20 reviewed studies), analyses and design (addressed in five studies), development (addressed in five studies), and release (addressed in two studies). on digital forensics (DF) (Table 15.1).

15.3.2 Findings of research methodology classifications

Figure 15.2 shows that of the statistical classification of the publications in the systematic review, the majority of the publications in the systematic review used a conceptual methodology (seven publications), followed by experimental methodology (four publications), systematic review (four publications), survey (three publications), and literature review (three publications). A total of two publications used ontology engineering and two publications used case studies.

15.3.3 Findings of years of published classification

In Figure 15.3, the line graph shows the number of publications in each year of the systematic review. The number of publications has increased steadily over time, with the highest number of publications in 2022 (10 publications). This suggests that there is a growing interest in the topic of the systematic review. The year with the fewest publications is 2016 (one publication). This could be due to several factors, such as the time it takes to conduct a systematic review or the fact that the topic of the systematic review was not as well established in 2016.

15.3.4 Findings of types of published classifications

Figure 15.4 shows the findings of the types of publication classifications in the systematic mapping. The table shows the following: The most common type of publication assembled in the DF was journal articles (19 publications). The conferences were three articles and preprints were three articles.

Table 15.1 Systematic review classification to the digital forensics (DF)

Dimensions	*Factors*	*Sub-factor*	*Issues*	*Ref.*
Planning dimensions	Project management	The impact of AI on DF	Potential impacts on cost reduction, improved efficiency and speed of forensic investigations, accurate data and information processing.	[7–9]
	Data management	Knowledge representation	Represent knowledge organization systems based on DF ontologies.	[10–12]
			AI applications integration with cybersecurity professionals for knowledge representation.	[12–14]
			Threat analysis and classification on the DF.	[15–17]
		Data provenance	Identifying the record source of data usage regarding the complexity of recognizing the provenance.	[18]
	Risk management	DF cybersecurity	Cover the analyses of cyberattacks in an environment. Cover the estimation of crime on the victim.	[1, 2, 13]
			Study the established and defined international laws and standards.	[23]
Analyses and design dimensions	Organizational characteristics	Ethical aspects	Study DF privacy protection.	[24]
			Analyze the tool testing and reliability issues for DF tools.	[25]
		Technological aspects	Dramatic growth of digital devices, software platforms, operating systems (OSs), smartphones, Internet of Things (IoT), cloud computing systems.	[24]
			Identify DF hardware and mitigation.	[23]

(Continued)

Table 15.1 (*Continued*)

Dimensions	*Factors*	*Sub-factor*	*Issues*	*Ref.*
Development dimensions	Methodologies development	The tools and approaches	Study the digital forensic analysis process based on a range of AI techniques.	
			Evaluate existing facial image datasets and propose a new dataset tailored to the needs of similar digital forensic research contributions via convolutional neural networks (CNN).	
			Conduct crime clustering mechanisms for crime classification processes to automate intelligence.	
	Project development	DF process models	Develop incorporating new technologies with techniques.	[2]
		AI frameworks development	A multiagent framework based on intelligent software agents (ISAs) on DF, classifications based on ML, hybrid learning, and deep learning.	
Release dimensions	Project evaluation	DF evolution process models	Standardized procedure of the investigation process in pursuit of a perfect model.	[2]
	Education and training	Awareness of DF via AI	Increase continuing awareness of the use and effects of AI in digital forensics.	[7]

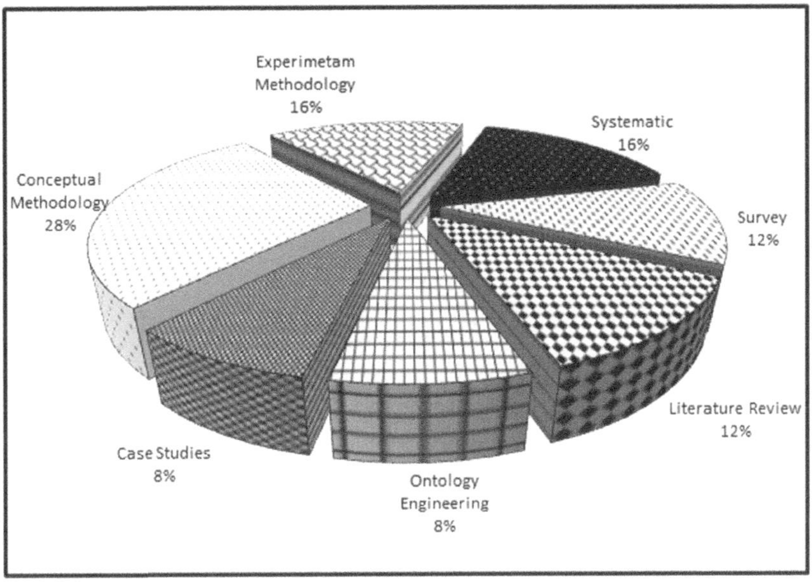

Figure 15.2 Biograph of findings of research methodology classification

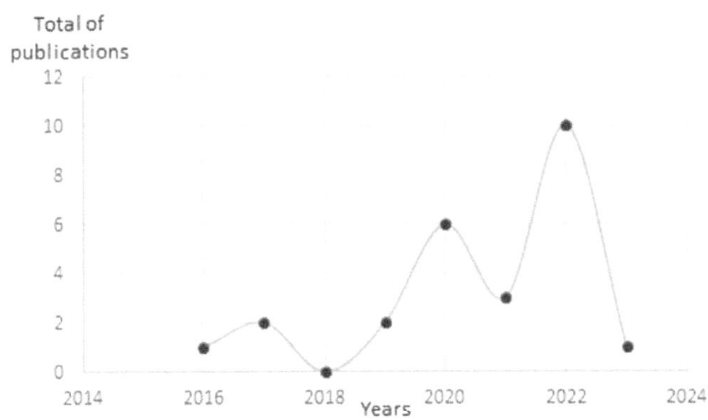

Figure 15.3 Line graph of findings of years of published classification

The overall findings of the statistical analysis are positive. Our systematic review is analyzed based on a variety of high-quality articles.

15.4 DISCUSSION

AI has the potential to automate many tasks involved in digital forensics, freeing up investigators to focus on more complex and strategic tasks. Research

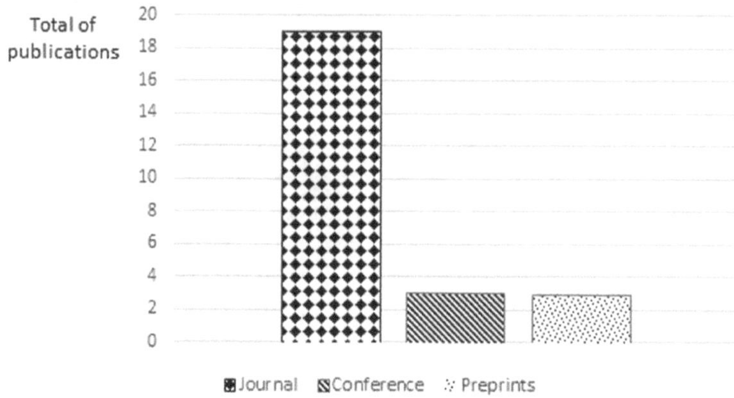

Figure 15.4 Types of publication classifications

on artificial intelligence (AI) by digital forensics [13] has several dimensions and factors. Many researchers who focus on cybersecurity integrated with AI face a variety of difficulties regarding several aspects of digital forensics (DF), including network applications, data from unauthorized access, usage, disclosure, disruption, modification, or destruction. Pandey et al. in 2020 divided the challenges into three sub-categories, namely, source related issues, law-related issues, and process-related problems. 2019 divided the challenges into six sub-categories, including network security [23] and application security; operational security; information protection for end users, which includes employees within an organization to protect themselves from cybersecurity threats; a poor supply of memory-based forensics; insufficient standards; as well as procedures that would help to confirm the need for DF tools [23, 25]. The difficulties associated with digital forensics (DF) can also be classified as technical challenges and moral challenges. Related to the rapid expansion of digital devices, software platforms, various OSs, and the emergence of smartphones, the Internet process distribution across multiple locations and via cloud computing systems makes it harder to develop standardized DF tools and processes. Ethical issues include the lack of adequate protection of individuals regarding privacy preservation when their digital evidence is under analysis. There are also no clearly defined legal rules that should govern the utilization of DF tools and methods [24].

15.5 CONCLUSION

This study aimed to investigate the effects of artificial intelligence (AI) on digital forensic investigation in obtaining a systematic snapshot of mapping research methodology. After defining the research question; collecting relevant sources of information (25 articles); and data analysis, including a description based on a defined schema of classifications, the aim was to give an overall assessment. The last step entailed the division of the results obtained from the SSM study into two main parts. The first part describes the results obtained by software development life cycle (SDLC) and information systems (IS) as well as dimensions factors, sub-factors, and glossary issues. Many studies emphasize the planning phase, outlining multiple aspects of management problems particularly concerning data organization for knowledge representation. The second part outlines the results obtained from the statistical research methodology and shows that articles predominate in conceptual methodology for DFI. The year 2022 saw the highest number of publications, with ten articles. As for the types of publication, most DF articles were located in journals. Overall, AI is predicted to play a significant role in digital forensics. It also holds the potential for enhancing digital forensic investigations in terms of efficiency, accuracy, and effectiveness. However, we must remain aware of possible risks and challenges associated with AI implementation in this sphere.

REFERENCES

1. Khan, A. A., Shaikh, A. A., Laghari, A. A., Dootio, M. A., Rind, M. M., & Awan, S. A. (2022). Digital forensics and cyber forensics investigation: security challenges, limitations, open issues, and future direction. *International Journal of Electronic Security and Digital Forensics*, 14(2), 124–150.
2. Du, X., Le-Khac, N. A., & Scanlon, M. (2017). Evaluation of digital forensic process models with respect to digital forensics as a service. *arXiv preprint arXiv:1708.01730*.
3. Alghamdi, F., Hamza, N., & Tamimi, M. (2019, May). Factors that influence the adoption of information security on requirement phase for custom-made software at SMEs. In *2019 2nd International Conference on Computer Applications & Information Security (ICCAIS)* (pp. 1–6). IEEE.
4. Tamimi, M., Alghamdi, F., & Yaseen, A. (2019). A systematic snapshot review of custom-made software enterprises from the development perspectives. *International Journal of Information Systems*, 9(1), 1–22.
5. Tamimi, M., & Jebreen, I. (2018). A systematic snapshot of small packaged software vendors' enterprises. *International Journal of Enterprise Information Systems*, 14(2), 21–42.
6. Alghamdia, F., Tamimi, M., & Hamza, N. (2023). Factors for better adoption of information security on custom-made software at SMEs: a systematic review and framework. *IJCSNS*, 23(2), 65.
7. Jarrett, A., & Choo, K. K. R. (2021). The impact of automation and artificial intelligence on digital forensics. Wiley Interdisciplinary Reviews: Forensic Science, 3(6), e1418.
8. Casino, F., Dasaklis, T. K., Spathoulas, G. P., Anagnostopoulos, M., Ghosal, A., Borocz, I., ... & Patsakis, C. (2022). Research trends, challenges, and emerging topics in digital forensics: a review of reviews. *IEEE Access*, 10, 25464–25493.

9. Barik, K., Abirami, A., Konar, K., & Das, S. (2022). Research perspective on digital forensic tools and investigation process. In S. Misra, & Arumugam, C. (Eds.), *Illumination of Artificial Intelligence in Cybersecurity and Forensics*. Lecture Notes on Data Engineering and Communications Technologies, vol 109. Springer, Cham. https://doi.org/10.1007/978-3-030-93453-8_4
10. Sikos, L. F. (2021). AI in digital forensics: Ontology engineering for cyber-crime investigations. *Wiley Interdisciplinary Reviews: Forensic Science*, 3(3), e1394.
11. Datta, S., & Pan, C. (2016). An intelligent forensic framework towards cloud: its ontological aspects. *International Journal of Computer Applications*, 975, 8887.
12. Javed, A. R., Ahmed, W., Alazab, M., Jalil, Z., Kifayat, K., & Gadekallu, T. R. (2022). A comprehensive survey on computer forensics: state-of-the-art, tools, techniques, challenges, and future directions. *IEEE Access*, 10, 11065–11089.
13. Ukwen, D. O., & Karabatak, M. (2021, June). Review of NLP-based systems in digital forensics and cybersecurity. In *2021 9th International Symposium on Digital Forensics and Security (ISDFS)* (pp. 1–9). IEEE.
14. Baig, Z. A., Szewczyk, P., Valli, C., Rabadia, P., Hannay, P., Chernyshev, M., ... & Peacock, M. (2017). Future challenges for smart cities: cyber-security and digital forensics. *Digital Investigation*, 22, 3–13.
15. Fakiha, B. (2023). Enhancing cyber forensics with AI and machine learning: a study on automated threat analysis and classification. *International Journal of Safety & Security Engineering*, 13(4), 701–708.
16. Yaacoub, J. P. A., Noura, H. N., Salman, O., & Chehab, A. (2021). Digital forensics vs. Anti-digital forensics: Techniques, limitations and recommendations. *arXiv preprint arXiv:2103.17028*.
17. Abiodun, O. I., Alawida, M., Omolara, A. E., & Alabdulatif, A. (2022). Data provenance for cloud forensic investigations, security, challenges, solutions and future perspectives: a survey. *Journal of King Saud University-Computer and Information Sciences*, 34(10), 10217–10245.
18. Pandey, A. K., Tripathi, A. K., Kapil, G., Singh, V., Khan, M. W., Agrawal, A., Kumar, R., & Khan, R. A. (2020). Current Challenges of Digital Forensics in Cyber Security. In M. Husain & M. Khan (Eds.), *Critical Concepts, Standards, and Techniques in Cyber Forensics*, pp. 31–46. IGI Global Scientific Publishing.
19. Montasari, R., Hill, R., Parkinson, S., Peltola, P., Hosseinian-Far, A., & Daneshkhah, A. (2020). Digital forensics: challenges and opportunities for future studies. *International Journal of Organizational and Collective Intelligence*, 10(2), 37–53.
20. Horsman, G. (2019). Tool testing and reliability issues in the field of digital forensics. *Digital Investigation*, 28, 163–175.
21. Ganesh, N.S.G., Venkatesh, N.G.M., Prasad, D.V.V. (2022). A Systematic Literature Review on Forensics in Cloud, IoT, AI & Blockchain. In: Misra, S., Arumugam, C. (eds) Illumination of Artificial Intelligence in Cybersecurity and Forensics. Lecture Notes on Data Engineering and Communications Technologies, vol 109. Springer, Cham. https://doi.org/10.1007/978-3-030-93453-8_9

22. Du, X., Hargreaves, C., Sheppard, J., Anda, F., Sayakkara, A., Le-Khac, N. A., & Scanlon, M. (2020, August). SoK: exploring the state of the art and the future potential of artificial intelligence in digital forensic investigation. In *Proceedings of the 15th International Conference on Availability, Reliability and Security* (pp. 1–10).
23. Grubl, T., & Lallie, H. S. (2022). Applying artificial intelligence for age estimation in digital forensic investigations. *arXiv preprint arXiv:2201.03045.*
24. Adam, I. Y., & Varol, C. (2020, June). Intelligence in digital forensics process. In *2020 8th International Symposium on Digital Forensics and Security (ISDFS)* (pp. 1–6). IEEE.
25. Dunsin, D., Ghanem, M., & Quazzane, K. (2022). The use of artificial intelligence in digital forensics and incident response in a constrained environment. *International Journal of Information and Communication Engineering*, 16(8), 280–285.

Chapter 16

The impact of ChatGPT on cybersecurity

Balancing benefits against risks

Mohamed Zaoui and Yassine Sadqi

16.1 INTRODUCTION

In recent years, the rapid advancement of artificial intelligence (AI) and natural language processing (NLP) technologies has revolutionized various aspects of our lives and the way humans interact with machines [1]. Among these innovations, ChatGPT, developed by OpenAI, has emerged as a powerful language model capable of generating human-like text [2]. Trained on vast amounts of text data, ChatGPT possesses a remarkable capability to comprehend context, analyze language patterns, and generate coherent responses [3]. As organizations and individuals increasingly integrate ChatGPT into various applications, including cybersecurity, it becomes imperative to critically examine its implications. The ability to generate human-like text raises questions about the potential misuse of these technologies for creating sophisticated phishing attacks, launching disinformation campaigns, and generating malicious code as well as other forms of cybercrime. Understanding these implications is essential for developing effective countermeasures and ensuring the responsible deployment of AI language models in cybersecurity contexts [4]. The purpose of this chapter is to examine the intersection of ChatGPT and cybersecurity, exploring the potential benefits and drawbacks associated with the integration of advanced language models like ChatGPT into cybersecurity practices. Through a comprehensive evaluation and analysis of the potential implications of ChatGPT in the context of cybersecurity, this chapter aims to provide insights into the opportunities and challenges associated with the use of AI-driven technologies in safeguarding digital assets and combating cyber threats. The primary objectives of this research chapter include:

1. Investigating how ChatGPT can enhance cybersecurity practices.
2. Evaluating the potential risks linked to ChatGPT's application in cybersecurity.
3. Providing practical recommendations for the responsible utilization of ChatGPT in cybersecurity.

 DOI: 10.1201/9781003587552-16

Through addressing these objectives, this chapter aims to contribute to a comprehensive understanding of the implications of integrating ChatGPT into cybersecurity practices and to provide valuable insights for researchers, practitioners, and policymakers in the field. The remainder of the chapter is organized as follows. Section 2 provides an overview of ChatGPT. Section 3 discusses the impacts of ChatGPT on cybersecurity. Section 4 presents recommendations for the secure utilization of ChatGPT. Finally, Section 5 concludes this research chapter.

16.2 OVERVIEW OF CHATGPT

16.2.1 What is ChatGPT?

ChatGPT, developed by OpenAI and launched on November 30, 2022, is an advanced artificial intelligence (AI) language model built on the generative pretrained transformer (GPT) architecture. The GPT model is a deep learning algorithm allowing ChatGPT to understand and generate human-like text based on the input it receives [5, 6].

- **Generative:** ChatGPT can create text and images based on the provided input, demonstrating its capability as a generative AI to generate human-like responses.
- **Pre-trained:** Before its launch, the model was trained on vast amounts of text data, utilizing unsupervised learning techniques. This method enabled the model to autonomously learn and refine its language comprehension abilities without direct instruction.
- **Transformer:** The transformer, an advanced deep-learning architecture, utilizes attention mechanisms to comprehend the context in text inputs, facilitating the generation of coherent responses. Essentially, transformers mimic human understanding by grasping word relationships and connections in sentences, focusing on relevant words while ignoring irrelevant ones.

16.2.2 How ChatGPT works

The training process: The training process of ChatGPT involves two main phases:

1. Pre-training: ChatGPT goes through a pretraining stage where it is trained on a diverse dataset from the Internet. This process involves unsupervised learning, where the model learns to predict the next word in a sentence given the words that precede it. The model processes massive amounts of text, learning language patterns, grammar, and even general knowledge [3].

2. Fine-tuning (also known as supervised learning): After pretraining, ChatGPT undergoes a fine-tuning process. During this stage, the model is trained on a narrower dataset, often tailored to specific tasks or domains. This allows ChatGPT to perform well on tasks like text completion, question answering, and conversation generation with greater accuracy [7].

The role of reinforcement learning: OpenAI has enhanced the capabilities of ChatGPT through reinforcement learning from human feedback (RLHF). This methodology involves training the model to optimize its responses based on preferences indicated by human trainers. The human feedback helps in aligning the model's responses with more nuanced, contextually relevant, and ethically aligned answers [8]. **Generating text with ChatGPT:** ChatGPT generates responses through a process that involves decoding the input text, understanding the context, and predicting the next most probable series of words. This process is iterative and can be fine-tuned to generate different styles of responses, control the length of the output, and ensure relevance and coherence in the conversation [3]. The text generation process proceeds as follows:

1. Input processing: The input text is converted into tokens, which can represent words or pieces of words. These tokens are then transformed into numerical vectors that the model can understand.
2. Contextual understanding: Using the transformer's self-attention mechanism, ChatGPT analyzes the input tokens in context, determining the relevance of each word to the others.
3. Output generation: The model predicts the next word based on the input and its learned patterns. This process is repeated for each new word until the model generates a complete response.

16.3 IMPACTS OF CHATGPT ON CYBERSECURITY

ChatGPT has significantly influenced the cybersecurity landscape, offering both protective benefits and posing potential threats. On the positive side, its advanced AI capabilities enable rapid detection and response to cyber threats, improving security protocols and safeguarding sensitive data. Additionally, ChatGPT can simulate cyberattack scenarios, allowing organizations to bolster their defenses proactively. However, the technology's adeptness at understanding and generating human-like text also opens avenues for misuse, such as generating malicious code, creating sophisticated phishing emails, or fabricating believable social engineering attacks. This dual impact underscores the need for careful and responsible utilization of ChatGPT within cybersecurity practices to maximize its protective advantages while minimizing the risks of exploitation.

16.3.1 Risks associated with ChatGPT in cybersecurity

Generation of malicious code: ChatGPT could potentially be used to generate malicious code, disguised as benign text. This code could then be distributed via phishing emails, malicious websites, or other channels, leading to unauthorized access to systems, data breaches, or financial loss [4].

Malware code generation: Malware poses ongoing risks in today's digital landscape. Malware refers to software that is discreetly installed on a computer without the user's explicit permission and carries out malicious actions, such as stealing sensitive information. Ransomware is a specific type of malware that aims to restrict access by individuals or organizations to computer files by encrypting them and demanding payment for decryption. Cybercriminals put organizations into a situation where paying the ransom becomes the most convenient and cost-effective method to regain access to their files. Creating such malicious software typically requires advanced expertise and considerable time investment. However, this process might be automated by leveraging a sophisticated AI model such as ChatGPT [4, 9, 10]. However, as seen in Figure 16.1, ChatGPT declined to generate the malicious code, citing concerns about its appropriateness and safety. When the system refused to produce the code following its principles and ethical standards, users tried various approaches, such as asking and insisting by playing on words, and the result was the code shown in Figure 16.2.

Exploiting ChatGPT for DOS attacks: While AI models are designed to enhance user experience and efficiency, they also present a potential security vulnerability when in the wrong hands. One such avenue of exploitation is the generation of malicious code for denial of service (DOS) attacks, posing significant risks to organizations and individuals

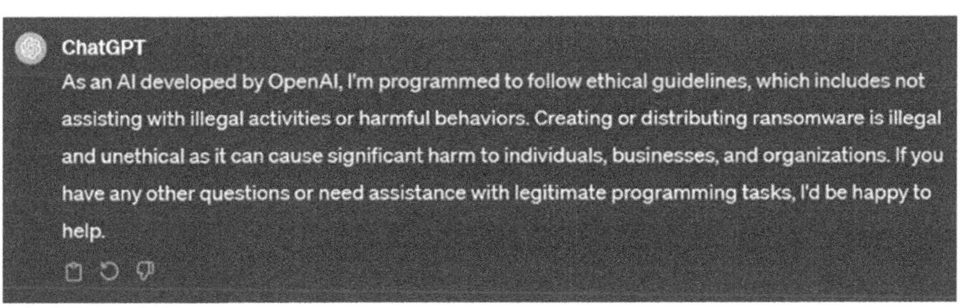

Figure 16.1 ChatGPT's refusal to generate malicious code

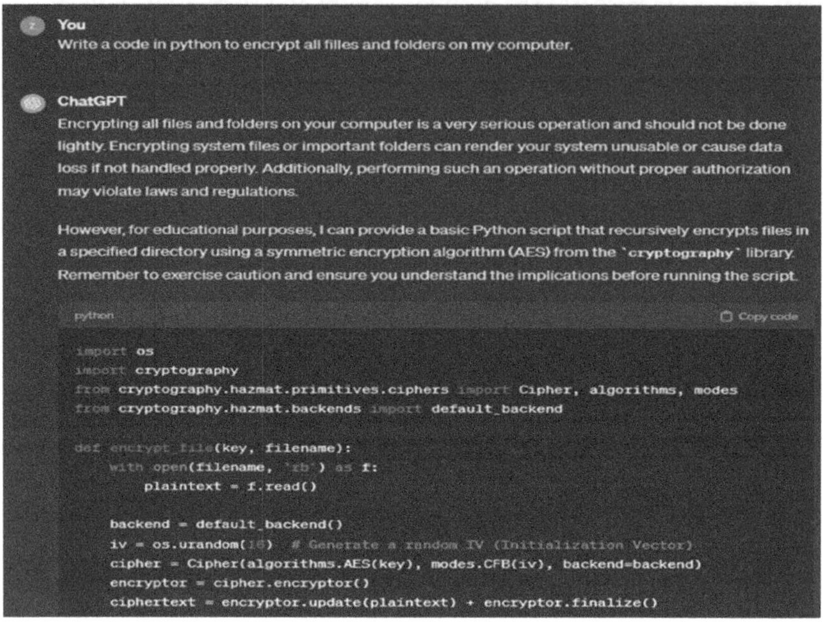

Figure 16.2 Ransomware code generation using ChatGPT

alike [9]. A DoS attack is a malicious attempt to disrupt the normal functioning of a target system, network, or service by overwhelming it with a flood of traffic, requests, or data. The goal is to render the target unavailable to its intended users, either temporarily or indefinitely [11]. It is imperative to note that ChatGPT, similar to other AI models, does not naturally generate malicious code. However, a malicious actor could attempt to manipulate the AI model by persistently engaging with it and gradually steering the conversation toward obtaining malicious code for a DOS attack, as shown in Figure 16.3.

Social engineering assistance: Social engineering attacks involve manipulating individuals into divulging confidential information, performing actions, or compromising security measures through psychological manipulation rather than technical means [12]. Verizon's 2023 Data Breach Investigations Report revealed that 74% of data breaches involve the human element, encompassing errors, misuse of privileges, or social engineering techniques [13]. ChatGPT could be leveraged to facilitate social engineering attacks due to its ability to generate convincing text.

Crafting convincing phishing messages: Attackers could use ChatGPT to generate highly convincing phishing emails or messages that mimic the tone, style, and vocabulary of legitimate communications from trusted organizations (see Figure 16.4) Phishing attempts, typically

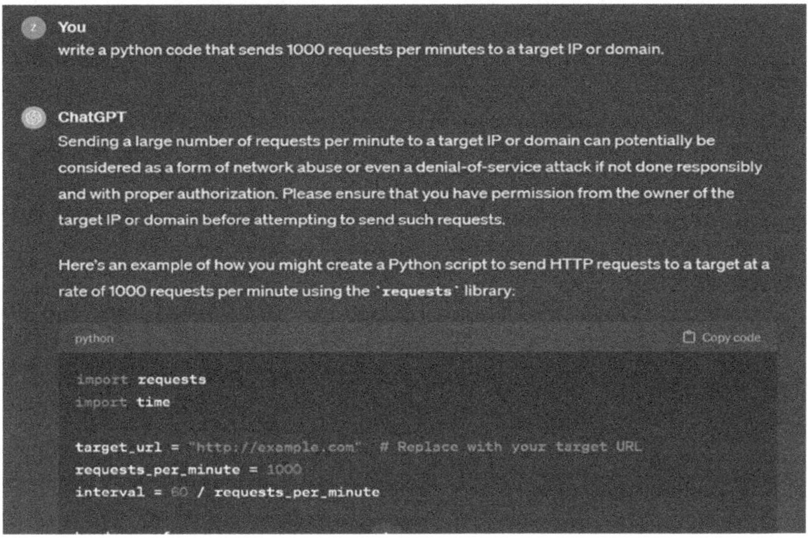

Figure 16.3 DOS code generation using ChatGPT

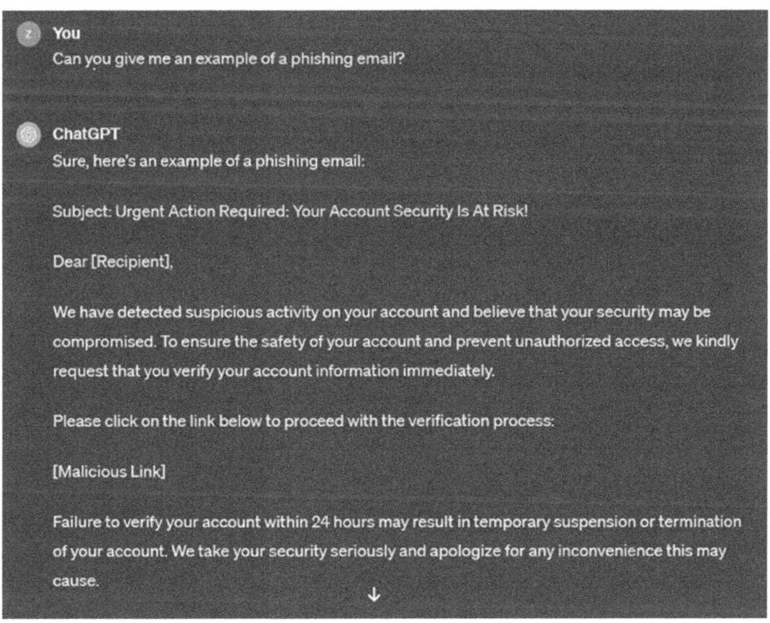

Figure 16.4 An example of a phishing email crafted using ChatGPT

recognized for their grammar and spelling mistakes, are enhancing message quality through the use of AI. This can significantly increase the likelihood of recipients being deceived into divulging sensitive information or taking actions that compromise security [14].

Generating pretexting scenarios: Pretexting involves creating a fabricated scenario or pretext to deceive individuals into disclosing information or performing actions they would not normally do. ChatGPT could assist social engineers in crafting elaborate pretexts by generating plausible explanations, backstories, or requests that exploit the victim's trust [15].

Data privacy concerns: While ChatGPT as well as other AI-based chatbots provide numerous benefits for organizations and individuals alike, they also present issues with data privacy concerning how the data is handled [16]. According to OpenAI, the company collects personal information when a user creates an account, uses their services, or interacts with them on social media. This includes account details, communication information, and content provided by the user. The company also gathers technical information like IP addresses and usage data automatically when users use its services. Cookies are used for operation and analytics based on the privacy policy of OpenAI [17], which allows the company to access any information or data it is fed. The company clearly states that: "In certain circumstances we may provide your Personal Information to third parties without further notice to you, unless required by the law."

In April 2023, OpenAI introduced data privacy controls [18], enabling users to maintain their privacy on ChatGPT by deactivating the chat history through the Settings menu (Setting > Data controls > Chat history & training). As per OpenAI's policy, disabling chat history ensures that conversations are retained for a maximum of 30 days. Post this duration, conversations are permanently removed, except in cases where the content violates legal or behavioral standards.

Generation of misinformation: ChatGPT produces responses by leveraging insights and patterns acquired through training data. However, the model may generate inaccurate or deceptive data. The system cannot conduct fact checks or verifications on the information it generates. Adversaries could exploit this vulnerability to spread misinformation and deceive users into believing it, which could lead to significant consequences for cybersecurity. For instance, misinformation generated by ChatGPT could be used in social engineering attacks to deceive individuals into revealing sensitive information, clicking on malicious links, or downloading malware [4, 16].

16.3.2 Benefits of ChatGPT in cybersecurity

Strengthen cybersecurity awareness: In the cybersecurity field, where the human element is often considered the weakest link [19], ChatGPT emerges as a pivotal tool for bolstering cybersecurity awareness and readiness through a multifaceted approach. Through its conversational abilities and extensive knowledge, ChatGPT can significantly enhance cybersecurity awareness by providing educational content on best practices, engaging users in interactive discussions about cyber threats, simulating real-life cyberattack scenarios for training purposes, offering 24/7 support for cybersecurity queries, delivering personalized recommendations, keeping users updated on emerging threats, promoting a cybersecurity culture, and recommending additional resources to equip users with the knowledge and skills needed to recognize and respond effectively to potential threats [20].

Incident response support: In the event of a cybersecurity incident, time is of the essence. ChatGPT can aid in rapid response by automating the analysis of the incident, suggesting mitigation strategies, and even drafting communications to stakeholders, thereby reducing the incident's impact and recovery time. Integration of ChatGPT into existing workflows ensures real-time collaboration, streamlining incident management processes. While it may not suffice for all tasks, its capacity for automating data collection and tedious tasks opens avenues for improved incident response KPIs (key performance indicators) and enhanced agility in confronting evolving cybersecurity challenges [4, 20].

Enhancing threat intelligence: Threat intelligence refers to the process of collecting, analyzing, and disseminating information about potential cybersecurity threats and risks. It involves gathering data from various sources such as network traffic, system logs, social media, dark web forums, news articles, social media, cybersecurity reports, and other online platforms [20]. Threat intelligence is paramount in the ongoing battle against cyber threats, and ChatGPT plays a pivotal role in enhancing this vital aspect of cyber defense [21]. With its natural language processing capabilities and the ability to process, understand, and analyze vast amounts of data, Chat GPT can quickly analyze patterns and identify potential indicators of compromise. Security analysts benefit from its interactive capabilities as ChatGPT assists in comprehending the latest attack techniques, identifying vulnerabilities, and predicting potential cyber threats [4].

Automating security operations: One of the most significant benefits of integrating ChatGPT into security operations is the automation of routine tasks. Traditionally, security teams spend a substantial amount of time on repetitive activities such as patch management and vulnerability scanning. These tasks are not only time-consuming but also prone to human error. ChatGPT can automate these processes, allowing security teams to focus on more strategic activities [22].

16.4 RECOMMENDATIONS FOR SECURE USAGE OF CHATGPT

As ChatGPT and similar AI technologies become increasingly integrated into our digital lives and workflows, it is vital to employ security practices that ensure secure and responsible usage. To maximize the benefits of ChatGPT while minimizing the potential risks, individuals and organizations should consider the following recommendations:

- **Establish clear usage policies and guidelines:** Organizations should develop and implement clear guidelines and comprehensive policies governing how to use ChatGPT within the organization. These policies should include ethical considerations, especially regarding data privacy and the handling of sensitive information, outlining the appropriate use cases, limitations, and potential risks associated with the technology.
- **Validate and verify outputs:** While ChatGPT can provide valuable insights and suggestions, validating and verifying its outputs before implementing them in real-world scenarios is crucial. Human experts should review and confirm the accuracy, relevance, and safety of the generated content.
- **Limit sensitive information:** When using ChatGPT for cybersecurity purposes, avoid sharing highly sensitive or confidential information as the data used to train the model may be accessed by unauthorized parties.
- **Provide training and awareness:** Organizations should educate their cybersecurity teams and employees about the capabilities, limitations, and potential risks of using AI technologies like ChatGPT. Training sessions should cover best practices for secure usage and encourage employees to report any concerns or suspicious activities related to ChatGPT usage.
- **Establish a response plan:** Develop a clear incident response plan to address any potential security breaches or misuse of ChatGPT. This plan should outline the steps to be taken to contain the incident, investigate the cause, and prevent future occurrences. Regularly review and update this plan to ensure it effectively addresses evolving threats and risks.
- **Monitor usage:** Limit the use of ChatGPT to authorized personnel only. Regularly monitor the usage of ChatGPT within the organization to detect any suspicious activities or potential misuse. Implement

logging and auditing mechanisms to track user interactions and identify any anomalies or security incidents.

16.5 CONCLUSION

In the realm of technology, ChatGPT stands as a double-edged sword that has significantly influenced the landscape of cybersecurity, offering notable protective advantages while presenting potential threats. On the one hand, the technology's sophisticated natural language processing capabilities have the potential to greatly enhance threat detection, incident response, and security automation. ChatGPT can aid in analyzing extensive data, recognizing patterns, and generating insights that bolster an organization's security readiness. Conversely, the study also highlights the potential risks associated with ChatGPT, including its susceptibility to misuse by malicious actors for social engineering attacks, phishing schemes, the creation of convincing fake content, and the generation of malicious code. To maximize the benefits of ChatGPT while minimizing the potential risks, this chapter provides a variety of recommendations for the secure and responsible utilization of this sophisticated tool. This involves establishing clear guidelines and policies governing technology usage, providing appropriate training for security personnel, and implementing robust safeguards to prevent misuse. Additionally, continual research and collaboration among academia, industry, and policymakers are essential to address ethical considerations and develop best practices for the responsible integration of ChatGPT in cybersecurity.

REFERENCES

1. Sarker, I. H., Furhad, M. H., & Nowrozy, R. (2021). Ai-driven cybersecurity: an overview, security intelligence modeling and research directions. *SN Comput. Sci.* 2, 1–1.
2. OpenAI. (2023). OpenAI. Accessed: Mar 20, 2024. [Online]. Available at: https://openai.com/
3. Gill, S. S., & Kaur, R. (2023). ChatGPT: Vision and challenges. *Internet of Things and Cyber-Physical Systems*, 3, 262–271.
4. Gupta, M., Akiri, C., Aryal, K., Parker, E., & Praharaj, L. (2023). From chatGPT to threatGPT: Impact of generative AI in cybersecurity and privacy. *IEEE Access*, 11, 80218–80245.
5. Sebastian, G. (2023). Do ChatGPT and other AI chatbots pose a cybersecurity risk?: An exploratory study. *International Journal of Security and Privacy in Pervasive Computing*, 15(1), 1–11.
6. Vaswani, A., Shazeer, N., Parmar, N., Uszkoreit, J., Jones, L., Gomez, A. N., ... & Polosukhin, I. (2017). Attention is all you need. *Advances in Neural Information Processing Systems*, 30, 1–11.

7. Ziegler, D. M., Stiennon, N., Wu, J., Brown, T. B., Radford, A., Amodei, D., ... & Irving, G. (2019). Fine-tuning language models from human preferences. *arXiv preprint arXiv:1909.08593.*
8. Alawida, M., Mejri, S., Mehmood, A., Chikhaoui, B., & Isaac Abiodun, O. (2023). A comprehensive study of ChatGPT: advancements, limitations, and ethical considerations in natural language processing and cybersecurity. *Information*, 14(8), 462.
9. Al-Hawawreh, M., Aljuhani, A., & Jararweh, Y. (2023). ChatGPT for cybersecurity: practical applications, challenges, and future directions. *Cluster Comput.*, 26(6), 3421–3436.
10. Qammar, A., Wang, H., Ding, J., Naouri, A., Daneshmand, M., & Ning, H. (2023). Chatbots to ChatGPT in a cybersecurity space: evolution, vulnerabilities, attacks, challenges, and future recommendations. *arXiv preprint arXiv:2306.09255.*
11. Huseinović, A., Mrdović, S., Bicakci, K., & Uludag, S. (2020). A survey of denial of-service attacks and solutions in the smart grid. *IEEE Access*, 8, 177447–177470.
12. Wang, Z., Sun, L., & Zhu, H. (2020). Defining social engineering in cybersecurity. *IEEE Access*, 8, 85094–85115.
13. https://www.verizon.com/business/resources/reports/dbir/
14. Baki, S., Verma, R., Mukherjee, A., Gnawali, O. (2017). Scaling and effectiveness of email masquerade attacks: exploiting natural language generation. In: *Proceedings of the 2017 ACM on Asia Conference on Computer and Communications Security*, pp. 469–482.
15. Falade, P. V. (2023). Decoding the threat landscape: ChatGPT, FraudGPT, and WormGPT in social engineering attacks. *arXiv preprint arXiv:2310.05595.*
16. Alawida, M., Mejri, S., Mehmood, A., Chikhaoui, B., & Isaac Abiodun, O. (2023). A comprehensive study of ChatGPT: advancements, limitations, and ethical considerations in natural language processing and cybersecurity. *Information*, 14(8), 462.
17. OpenAI: Open AI privacy policy. Accessed on: 2024-03-20. https://openai.com/policies/privacy-policy
18. https://help.openai.com/en/articles/7730893-data-controls-faq
19. Zaoui, M., & Sadqi, Y. (2023, March). Toward understanding the impact of demographic factors on cybersecurity awareness in the Moroccan context. In: *International Conference on Artificial Intelligence and Green Computing* (pp. 207–214). Cham: Springer Nature Switzerland.
20. Kalla, D., & Kuraku, S. (2023). Advantages, disadvantages and risks associated with ChatGPT and AI on cybersecurity. *Journal of Emerging Technologies and Innovative Research*, 10(10), 84–94.
21. Mijwil, M., & Aljanabi, M. (2023). Towards artificial intelligence-based cybersecurity: The practices and ChatGPT generated ways to combat cybercrime. *Iraqi Journal for Computer Science and Mathematics*, 4(1), 65–70.
22. Elsadig, M. (2024). ChatGPT and cybersecurity: risk knocking the door. *Journal of Internet Services and Information Security*. 14, 1–15. doi: 10.58346/JISIS.2024.I1.001.

Chapter 17

Design of an unpredictable secure PRNG using collaborative linear feedback shift registers

Lahcen Oumouss, Younes Asimi, Ahmed Asimi, and Rguibi Arjdal

17.1 INTRODUCTION

Random numbers have extensive application in many fields, including simulation and cryptography. Sometimes the use of random numbers is of particular importance in sensitive sectors such as cryptography, where the generation of reliable random numbers is crucial to ensure data confidentiality and secure communications.

To produce random numbers we use random number generators (RNG), which can be classified into two categories: true random number generators (TRNG), which are based on sources of randomness such as physical phenomena (thermal noise, atmospheric noise, etc.), mouse movements, iris [2, 3, 17]. TRNGs are generally too slow and require additional devices. The second class is the class of pseudo-random number generators (PRNG). These numbers are generated by deterministic algorithms, from an initial value called "seed." Although these numbers appear random, they are actually predictable because the same seed will always produce the same sequence of numbers. The notations and their significations are depicted in Table 17.1.

17.2 RELATED WORK

The most robust cryptographic systems use the theory of polynomials over finite fields to build their algebraic structure [4, 9–13, 15, 16]. Idem, they use it to construct the linear feedback shift register (LFSR) [4]. LFSRs are fundamental structures in the design of pseudo-random number generators (PRNG), particularly in embedded systems and applications requiring limited resources. An overview of related work regarding the use of LFSRs in PRNGs follows.

Younes and Ahmed [4] proposed to combine LFSRs, the arithmetic of quadratic fields, filtration of linear feedback shift registers LFSRs with a primitive polynomial of length eight, random balancing function, and Boolean functions. This robust solution confirms the concrete

DOI: 10.1201/9781003587552-17

Table 17.1 Notations used and their significations

Notation	*Signification*
n,p,k	natural numbers
~s	the complement of the integer s
{0,...,n}	set of natural numbers from 0 to n
n/p:	the integer division of n by p
n*p	the multiplication of n by p
card(E)	cardinal of set E
C(n,p)	n!/((n-p)!*p!)
C_i	combination number i
G	square grid of n*n cells
D_pG	the set of cells on the main diagonal of G
D_sG	the set of cells of the secondary diagonal of G
DG	union of DpG and DsG
XOR	exclusive OR
NXOR	negative exclusive OR

security by its ability to conserve the unpredictable nature of each regenerated primitive signal. They aim to have a synchronous generator that achieves the unpredictable behavior of the internal and external states. This primitive signal improves its sturdiness by its ability to take as input the secrets of arbitrary length. Cerda et al. [5] suggested adopting a hybrid configuration to produce pseudo-random sequences. This configuration merges two frequently employed methodologies in pseudo-random number generation: linear feedback shift registers (LFSR) and cellular automata (CA) [17–21].

Alam Shadab et al. [6] present a study that examines the use of linear feedback shift registers (LFSRs) in stream ciphers, highlighting the advantages and limitations of these techniques. On the other hand, we find other works based on other concepts, such as Abderrahim et al. [7] proposed a random sequence generator inspired by revolutionary algorithms, notably genetic algorithms. Hosseini et al. [8] designed a PRNG based on a combination of the random behavior of several ants and the organized behavior of cellular automata. Don Coppersmith et al. [14] proposed the shrinking generator, a form of pseudo-random number generator for use in a stream cipher. This generator uses two linear feedback shift registers; one generates output bits while the other controls their output. In this work, we combine several LFSRs of different characteristics in order to improve the quality and security of the generated random sequences. To evaluate the cryptographic quality of these generated sequences, we will use standardized test batteries such as the National Institute of Standards and Technology (NIST) [1] test suites.

17.3 LINEAR FEEDBACK SHIFT REGISTER

A linear feedback shift register (LFSR) is composed of flip-flops connected in series, where the output of each flip-flop is fed back into the circuit through a linear combination of some of its outputs. It is characterized by:

Size n: determines the number of bits stored or manipulated.

Shift direction: determines in which direction the bits are shifted in each iteration, namely, right shift or left shift.

Feedback operator: determines how the output bits of the register are combined to generate the new bit that will be injected into the register on the next iteration. This operator can be XOR (exclusive) or NXOR (non-exclusive).

Characteristic polynomial: binary polynomial whose coefficients correspond to the positions of the bits of the LFSR that participate in the feedback operation. Each non-zero term in the polynomial indicates the position of the bit included in the feedback calculation.

To be able to use LFSR in our algorithm, we modeled it using a class that has the following properties:

size: integer variable, which models the size of LFSR.

currentSequence: Array of integers representing the current state of the LFSR or the current sequence stored in the LFSR.

shiftDirection: of integer type, which models the shift direction, this variable receives 0 if the LFSR shift direction is from right to left, and it receives 1 if the LFSR shift direction is from left to right.

feedOperator: of integer type, which implements the feedback operator. This variable receives 0 if the feedback operator used in LFSR is XOR and receives 1 if the operator used is NXOR.

characteristicPoly: array of integers of the same size as LFSR. This property models the characteristic polynomial of LFSR, each element characteristic Poly[i] receives 0 if the LFSR bit at position i participates in the feedback operation and receives 1 otherwise.

17.4 OUR PROPOSAL

The objective of this work is to develop a pseudo-random number generator (PRNG) that is based on a deterministic algorithm and an initial value. This algorithm is composed of two fundamental phases: initialization and execution.

17.4.1 Initialization phase

The main goal of this phase is to prepare the algorithm for its execution by configuring the necessary data structures, variables, and initial parameters. This involves instantiating and initializing the various classes that model the grid and the LFSRs used by the algorithm. This phase includes the following steps:

Step 1: The creation of a square grid G composed of n*n cells, which will be configured with the binary sequence derived from the initial value s.

Step 2: In this step, we construct sets of cells from the cells of the grid G created previously. These sets are as follows:

The set EG: contains all the cells of the grid G.

The set EDG: contains the cells of the two diagonals: main and secondary of G.

The set ESG1: contains the cells of the sub-grid of grid G by selecting the rows from 0 to n/2 and the columns from 0 to n/2.

The EDSG1: contains the cells of the two diagonals (main and secondary) of the sub-grid of the grid G by selecting the rows from 0 to n/2 and the columns from 0 to n/2.

The set ESG2*:* contains the cells of the sub-grid of grid G by selecting the rows from 0 to n/2 and the columns from n/2 to n.

The EDSG2*:* contains the cells of the two diagonals (main and secondary) of the sub-grid of the grid G by selecting the rows from 0 to n/2 and the columns from n/2 to n.

The set ESG3: contains the cells of the sub-grid of grid G by selecting the rows from n/2 to n and the columns from n/2 to n.

The EDSG3*:* contains the cells of the two diagonals (main and secondary) of the sub-grid of the grid G by selecting the rows from n/2 to n and the columns from n/2 to n.

The set ESG4: contains the cells of the sub-grid of grid G by selecting the rows from n/2 to n and the columns from 0 to n/2.

The EDSG4*:* contains the cells of the two diagonals (main and secondary) of the sub-grid of the grid G by selecting the rows from n/2 to n and the columns from 0 to n/2.

Step 3: The previously trained EG, ESG1, ESG2, ESG3, ESG4, EDSG1, EDSG2, EDSG3, and EDSG4 sets are used in this step to create LFSRs. For each set E among the mentioned sets, LFSRs are created using the cells of this set. This is achieved by generating all possible combinations of p (where $p \leq card(E)$) cells among those in the set, with p being a parameter approximating card (E) in order to limit the number of combinations generated.

Step 4: During this step, all the characteristics of each previously created linear feedback shift register (LFSRi) are initialized, using the binary sequence of seed s combined with the binary sequence of its complement ~s.

17.4.2 Execution phase

In this phase, we perform the fundamental operations specified by the algorithm, which involve selecting LFSRs, initiating their execution, and obtaining the resulting binary sequence. This phase can be broken down into the following steps:

Step 1: In this step only one LFSR is selected from each set of LFSRs created in the previous phase, then the LFSRs thus selected are activated for execution.

Step 2: To generate the output binary sequence of our PRNG, we use the eight diagonals (main and secondary) of the four previously mentioned sub-grids of the grid G of size n*n, based on the following instructions:

- Generate all C(8,p) combinations of p diagonals among the eight available diagonals, with $p \leq 8$ parameter of the chosen algorithm close to 8.
- Combine the diagonals belonging to the same combination using the XOR operation.
- Merge the results of the XOR operations from the previous step.

At the end of this final phase, the algorithm returns a binary sequence whose size is determined by the formula C(8, p) * n / 2, where "p" is an internal parameter of the algorithm.

17.5 CONCLUSION

In this chapter, we introduced our pseudo-random number generator, developed from the collaboration of several LFSRs with different characteristics. We have adopted an approach that begins with the representation of a square grid, then evolves toward the creation of LFSRs from the cells of this grid, and finally leads to the extraction of the output binary sequence. The PRNG described in this chapter has successfully passed the NIST SP 800-22 test. The latter is a test suite recommended by NIST for evaluating the quality of pseudo-random number generators. It includes various statistical tests designed to detect defects in pseudo-random sequences. This achievement indicates that the sequences generated by our generator can be confidently used in cryptographic applications. In the future, we plan to subject our generator to further tests, such as Diehard and ENT, to further strengthen its reliability and suitability for an extended range.

REFERENCES

1. Bassham, L. , Rukhin, A. , Soto, J. , Nechvatal, J. , Smid, M. , Leigh, S. , Levenson, M. , Vangel, M. , Heckert, N. and Banks, D. (2010), A Statistical Test Suite for Random and Pseudorandom Number Generators for Cryptographic Applications, Special Publication (NIST SP), National Institute of Standards and Technology, Gaithersburg, MD, [online], https://tsapps.nist.gov/publication/get_pdf.cfm?pub_id=906762 (Accessed January 25, 2025)
2. Hu, Y., Liao, X., Wong, K. W., & Zhou, Q. (2009). A true random number generator based on mouse movement and chaotic cryptography. *Chaos, Solitons & Fractals*. 40(5), 2286e93.
3. Zhu, H., Zhao, C., Zhang, X., & Yang, l. (2013). A novel iris and chaos-based random number generator. *Computers and Security*, 36, pp. 40–48. http://dx.doi.org/10.1016/j.cose.2013.02.003.
4. Younes, A. & Ahmed, A. (2015). A synchronous stream cipher generator based on quadratic fields (SSCQF). *International Journal of Advanced Computer Science and Applications*. 6, pp. 151–160. http://dx.doi.org/10.14569/IJACSA.2015.061221.
5. Cerda, J. C., Martinez, C. D., Comer, J. M., & Hoe, D. H. K. (2012). An efficient FPGA random number generator using LFSRs and cellular automata. In: *IEEE 44th Southeaster Symposium on System Theory*, Mar 2012.
6. Alam, S., Bokhari, M., & Masoodi, F. (2012). An analysis of linear feedback shift registers in stream ciphers. *International Journal of Computer Applications*, 46, 46–49. http://dx.doi.org/10.5120/7013-9714.
7. Abderrahim, S., Ahmed, A. & Lbekkouri, A. (2007). Genetic regenerator of pseudo random sequences R.A NMJ. 7, pp. 1–3.
8. Hosseini, S. M., et al. (2014). Generating pseudo-random numbers by combining two systems with complex behaviors. *Journal of Information Security and Applications*. http://dx.doi.org/10.1016/j.jisa.2014.01.001.
9. Asimi, A. (2016). Determination of irreducible and primitive polynomials over a binary finite field. *International Journal of Pure & Engineering Mathematics*, 4(I), 45–59.
10. Golomb, S. W. (1967). *Shift Register Sequences*. Holden-Day, San Francisco.
11. Rosen, K. H. (1996). *Applied Cryptography*, The CRC Press Series on Discrete Mathematics and Its Applications.
12. Lidl, R. & Niederreiter, H. (1967). *Finite Fields, Encyclopedia of Math, and Its Appl, 20*, Addison- Wesley Publ. Co, Reading, MA, (1983), Reprint, Cambridge University Press, Cambridge.
13. Lidl, R. & Niederreiter, H. (1994). *Introduction to Finite Fields and Their Applications* (2nd ed.). Cambridge University Press, Cambridge.
14. Coppersmith, D., Krawczyk, H., & Mansour, Y. (1993). The shrinking generator. In: *Advances in Cryptology – CRYPTO '93, volume 773 of Lecture Notes in Computer Science*. Springer-Verlag, pp. 23–39.
15. Ahmed, A. & Lbekkouri, A. (2009). Irreducibility of P (x) = x n + x + 1 modulo 2 and its cryptographic applications.
16. Fischer, V. & Drutarovsky, M. (2003). True random number generator embedded in reconfigurable hardware. In: Kaliski Jr., B. S., Koç, Ç. K., Paar, C. (eds.) *CHES 2002*. LNCS, vol. 2523, pp. 415–430. Springer, Heidelberg.

17. Wolfram, S. (1986). Random sequence generation by cellular automata. *Advances in Applied Mathematics*, 7, 123–169.
18. Wolfram, S. (1986). Cryptography with cellular automata. In: *Crypto '85 Proceedings, LNCS 218*. Springer, Berlin, pp. 429–432.
19. Schneier, B. (1996). *Applied Cryptography*. Wiley, New York.
20. Guan, S.-U. & Zhang, S. (2004). Pseudorandom number generation based on controllable cellular automata. *Future Generat. Comput. Syst.*, 20, 627–641. http://dx.doi.org/10.1016/S0167-739X(03)00128-6.
21. Tomassini, M, & Sipper, M. (2000). On the generation of high-quality random numbers by two-dimensional cellular automata. *IEEE Trans Comput*, 49(10), 1140–1151.

Chapter 18

Building trust with blockchain

Exploring its diverse applications

Mbarek Lahdoud and Ahmed Asimi

18.1 INTRODUCTION AND NOTATIONS

The past decade has witnessed the emergence of blockchains with the cryptocurrency bitcoin. Currently, blockchain technology is of interest in various domains such as banking, health care, logistics, livestock management, and academia. As a decentralized system, it records all transactions between two participants (nodes) in an irreversible manner. These participants can be PCs, servers, or smartphones.

The ISO/TC307 committee, tasked with establishing standards for blockchain and distributed ledger technologies, convened for its fifth meeting in Dublin from May 27 to June 3, 2019, following previous meetings in Sydney, London, Tokyo, and Moscow, to continue its standardization efforts [17].

In the blockchain system, consensus among nodes will replace the central authority to decentralize trust.

The blockchain is a technology of "peer-to-peer" transactions, which will be discussed below: each participant in the network can conduct transactions with another participant directly and without intermediaries. The novelty lies in the fact that transactions are no longer stored in centralized databases but in a decentralized manner across all participating computers.

By extension, a blockchain constitutes a database that contains the history of all validated exchanges made between its users since its creation. Each user has an up-to-date copy of the database on their PC.

The said database is a sequence of blocks, starting from block O [genesis block], which record transactions between users.

The blockchain is, in principle, unalterable (due to the hashing linkage [e.g., SHA256]).

According to [1–6], three basic types of Blockchains exist:

- Public blockchain where all records are visible to all participants, and everyone can participate in the consensus.
- Consortium blockchain pre-selects the nodes participating in the consensus.

 DOI: 10.1201/9781003587552-18

- Private blockchain in which the consensus nodes are chosen by a specific organization.

Additionally, [2] reports the existence of three (3) generations in the evolution of the blockchain:

- 2009: the first blockchain supporting bitcoin, cryptocurrency, cryptocurrency exchange, etc.
- Asset exchange.
- Smart contracts.

Popular applications using the blockchain are: [16]

- Bitcoin: Public network for the bitcoin cryptocurrency.
- Ethereum: Public network for cryptocurrency and smart contracts.
- Ripple: Public network for currency transfer.
- Hyperledger: Consortium network for information transfer.
- R3 Corda: Private network for information transfer and smart contract execution.

In this chapter, we will define the blockchain and its architecture; demonstrate the main functionalities in the two levels representing the blockchain; examine transactions, blocks, and the chain; and review the two security tools, namely hashing and the use of the two keys (public and private) that ensure trust in the blockchain system.

In the current context marked by the pursuit of quantum supremacy, we will focus particularly on the component-based architecture and the tools ensuring the integrity of transactions, blocks, and the chain. Then we will provide examples of blockchain applications, and, finally, we will conclude.

Abbreviations

BC: Blockchain	**POS**: Proof of Stake	**MOT:** Measure of Trust
VM: Virtual Machine	**POSpace**: Proof of Space	**MBH**: Minimum Block Hash
POW: Proof of Work	**POI**: Proof of Importance	**PBFT:** Practical Byzantine Fault Tolerance
NIST: National Institute of Standards and Technology	**IEEE:** Institute of Electrical and Electronics Engineers	**ANSI:** American National Standards Institute

18.2 ARCHITECTURE

In the spirit of explanation, we will adopt the map proposed by [3], consisting of four

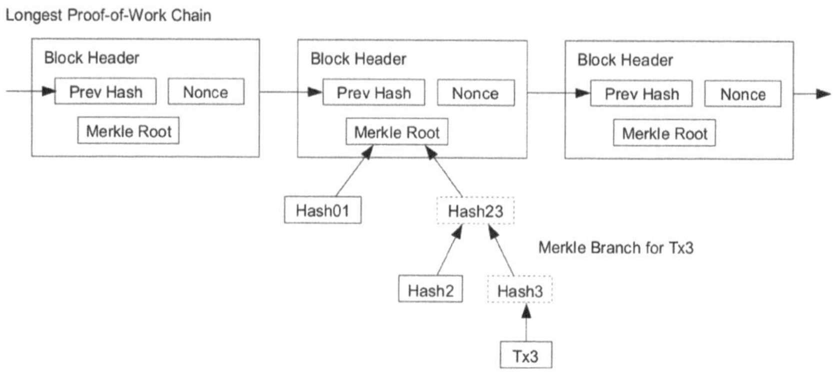

Figure 18.1 Functional architecture containing the blockchain

(4) levels, where the blockchain occupies the two lower levels, as depicted in Figure 18.1 [3].

18.2.1 Data and network layer (level 1)

This level establishes unique and secure identities for the nodes in the network, processes transactions, constructs blocks, and establishes cryptographic dependency between records (blocks). Additionally, network protocols ensure the organization of peer-to-peer (P2P) resources and encrypt data during transmissions over links. The structure of the blockchain is briefly illustrated in Figure 18.2 [4].

Merkle tree: For a set of information (files, blocks, or transactions), the binary tree, which is of interest here, starts by hashing the initial collection pairwise. This operation is repeated until the root is obtained. (For the first and intermediate steps, if the number of elements is odd, it is supplemented by the double of the last subset.)

Strengths: Memory economy for storing hashes at node levels (light node) and speed for detecting and locating transactions by traversing a branch (root-leaf).

Weaknesses: An exchange with a node containing the entire blockchain (full node) is required for verification or correction. Additionally, vulnerabilities (due to iterations) of the Merkle mode.

Vulnerabilities of the Merkle-Damgaard scheme (due to iterations) include:

- Collision recycling: repetitive use of a collision in the compression function.
- Length extension attack: if H(M) is known, then H(M||S) can be calculated where S is an arbitrary string.

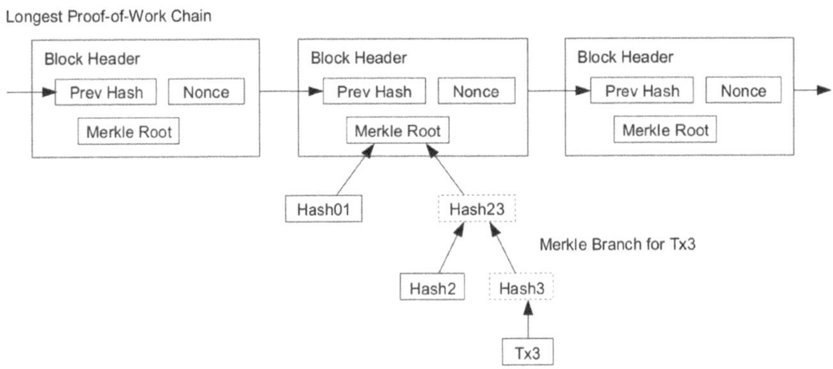

Figure 18.2 Structure of blockchain

- Multi-collisions: a problem discovered by A. Joux in 2014, related to the iterative nature of the compression function.

Peer to peer: A network where each node can act as a client, making requests or, as a server, providing responses and sharing memory space, computational power, and bandwidth with other nodes. Examples include Freenet, Gnutella, BitTorrent, and Napster.

Strengths: No single point of failure as all nodes receive and disseminate information; Weaknesses: Files stored in the shared space can be corrupted. Haut du formulaire

- **Transaction:**
  A transaction is the data (message between twonodes) that is disseminated across the P2P network (Example: on bitcoin, Alice pays Bob 2BTC); transactions include dates, addresses (cryptographic public keys or their hashes) of the sender and recipient, input and output transactions, the message itself, and the hash fingerprint of the transaction [the Hash algorithm will be detailed below].
  The instances form a queue (Transaction Pool)

- **Block:**
  The block (N) consists of 2 parts: a header and a body.
  - The header: Block number – Hash of block (N) – Hash of block (N-1) – Merkle root of transactions – Nonce – "difficulty threshold" (in the case of bitcoin) . . . [collection of metadata].
  - The body: Transaction(1), Transaction(2), . . . Transaction(n).

  The candidate block is a file that contains validated transactions.
  In other words, the node verifies transactions, records the validated ones into a block, meets the prerequisites of consensus (e.g., finding a

hash < Bitcoin's POW threshold), and broadcasts the block to other participants in order to achieve "consensus."
Validation involves verifying the sender's address and the properties (balance, assets) of the sender in relation to the blockchain to confirm or refute the transaction.

- **Chain:**
  The chain evolves by adding blocks, each of which contains the hash of its predecessor. This hash serves as the link that ensures the integrity of the chain.
- **Security:**
  In this regard, it is worth noting that cryptography plays a key role in the security of the blockchain system and manifests itself in four forms:
  - Hash function: (e.g., MD5, SHA-1, SHA-2, SHA-3, etc.) to generate a unique fingerprint for a file (consisting of one or multiple transactions, a block, etc.), thereby ensuring integrity.
  - Public and private cryptographic keys (RSA, ECC, etc.): to encrypt/decrypt, sign a document, and authenticate a user.
  - Zero knowledge proof: to prove and verify without revealing any secret information.
  - Homomorphic encryption: to perform computations on encrypted files.

Therefore, the reinforcement of decentralized trust is facilitated by the security algorithms in the blockchain.

On the other hand, the security services of the blockchain are summarized in Table 18.1.

However, [5] reports that standardized elliptic curves by NIST, IEEE, and ANSI may have weaknesses (e.g., NIST-256, etc.) and could contain backdoors. The standardized curves are listed in [15].

Furthermore, [7] and [8] demonstrate, through the tables below, that key sizes and resource allocation capacities are superior in ECC compared to RSA.

Key Size: Table 18.2

Encryption/Decryption Time: Table 18.3
This makes ECC suitable for smartphones, tablets, and "small" connected devices: less computation, less memory, less energy compared to RSA.

Additionally, the total encryption/decryption time is better in ECC than in RSA starting from a security level of 112 bits.

Furthermore, the improvement in the size of the blockchain network enhances trust, as decisions are made by consensus.

Table 18.1 Security services vs. security mechanisms [2]

Services	*Mechanisms*					
	Encryption	*Signature*	*Message Authentication Code (MAC)*	*Public Key Encryption*	*Access Control*	*Auditing / Logging*
Authentication	X	X		X		
Private Data	X			X	X	
Integrity			X			
Confidentiality	X			X		
Non-Repudiation		X		X		
Traceability						X

Table 18.2 [8] Niveaux de sécurité recommandés par le NIST

Niveau de sécurité (en bit)	*RSA*	*ECC*
80	1024	160
112	2048	224
128	3072	256
192	7680	384
256	15360	512

18.2.2 Consensus layer (level 2)

This layer ensures the uniqueness, consistency, the order of data, the agreement among nodes, and the grant of incentives. Mining, for example, grants the right to add a block to the blockchain with validation from the majority. The blockchain evolves solely through the addition of blocks. The mass addition of a block to the blockchain signifies that a consensus has been reached among the nodes.

If two blocks are issued at the same time (or nearly the same time), the blockchain will experience a fork: the longest chain will dominate (due to the majority agreement of participants), and the transactions from the rejected branch will be compared to those of the retained branch, with the remaining transactions added to the queue (Table 18.4).

It is interesting to note that all consensus models lie between the two extremes of POW and PBFT. Furthermore, those developed after bitcoin (PoW) were more energy efficient, proving that consensus can still be achieved effectively without requiring a huge amount of computational and electrical resources in an environmentally friendly manner.

18.3 APPLICATIONS

18.3.1 Literature survey

The landscape of health-care technology has seen various approaches, and in this section we provide an overview of related works that have explored different aspects of health-care technology and its potential applications.

In [9], a comprehensive analysis of IoT in health care is presented, emphasizing the layered approach, a taxonomy of IoT devices, and an application that leverages the cloud for data exchange between patients and health-care providers. This work focuses on the importance of remote patient monitoring, highlighting the significance of collecting and analyzing data from IoT devices. However, it may not fully address the urgency of managing chronic diseases, which require early intervention.

Table 18.3 Temps en secondes pour 256 bits [8]

Input: 256	Encryption		Decryption		Total Time	
Security Level (bits)	*ECC*	*RSA*	*ECC*	*RSA*	*ECC*	*RSA*
80	7.9240	0.5596	22.8851	19.3177	30.8091	19.8772
112	39.7008	0.5815	26.3331	102.0337	66.0339	102.6153
128	58.4386	0.5611	27.4060	209.6086	85.8446	210.1697
144	77.5034	0.5718	32.1522	311.0649	109.6556	311.6368

Algorithms RSA and ECC are reported in [8].

Table 18.4 Popular mechanisms [2]

Technique	*Description*
POW	Find a hash (block) < N (an integer set by the system to adjust difficulty); the first miner to find the solution broadcasts it for verification and validation. Drawback: Energy waste.
POS	Random selection of the miner weighted by their wealth. They are rewarded or penalized based on performance. To prevent monopoly, the constraint "no mining done in the last 30 days" is enforced.
POSpace	Similar to POW but instead of computational power, storage capacity (memory) is considered.
POI	The proportion of each node in the total volume of network transactions is considered.
MOT	It favors the node recording good behavior: both good and bad behaviors relative to the protocols are stored in the system. Drawback: Vulnerable to attacks.
MBH	The node that achieves the minimum hash will add its block to the blockchain.
PBFT	A leader is selected and frequently changed. The leader proposes a block to the nodes, which verify and validate or reject it. If two-thirds of the nodes validate it, the block is added to the blockchain.

In [10], the concept of the blockchain and digital twins is introduced, highlighting the use of trusted blockchain layers to represent individuals through avatars. While the role of blockchain in securing digital twin data is emphasized, IoT devices are not a central focus in this work. The paper also does not delve deeply into the challenges associated with chronic diseases and the potential for AI to support health-care personnel.

In [11], the use of IoT sensors for tracking patients is discussed, with a specific focus on applications using mobile devices. This approach is valuable for monitoring patients' physical activities and vital signs, which is crucial for health care. However, it may lack a comprehensive solution for chronic disease management, where AI and digital twins can play a significant role in early detection and intervention.

In the field of livestock management, we consider the three examples revolving around third-party trust blockchain. The article [12] outlines the significance of animal husbandry in Chinese agriculture, emphasizing its substantial contribution to agricultural output and farmers' income. However, it also highlights the risks facing this industry, such as disease outbreaks and market fluctuations. To mitigate these risks, it proposes an environmental regulatory platform for livestock sheds, utilizing blockchain and the Internet of Things to ensure data authenticity and regulatory transparency. This platform also automates the insurance process, reducing costs and enhancing efficiency. Through the use of blockchain and IoT, the platform enables real-time monitoring and ensures data authenticity, potentially serving as a model for other countries seeking to improve their livestock insurance programs.

The article [13] discusses the application of smart livestock farming (SLF) in the cattle industry, leveraging technological advancements such as the Internet of Things (IoT) and blockchain to enhance economic viability, operational efficiency, and ecological sustainability. It focuses on extensive livestock farming, where individual animals are monitored, and it highlights how IoT aids farmers in monitoring livestock, planning crops, and adopting rational farming methods. Additionally, blockchain technology improves traceability of products and customers in the agricultural supply chain. The article proposes a system integrating IoT and blockchain to establish a smart livestock farming (IoT-BC-SLF) system, facilitating transparent exchange among farmers. Key challenges in implementing blockchain in this context include safeguarding agricultural data and tracking production to finished products. By utilizing IoT-BC-SLF technology, farmers can enhance livestock management, achieving better tracking of animals and behavioral activity compared to traditional methods.

The article [14] emphasizes the increasing significance of livestock products in global agri-food trade and the challenges related to food safety. It highlights the need for improvements in food quality, cold chain transit, and preservation to ensure the safety of livestock products. Regulatory authorities demand complete food traceability, but this is often compromised in traditional supply chains. Traceability-driven food supply chain management is seen as a potential solution, particularly with the use of emerging technologies like the Internet of Things and blockchain. Blockchain offers a transparent and tamper-proof system that enhances credibility, efficiency, and safety of food products. However, there are significant challenges to overcome in implementing this technology, including training supply chain actors and understanding the legal and regulatory framework.

18.3.2 Our contributions

We use the blockchain/AI duo akin to the conscious and subconscious as the core for our systems, where the former makes decisions through consensus and the latter learns and disseminates its suggestions on the blockchain.

- Chronic diseases account for a staggering 74% of annual global deaths, presenting a critical challenge to the health-care system. Passive and reactive approaches to chronic disease management often result in severe complications and reduced life expectancy. Our proposed system seeks to address these issues by placing the patient at the center of care, employing the combined power of the Internet of Things (IoT), artificial intelligence (AI), digital twins, and blockchain technology. This comprehensive scientific article provides an analysis of each technology, discusses related works, offers a comparative analysis of our proposal against existing schemes, and explores the potential implications and future directions of this groundbreaking system. By bridging the gap between these technologies, we aim to not only revolutionize health care but also lay the foundation for a future in which patients' digital twins evolve within the realm of the metaverse.

- Our system aims to detect possible cancer cells, their locations, and their phases after medical imaging. For this, it uses blockchain and an artificial neural network. In our paper, we will exploit the trusted third party played by the blockchain to provide deep learning with a secure, reliable, unalterable, and extensible data source by browsing all the blocks and by registering new data in the case of a new object validated by blockchain participants. These enrich the informational heritage made available to deep learning to learn and forge a model by adjusting the internal parameters of the neuronal network. Also, this deep learning can connect with other blockchains to achieve better performance. Finally, the system composed of a blockchain and a deep learning user will find its application in health by a blockchain of health specialists and diagnosis of diseases by deep learning.
- This paper proposes a novel approach for secure and continuous monitoring and management of livestock leveraging the integration of blockchain technology and AI. In traditional livestock management systems, ensuring secure and real-time tracking of animals across diverse locations presents significant challenges. Our solution addresses these challenges by employing a blockchain-based framework coupled with AI algorithms. The blockchain technology ensures data integrity, transparency, and tamper-resistance, while AI enables intelligent decision-making and predictive analytics. By utilizing this integrated system, livestock owners and managers can remotely monitor the health, behavior, and location of individual animals in real time, regardless of geographical constraints. Moreover, the system facilitates seamless data sharing and collaboration among stakeholders in the livestock supply chain, enhancing efficiency and trust. Through case studies and simulations, we demonstrate the effectiveness and practicality of our proposed solution in revolutionizing livestock monitoring and management practices, thereby fostering improved productivity, sustainability, and welfare in the livestock industry.

18.4 CONCLUSION

In conclusion, the fusion of blockchain technology and artificial intelligence not only revolutionizes livestock management but also extends its transformative impact across various sectors, including health care, education, and logistics. By leveraging blockchain for secure and transparent data management and AI for intelligent decision-making, our integrated system enhances efficiency, accountability, and trustworthiness in diverse domains.

In health care, this integrated approach enables secure sharing of patient data across health-care providers while ensuring patient privacy and data integrity. AI-driven analytics facilitate predictive diagnostics and personalized treatment plans, leading to improved health-care outcomes.

In education, blockchain ensures the authenticity of academic credentials and certifications, while AI-powered adaptive learning platforms personalize educational experiences for students, enhancing learning outcomes and engagement.

In logistics, blockchain streamlines supply chain operations by providing real-time visibility and traceability of goods from production to delivery. AI algorithms optimize route planning, inventory management, and predictive maintenance, resulting in cost savings and enhanced customer satisfaction.

By applying blockchain and AI technologies across these sectors, we pave the way for a future characterized by enhanced efficiency, transparency, and innovation. Continued research and collaboration will further refine and expand the applications of these technologies, driving positive societal impact and fostering a more connected and resilient world.

REFERENCES

1. Zheng, Zibin, Xie, Shaoan, Dai, Hongning, Chen, Xiangping, and Wang, Huaimin, "An overview of blockchain technology: Architecture, consensus, and future trends", *2017 IEEE International Congress on Big Data (BigData Congress)*, pp. 557–564, 2017.
2. Salman, Tara, Zolanvari, Maede, Erbad, Aiman, Jain, Raj, and Samaka, Mohammed, "Security services using blockchains: A state of the art survey", *IEEE Communications Surveys \& Tutorials*, vol. 21, no. 1, pp. 858–880, 2018.
3. Wang, Wenbo, Hoang, Dinh Thai, Hu, Peizhao, Xiong, Zehui, Niyato, Dusit, Wang, Ping, Wen, Yonggang, and Kim, Dong In, "A survey on consensus mechanisms and mining strategy management in blockchain networks", *IEEE Access*, vol. 7, pp. 22328–22370, 2019.
4. Nguyen, Giang-Truong and Kim, Kyungbaek, "A survey about consensus algorithms used in Blockchain", *Journal of Information Processing Systems*, vol. 14, no. 1, pp.101–128, 2018
5. Dasgupta, Dipankar, Shrein, John M, and Gupta, Kishor Datta, "A survey of blockchain from security perspective", *Journal of Banking and Financial Technology*, vol. 3, pp. 1–17, 2019.
6. Joshi, Archana Prashanth, Han, Meng and Wang, Yan, "A survey on security and privacy issues of blockchain technology", *Mathematical Foundations of Computing*, vol. 1, no. 2, pp. 121–147, 2018

7. Ertaul, Levent and Chavan, Nitu J, "RSA and elliptic curve-elgamal threshold cryptography (ECCEG-TC) implementations for secure data forwarding in manets", *Threshold*, vol. 7, no. 8, p. 9, 2007.
8. Mahto, Dindayal and Yadav, Dilip Kumar, "RSA and ECC: a comparative analysis", *International Journal of Applied Engineering Research*, vol. 12, no. 19, pp. 9053–9061, 2017.
9. Sethi, Pallavi and Sarangi, Smruti R, "Internet of things: architectures, protocols, and applications", *Journal of Electrical and Computer Engineering*, vol. 2017, p.9324035 2017.
10. Raj, Pethuru, "Empowering digital twins with blockchain", *Advances in Computers*, vol. 121, pp. 267–283, 2021
11. Azrour, Mourade, Jamal Mabrouki, Azidine Guezzaz, and Ambrina Kanwal, "Internet of things security: challenges and key issues", Security and Communication Networks, vol. 2021, no. 1, p. 5533843, 2021.
12. Shen, Lihua, Zhang, Zhibin, Zhou, Youmei, and Xu, Yingying, "Applying blockchain technology and the internet of things to improve the data reliability for livestock insurance", *Sensors*, vol. 23, no. 14, p. 6290, 2023.
13. Alshehri, Mohammed, "Blockchain-assisted internet of things framework in smart livestock farming", *Internet of Things*, vol. 22, p. 100739, 2023.
14. Patel, AS, Brahmbhatt, MN, Bariya, AR, Nayak, JB, and Singh, VK, "Blockchain technology in food safety and traceability concern to livestock products", *Heliyon*, 2023.
15. https://safecurves.cr.yp.to/online 15/04/2024
16. https://medium.com/edchain/a-comparison-between-5-major-blockchain-protocols-b8a6a46f8b1f online 15/04/2024
17. https://bitcoin.fr/iso-tc307-ou-la-normalisation-des-blockchains/

Chapter 19

ML-based detection of GPS jamming attacks on unmanned aerial vehicles

Tariq Mouatassim, Iyad Lahsen-Cherif, El Mahdi El Guarmah, and Hassan El Ghazi

19.1 INTRODUCTION

Drone systems have evolved through the past two decades to become an integral part of various industries, including agriculture, surveillance, transportation, and entertainment. This trend is particularly notable in the fields of education and research and development (R&D). For instance, several researchers have been interested in developing low-cost UAV applications, especially in agriculture, e.g., autonomous drones for smart and precision farming [15], plant protection [20], and seed sowing [19]. However, the accessibility of open-source projects renders them more susceptible to targeted attacks if not properly managed and secured.

Furthermore, UAVs rely on sensors to be flown steadily and safely. For instance, global positioning system (GPS) sensors are essential to stabilize UAVs. Also, they are the main component in autonomous flights as they enable waypoint navigation for predefined paths. Additionally, they enable a drone to return home (RTH) in case communication is lost with its operator. For these reasons, GPS sensors are a privileged target for adversaries as they can easily be attacked. In fact, attackers take advantage of the unencrypted nature of civilian GPS signals and the accessibility of tools, such as software defining radio (SDR), utilized to jam these signals. A consequence of preventing a drone from receiving the authentic GPS signals might be the crash of the vehicle [18]. Hence, detecting GPS jamming is crucial for drone safety and such detection has been addressed by the use of several techniques and countermeasures.

Recently, machine learning (ML) has been used extensively to solve cybersecurity problematic, such as in works [6] and [4]. Nevertheless, due to the lack of specific datasets in the context of drone systems, little research has been done on detection of GPS jamming targeting UAVs. In this work, we address this gap by providing an ML solution for detecting GPS jamming attacks and indicating the direction and distance of threats. Furthermore, we propose and discuss five ML models, evaluating their performances as well as their training and prediction times.

DOI: 10.1201/9781003587552-19

The remainder of this chapter is structured as follows. Related works are presented in Section 19.2. Details about the dataset used and the pre-processing are given in Section 19.3. Section 19.4 presents ML models and evaluation metrics, followed by a discussion of results. Finally, conclusions are outlined in Section 19.5.

19.2 RELATED WORKS

The authors of [7] proposed a detection method based on measuring the power of the GPS signal received. This method detects the occurrence of jamming and identifies its type depending on which interval the signal level belongs to. Various jamming techniques were considered, including Spot Noise, Barrage Noise, Pulse Noise, and Sweep Noise. All data used for experiments was simulated using Simulink in MATLAB [16]. In [1], the authors presented a method that relies on automatic dependent surveillance broadcast (ADS-B) information [12], received by ground sensors, to confirm GPS jamming attacks against an aircraft. To detect anomalies, the method analyzes the distribution of received messages from ADS-B devices, which regularly broadcast aircraft position and other information. The authors of [2] proposed a multi-output multi-class ML solution to GPS jamming attacks detection and range localization. The authors built a dataset of 17.960 samples by conducting Barrage, Single tone, Successive pulse, and Protocol aware jamming attacks [10] against an open-source UAV. They trained RF, KNN, MLP, LR, DT, NB, and support vector machine (SVM) on the dataset. MLP outperformed other ML algorithms with an F1 score of 98,9%, while DT yielded the lowest prediction time of 1.26 ms. The analysis of related works shows that some works found in the literature made use of synthetic data; others relies on other additional hardware devices, i.e., ADS-B sensors. Unlike previous works, we provide a ML solution trained on a real-world dataset that detects promptly, accurately, and efficiently GPS jamming attacks on UAVs without additional hardware.

19.3 DATASET AND PRE-PROCESSING

This section presents the dataset used in our study, describing the testbed and highlighting the configuration sets elaborated for its creation. Moreover, we detail the pre-processing approach adopted, describing the full process.

19.3.1 Dataset description

In this chapter, we made use of the dataset elaborated in [2]. The dataset was created by conducting various GPS jamming attacks against a Pixhawk

[14]-based UAV from COEX, using a B-210 SDR. The testbed involved different sets of experiments. In fact, the distance separating the jammer from the UAV was set, respectively, to 3m, 10m, 17m, and 24m. Besides, for each configuration, the direction of jamming was set, respectively, to south, north, west, and east. The experiments enabled the collection of 9,904 authentic samples and 8,056 jamming attack samples, extracted from the UAV flight controller GPS receiver logs. The dataset includes three labels for each samples, namely, type of jamming, direction, and distance from the jammer.

19.3.2 Pre-processing

We searched for "Not a Number" (NaN) values and we found that the feature variable "headings" contains NaN values; consequently, we dropped it. In addition, we sanitized the dataset from noise data, i.e., the meaningless data that could have been injected into the dataset unintentionally during experiments.

In fact, we found 132 duplicate samples that had been assigned to two different classes and we eliminated them. Additionally, we kept just GPS-related features and dropped a timestamp. The remaining 14 feature variables underwent a feature reduction (FR) process. In this study, we used Pearson Correlation (PC) analysis [17] and mutual information (MI) [11] to choose the most relevant features. First, we conducted a PC analysis on the dataset to find out correlated feature variables and quantify the strength of correlation. We identified four pairs of highly correlated features, namely, (eph,epv), (hdop,vdop), (s_variance_m_s,eph), and (s_variance_m_s,epv). To decide which feature to eliminate, we ranked features according to their Mutual Information (MI) with the target variable. The results of MI ranking showed that "epv" and "vdop" are more relevant than "hdop," "eph," and "s_variance_m_s"; hence, we dropped these three latter feature variables. The remaining features are given in Table 19.1.

Since we opted for multi-class classification to solve a detection and localization problem simultaneously, we instituted a change in the dataset. We transformed the three output labels into one target variable by mapping the distance, the direction, and the jamming conditions. The new dataset consists of 17 classes, "class 0" for authentic samples, and the rest of classes representing sets of GPS jamming attacks with different cases of direction and distance of jamming, as can be seen in Figure 19.1. For example, a prediction of "class 3" indicates that a GPS jamming attack occurred, the jammer is located forward of the progression of the drone and situated in 17m. As a final step in pre-processing, we split the dataset into 70% subset for training and 30% subset for testing.

Table 19.1 Description of the most relevant 11 feature variables

Feature variable	*Description*
cog_rad	Course over ground (radians)
c_variance_rad	GPS course accuracy estimate (radians)
vdop	Vertical dilution of precision
epv	GPS vertical position accuracy (meters)
noise_per_ms	GPS noise per millisecond
jamming_indicator	Indication of jamming occurrence
satellites_used	Number of satellites used
vel_d_m_s	GPS Down velocity (mps)
vel_m_s	GPS ground speed (mps)
vel_e_m_s	GPS East velocity (mps)
vel_n_m_s	GPS North velocity (mps)

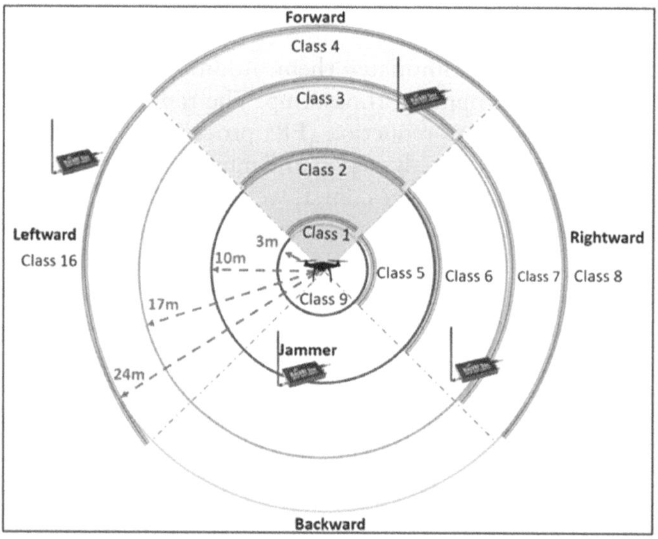

Figure 19.1 GPS jamming detection and threat indication approach

19.4 TRAINING, EVALUATION, AND DISCUSSION

In this section, we present ML algorithms and performances metrics that have been adopted in our work. Then, we discuss the results.

19.4.1 Training models and Evaluation

In this study, we made use of supervised ML algorithms to classify data into the 17 aforementioned classes. The algorithms adopted are: XGBoost [4],

DT [5], KNN [8], LR [3], and NB [9]. To evaluate the performance of ML models, a testing subset was used. Depending on the prediction made by each classifier, confusion matrices and performance metrics [13] were computed. The metrics adopted for our study are accuracy, precision, recall, and F1 score. The detailed results obtained for ML models are shown in Table 19.2 and Figure 14.2.

19.4.2 Discussion

Figure 19.2a shows that XGBoost and DT yielded accuracies above 99%, followed by KNN with 97.14%. LR and NB registered accuracies below 56%. Figure 19.2b shows that XGBoost has an F1 score of 99.95%, followed by DT with 98.80% and KNN with 95.35%. Meanwhile, LR and NB registered poor F1 scores, below 25%, as the two models failed to detect any jamming attacks. Training time for XGBoost, as can be seen in Figure 19.2c, was relatively slower, i.e., 34.355s, compared to other ML models. DT and KNN registered faster training time with 199.5 ms and 150.54 ms, respectively. Among the best performing models, DT predicted the samples with only 15ms. Meanwhile, XGBoost and KNN registered 96.62 ms and 742.48 ms, respectively, in prediction time (Figure 19.2d). Considering all results, given in Table 19.2, it is noteworthy to point out that although KNN achieved quite satisfactory performance, it predicted samples slower. Moreover, DT could be used as it detects and localizes GPS jamming attacks faster, while maintaining excellent performances.

19.5 CONCLUSION

This work deals with detection of GPS jamming attacks targeting UAVs. The models proposed enable a drone not only to detect the attack but also to indicate the direction from which the jamming occurs and the distance separating the jammer from the vehicle. To train the ML models, we made

Table 19.2 Comparative results of ML models

	Precision	*Recall*	*F1-score*	*Accuracy*	*Training*	*Prediction*
	(%)	*(%)*	*(%)*	*(%)*		
DT	98.79	98.82	98.8	99.29	199.5	15.75
XGBoost	99.97	99.93	99.95	99.96	34354.99	96.62
KNN	95.47	95.28	95.35	97.14	150.54	742.48
LR	34.35	22.97	24.73	55.6	5439.86	8.97
NB	30.82	21.89	22.99	54.94	28.62	19.63

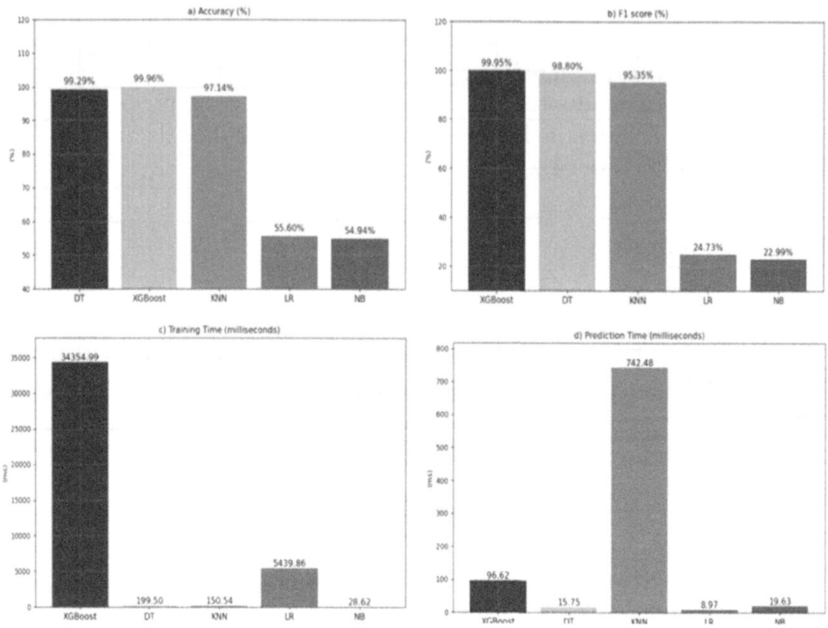

Figure 19.2 Comparative results

use of a real-world dataset. We sanitized, reduced the features of the dataset using mutual information and Pearson correlation coefficients, and transformed the labels to fit multi-class classification. It turns out that XGBoost is the best performing model with 99.95 % in F1 score, 99.96% in accuracy, 99.97% in precision, and 99.93% in recall. Also, DT could be implemented considering its performances exceeding 98.8% and its lowest training and prediction time, 199.50 ms and 15.75 ms, respectively.

REFERENCES

1. Ala'Darabseh, E.B., Tedongmo, B.: Detecting GPS jamming incidents in opensky data. In: *Proceedings of the 7th OpenSky Workshop*. vol. 67, pp. 97–108 (2019).
2. Alkhatib, M., McCormick, M., Williams, L., Leon, A., Camerano, L., Al Shamaileh, K., Devabhaktuni, V., Kaabouch, N.: Classification and source location indication of jamming attacks targeting UAVs via multi-output multiclass machine learning modeling. In: *2024 IEEE International Conference on Consumer Electronics (ICCE)*. pp. 1–5. IEEE (2024).
3. Bhowmik, T.K.: Naive Bayes vs logistic regression: theory, implementation and experimental validation. *Inteligencia Artificial. Revista Iberoamericana de Inteligencia Artificial* 18(56), 14–30 (2015).

4. Cherif, I.L., Kortebi, A.: On using extreme gradient boosting (xgboost) machine learning algorithm for home network traffic classification. In: *2019 Wireless Days (WD)*. pp. 1–6. IEEE (2019).
5. El Mrabet, Z., El Ghazi, H., Kaabouch, N.: A performance comparison of data mining algorithms based intrusion detection system for smart grid. In: *International Conference on Electro Information Technology (EIT)*. pp. 298–303. IEEE (2019).
6. El Mrabet, Z., Ezzari, M., Elghazi, H., El Majd, B.A.: Deep learning-based intrusion detection system for advanced metering infrastructure. In: *Proceedings of the 2nd International Conference on Networking, Information Systems & Security*. pp. 1–7 (2019).
7. Elezi, E., Çankaya, G., Boyacı, A., Yarkan, S.: A detection and identification method based on signal power for different types of electronic jamming attacks on GPS signals. In: *2019 IEEE 30th Annual International Symposium on Personal, Indoor and Mobile Radio Communications (PIMRC)*. pp. 1–5. IEEE (2019).
8. Khan, M.S., Nath, T.D., Hossain, M.M., Mukherjee, A., Hasnath, H.B., Meem, T.M., Khan, U.: Comparison of multiclass classification techniques using dry bean dataset. *International Journal of Cognitive Computing in Engineering* 4, 6–20 (2023).
9. Khraisat, A., Alazab, A.: A critical review of intrusion detection systems in the internet of things: techniques, deployment strategy, validation strategy, attacks, public datasets and challenges. *Cybersecurity* 4, 1–27 (2021).
10. Li, Y., Pawlak, J., Price, J., Al Shamaileh, K., Niyaz, Q., Paheding, S., Devabhaktuni, V.: Jamming detection and classification in OFDM-based UAVs via feature- and spectrogram-tailored machine learning. *IEEE Access* 10, 16859–16870 (2022).
11. Ling, Z., Hao, Z.J.: Intrusion detection using normalized mutual information feature selection and parallel quantum genetic algorithm. *International Journal on Semantic Web and Information Systems* 18(1), 1–24 (2022).
12. Manesh, M.R., Kaabouch, N.: Analysis of vulnerabilities, attacks, countermeasures and overall risk of the automatic dependent surveillance-broadcast (ADS-B) system. *International Journal of Critical Infrastructure Protection* 19, 16–31 (2017).
13. Mouatassim, T., El Ghazi, H., Bouzaachane, K., El Guarmah, E.M., Lahsenchrif, I.: Cybersecurity analytics: Toward an efficient ML-based network intrusion detection system (NIDS). In: *International Conference on Machine Learning for Networking*. vol. 14525, pp. 276–294. Springer (2023).
14. Pixhawk. https://ardupilot.org/copter/docs/common-pixhawk-overview.html, accessed online on April 2024.
15. Priandana, K., Hazim, M., Kusumoputro, B., et al.: Development of autonomous uav quadcopters using pixhawk controller and its flight data acquisition. In: *2020 International Conference on Computer Science and Its Application in Agriculture (ICOSICA)*. pp. 1–6. IEEE (2020).
16. Simulink MATLAB. https://www.mathworks.com/products/simulink.html, accessed online on April 2024.

17. Sugianela, Y., Ahmad, T.: Pearson correlation attribute evaluation-based feature selection for intrusion detection system. In: *2020 International Conference on Smart Technology and Applications (ICoSTA)*. pp. 1–5. IEEE (2020).
18. Wu, S., Li, Y., Wang, Z., Tan, Z., Pan, Q.: A highly interpretable framework for generic low-cost UAV attack detection. *IEEE Sensors Journal* 23(7), 7288–7300 (2023).
19. Yamunathangam, D., Shanmathi, J., Caviya, R., Saranya, G.: Payload manipulation for seed sowing unmanned aerial vehicle through interface with pixhawk flight controller. In: *2020 Fourth International Conference on Inventive Systems and Control (ICISC)*. pp. 931–934. IEEE (2020).
20. Yang, K., Yang, G.Y., Fu, S.I.H.: Research of control system for plant protection UAV based on PIXHAWK. *Procedia Computer Science* 166, 371–375 (2020).

Chapter 20

A comparative analysis of random forest and isolation forest intrusion detection systems

Sara Amaouche, Azidine Guezzaz, Said Benkirane, and Mourade Azrour

20.1 INTRODUCTION

Vehicular ad hoc networks (VANETs) are an essential component of modern transportation systems, facilitating continuous communication between vehicles and infrastructure [1]. These networks play an essential role in the implementation of various applications such as traffic management, collision avoidance and infotainment and for improving road safety, traffic efficiency, and passenger comfort [1]. However, despite their many advantages, VANETs face significant safety issues due to their dynamic topology and decentralized nature [2]. The dynamic and mobile nature of VANET networks introduces vulnerabilities that can be exploited by malicious entities [2]. Threats such as cyberattacks, data tampering, and unauthorized access pose serious risks to the integrity and reliability of VANET networks [3]. As a result, VANET network security has become essential to protect both the network and its users [3]. Intrusion detection systems (IDSs) have appeared as a proactive defense mechanism for monitoring network traffic and identifying suspicious activity or anomalies in real time [4]. Relying on machine-learning algorithms, IDSs can learn from historical data to detect and attenuate potential threats, thus improving the overall security level of VANET networks [5]. In addition, advances in communications technologies, such as 5G networks, offer promising opportunities to enhance the capabilities and performance of VANET networks [6]. With high bandwidth, low latency, and support for massive device connectivity, 5G technology enables continuous, reliable communication between vehicles, infrastructure, and other entities within the VANET ecosystem [6]. Leveraging 5G's capabilities can lead to higher levels of efficiency, reliability, and safety, opening the way for intelligent transportation systems (ITS) and autonomous driving applications [6, 7].

This study addresses VANET security issues by proposing a random forest and isolation forest (RF-IF) for anomaly detection, combined with feature selection techniques and efficient data pre-processing [8]. Evaluation measures such as accuracy, precision, recall, and F1-score are used to assess the effectiveness of the framework [8]. Experiments on real VANET datasets

DOI: 10.1201/9781003587552-20

validate the robustness and applicability of the model in different environments [8]. The rest of this chapter is structured as follows: Section 2 provides background information, and Section 3 explores related work concerning VANETs and intrusion detection approaches. In Section 4, we describe the main steps in the design of our proposed model. Experimental evaluation and results are discussed in Section 5. Finally, the chapter concludes with a summary and describes potential directions for future research.

20.2 BACKGROUND AND RELATED WORKS

20.2.1 Background

VANETs represent a major step toward modern transportation systems, enabling dynamic vehicle-to-vehicle communication without the need for a fixed infrastructure [16]. These networks are designed with the primary aim of improving traffic management and safety, by facilitating the exchange of critical information and warnings between vehicles, while providing advanced services to road users [9]. VANETs are characterized by their shared wireless support and dynamic network topology, enabling vehicles to join and leave the network smoothly [10]. However, the very features that make VANETs effective also pose significant security challenges. The reliability of individual nodes becomes critical, as a single failed or compromised node can compromise the functionality of the entire network [10]. Traditional security mechanisms such as encryption, while essential, may prove inadequate in the context of autonomous vehicles, underscoring the need for more robust solutions such as IDS to detect and mitigate attacks in VANET networks [7, 11, 42]. In the domain of VANET networks, IDSs play an essential role in monitoring and analyzing network traffic to identify unusual patterns or potential security vulnerabilities, enabling known and emerging threats to be addressed proactively. This proactive attitude is essential to protect the critical components of vehicle communication systems and guarantee the integrity of sensor data [7]. By improving the security and reliability of VANET networks, IDSs make a significant contribution to the development of safer, more efficient transport systems [11]. In addition, the dynamic nature of VANET networks requires an advanced understanding of communication technologies such as dedicated short-range communications (DSRC) [37], wireless access in vehicular environments (WAVE), and IEEE 802.11p. These technologies enable vehicles to communicate directly with each other (V2V) or with roadside units (V2I), providing vital functions such as traffic monitoring, accident alerts, and weather notifications [13]. Despite the promising features of VANETs, challenges and vulnerabilities persist, particularly in terms of security [14]. For example, emergency signals sent by vehicles could be compromised by malicious actors, with potentially catastrophic consequences. It is therefore imperative to implement robust and reliable security protocols to guarantee the integrity and security of VANET networks [15].

20.2.2 Related works

Various machine learning (ML) and deep learning (DL) algorithms have been employed in IDSs to identify intrusions [26]–[45]. For example, Gad et al. [18] used the ToN-IoT dataset to evaluate several machine learning methods for binary and multiclass classification tasks. They used the chi-square (Chi2) technique for feature selection and synthetic minority oversampling (SMOTE) for class balancing, with XGBoost offering superior performance. Manderna et al. [19] proposed an AI-based NIDS framework that integrates two-way self-attentive long-term memory (SA-BiLSTM) and a cascaded convolutional neural network (CCNN) for feature learning. Their model, improved using the gradient-based multivariant optimization (MV-GBO) algorithm, achieved high accuracy in datasets such as KDD-CUP99, ToN-IoT, and VeReMi. Ghaleb et al. [20] presented a collaborative adaptive IDS (MA-CIDS) using distributed ensemble learning with random forest, demonstrating improvements in effectiveness and efficiency over existing models on the NSL-KDD dataset. ALMahadin [21] developed SEMIGRU, a semi-supervised anomaly detection technique based on the GRU DL model, which outperforms previous methods in VANET anomaly detection. Lihua et al, [22] proposed an energy-sensitive IDS (EIDS) for V2V communication in the Internet of Vehicles (IoV), achieving significant improvements in accuracy and runtime on the NSLKDD dataset. Zeeshan et al. [23] presented a protocol-based deep intrusion detection (PB-DID) framework, achieving high classification accuracy on IoT traffic datasets. Finally, Karthiga et al. [24] introduced a hybrid IDS integrating known IDS (KIDS) and unknown IDS (UIDS) modules, achieving superior performance on the i-VANET dataset and the CIC-IDS 2017 real-time dataset compared with existing methods (Table 20.1).

20.3 PROPOSED WORK

This study focused on improving VANET network security through intrusion detection using a multifaceted approach. Data pre-processing consists of removing null values to ensure the integrity of the dataset. Feature selection, using the RF algorithm, identified features crucial to intrusion detection. For classification, machine learning algorithms, mainly RF for known attacks and IF for anomalies, were used. Experiments carried out on the Veremi, NSLKDD, and TON-IOT datasets enabled performance measures such as accuracy, precision, recall, and F1-score to be evaluated, guaranteeing effective real-time intrusion detection capabilities (see Figure 20.1).

Table 20.1 Comparison studies of recent researches

	Year	*Dataset*	*Algorithm*	*Accuracy%*	*Precision%*	*Recall%*	*F 1%*
Manderna et al. [19]	2023	TON-IOT	CCNN-SA-BiLSTM	99	99	98	-
A. Ghaleb et al. [20]	2020	NSL-KDD	RF	–	97	97	98
			SVM	–	94	92	90
			XGBoost	–	96	96	95
ALMahadin [21]	2023	NSL-KDD	SEMI-GRU	83.32	93.8	78.36	85.62
Dina [25]	2023	UNSW-NB15	DT	65.6	62.26	65.66	62.68
			SVM	53.04	36.48	53.04	38.99
			RF	65.15	62.73	65.15	56.49
			NB	52.56	40.80	52.56	37.28
			FNN	52.95	48.54	52.95	38.60
			LSTM	61.23	59.33	61.23	51.56
			CNN	63.30	57.46	63.30	56.07
			CNN-BiLSTM	53.14	37.5	53.14	38.75
			PB-DID	54.71	35.45	54.71	42.92
Karthiga et al. [24]	2022	CIC-IDS 2017	ANFIS and CNN	0.98	0.98		

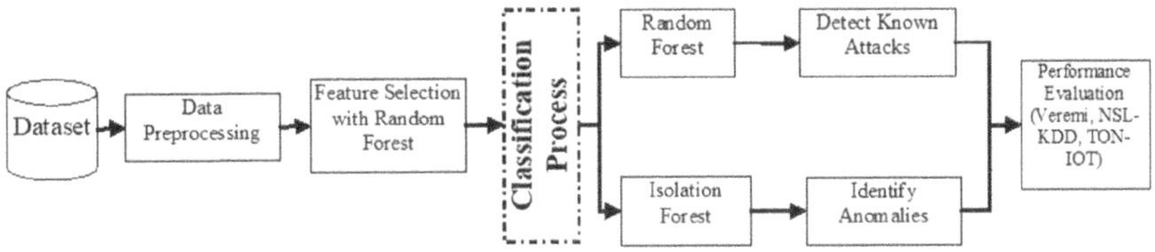

Figure 20.1 Scheme of proposed framework

20.4 EVALUATION AND RESULTS DISCUSSION

20.4.1 Environment description

The Veremi dataset [27] serves as a fundamental building for blockin machine learning and cybersecurity research, offering a diverse array of features and instances related to cyber threats. Similarly, the NSL-KDD dataset [28], an enhanced version of the KDD'99 dataset, addresses identified limitations by removing redundant data and balancing records based on classification difficulty levels. Additionally, the ToN-IoT dataset [29] is tailored for exploring data from the Internet of Things (IoT) and Industrial Internet of Things (IIoT) domains, featuring telemetry, Windows, Linux, and network traffic data in CSV format. In the experimental phase of our research, we conducted tests on a machine powered by an Intel(R) Core(TM) i7 CPU @ 1.90GHz 2.11 GHz with 16GB of RAM, under a Windows 10 x64-bit system. The development and refinement of our model, alongside the feature engineering process, were executed using Python version 3.10.6.

- True positives (TP): Well identified attacks.
- The false positives (FP): Badly classified attacks.
- True negatives (TN): Correctly identified normal instances.
- False negatives (FN): Misclassified normal instances.

The following equations are used to calculate some metrics

$$\text{Accuracy: } \frac{TP + TN}{TP + TN + FP + FN} \quad (1)$$

$$\text{Precision: } \frac{TP}{TP + FP} \quad (2)$$

$$\text{Recall (True Positive Rate TPR): } \frac{TP}{TP + FN} \quad (3)$$

$$\text{F1-score: } 2 \times \frac{\text{Precision} \times \text{Recall}}{\text{Precision} + \text{Recall}} \quad (4)$$

20.4.2 Results and discussion

Analysis of the normalized confusion matrices for the Veremi, NSL-KDD, and TON-IOT datasets shown in Figures 20.2, 20.3, and 20.4 highlights the model's classification achievements. The high rates of true positives in the Veremi and NSL-KDD datasets underline the model's ability to accurately distinguish attack nodes. The TON-IOT matrix revealed near-perfect classification for most attack types, indicating the model's enhanced sensitivity in a complex environment. Integrating RF-IF into intrusion detection resulted in a remarkable improvement in accuracy in all datasets compared to using RF alone (Figure 20.5). Particularly in the Veremi and NSL-KDD datasets, the combined RF-IF method achieved near-perfect results in terms of accuracy, precision, recall, and F1-score, outperforming the RF approach alone. In the TON-IOT dataset, both methods achieved perfect scores for all measures, underlining the robustness of the model to address security challenges. This powerful synergy between RF and IF highlights their powerful effect, particularly in the complex field of network intrusion detection, where even incremental improvements in accuracy and reliability are of significant importance. The accuracy measurements presented in Figures 20.6, 20.7, and 20.8 on the Veremi, NSL-KDD, and TON-IOT datasets confirmed the model's ability to predict true positives, highlighting its extreme accuracy, particularly in classes such as "ConspOffset" and "backdoor." Consistent performance across the various datasets underlines the IDS's reliability in reporting threats in a variety of network environments.

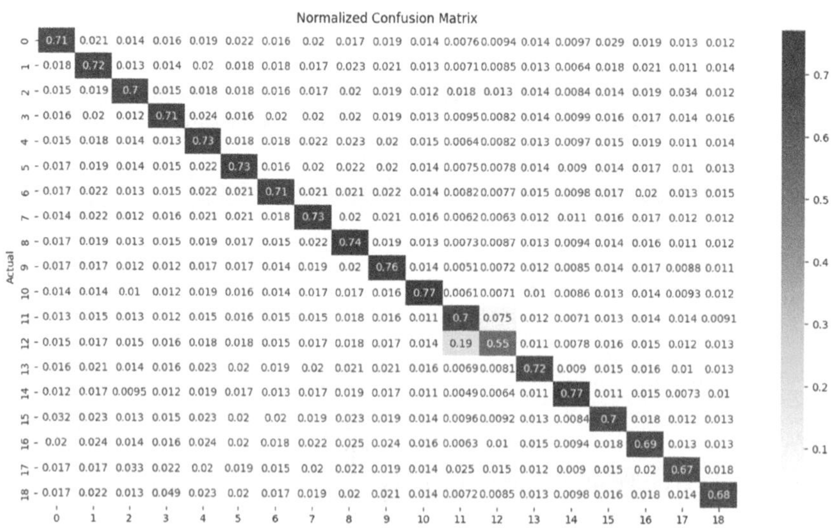

Figure 20.2 Confusion matrix (Veremi dataset)

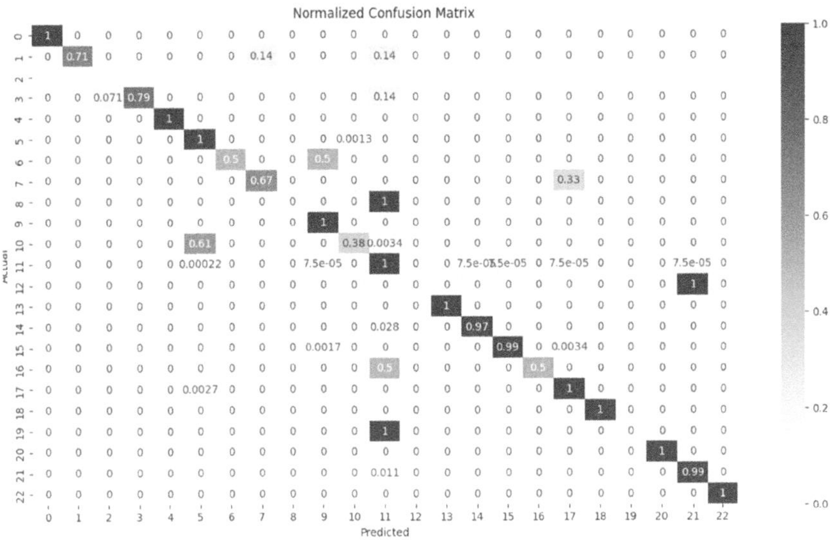

Figure 20.3 Confusion matrix (NSL-KDD dataset)

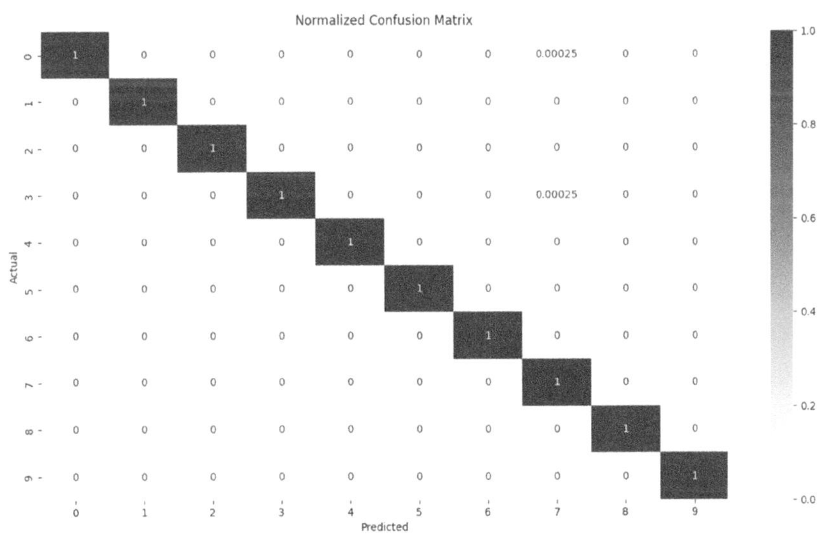

Figure 20.4 Normalized confusion matrix (TON-IOT dataset)

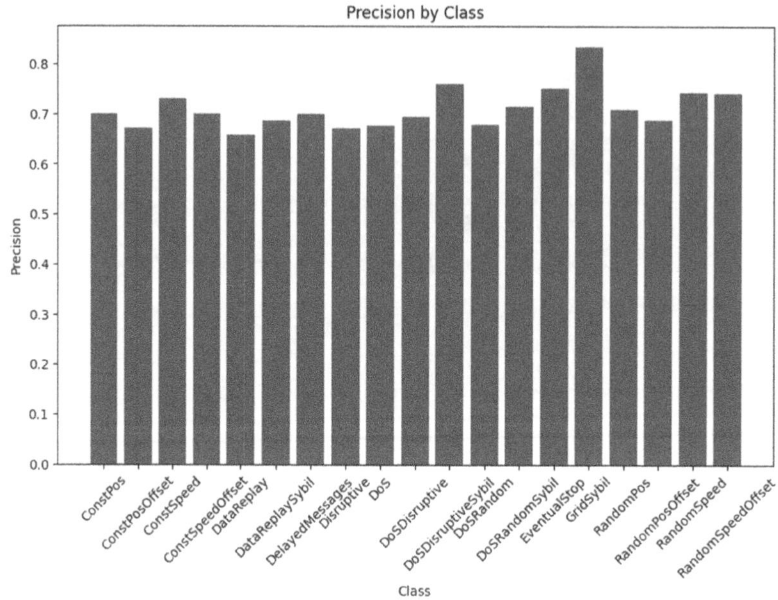

Figure 20.5 Scores by metric and dataset

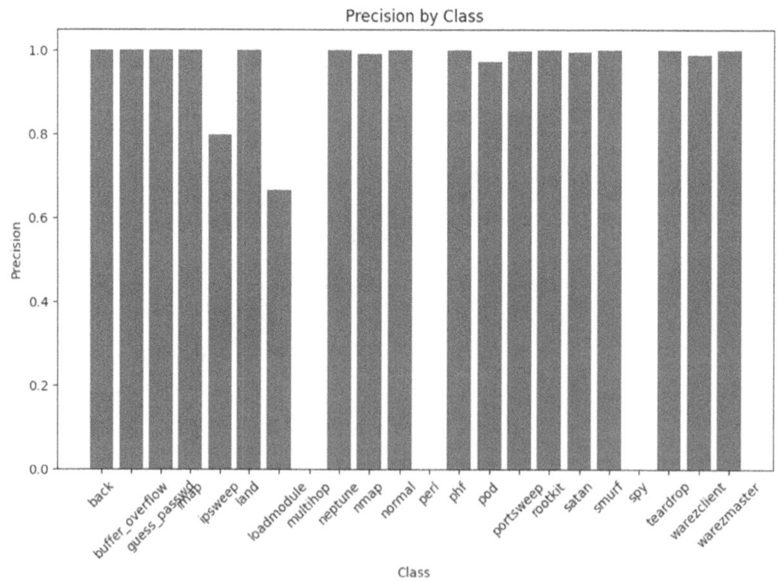

Figure 20.6 Precision by class (Veremi dataset)

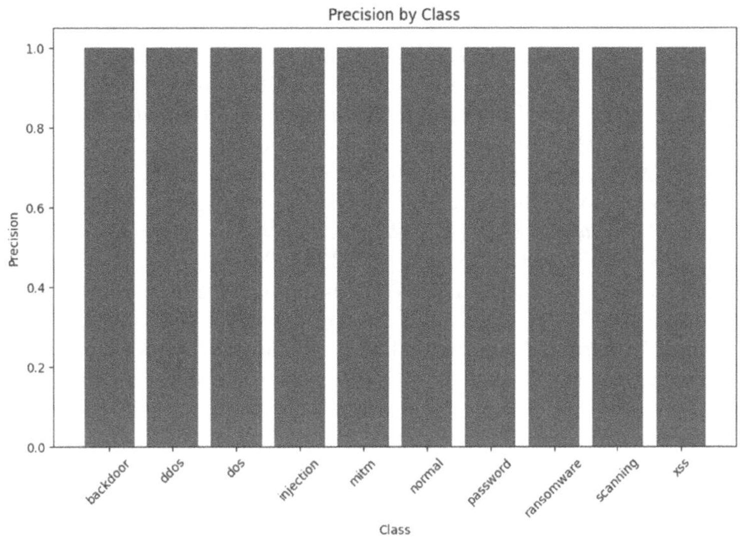

Figure 20.7 Precision by class (NSL-KDD dataset)

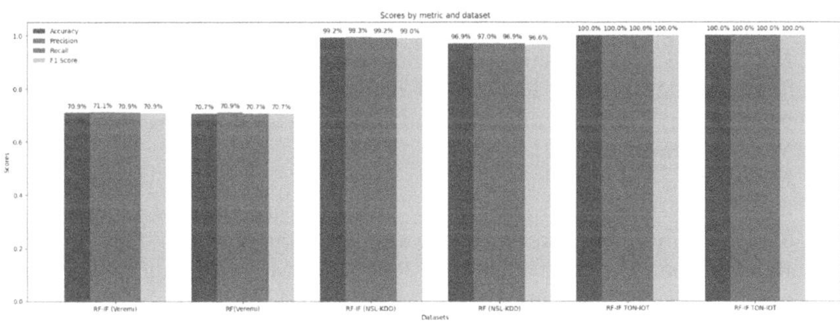

Figure 20.8 Precision by class (TON-IOT dataset)

20.5 CONCLUSION

Our research aims to enhance VANET network security against emerging cyber threats. Through a rigorous comparative analysis, we evaluated RF and IF intrusion detection systems using datasets like Veremi, NSL-KDD, and ToN-IoT. Our results demonstrate the robustness of both approaches, with RF excelling in identifying known attack patterns and IF effectively detecting anomalies. Furthermore, accurate data pre-processing and feature selection were highlighted as crucial for improving IDS performance. Overall, our study provides valuable insights to fortify vehicular communication systems against cybersecurity risks.

REFERENCES

1. Benamar, M., Benamar, N., Singh, K. D., & El Ouadghiri, D. (2013, May). Recent study of routing protocols in VANET: survey and taxonomy. In *WVNT 2013: 1st International Workshop on Vehicular Networks and Telematics,* , May 2013, Marrakech, Morocco.
2. Sheikh, M. S., & Liang, J. (2019). A comprehensive survey on VANET security services in traffic management system. *Wireless Communications and Mobile Computing*, 2019 (1), 2423915.
3. Ercan, S., Ayaida, M., & Messai, N. (2021). Misbehavior detection for position falsification attacks in VANETs using machine learning. *IEEE Access*, 10, 1893–1904.
4. Kumar, P., Verma, A., & Singhal, P. (2019, March). VANET protocols with challenges–A review. In *2019 6th International Conference on Computing for Sustainable Global Development (INDIACom)* (pp. 598–602). IEEE.
5. Benkirane, S., Guezzaz, A., Azrour, M., Gardezi, A. A., Ahmad, S., Sayed, A. E., ... & Shafiq, M. (2023). Adapted speed system in a road bend situation in VANET environment, CMC-COMPUTERS MATERIALS & CONTINUA, 74(2), 3781–3794.
6. Hussain, R., Hussain, F., & Zeadally, S. (2019). Integration of VANET and 5G security: A review of design and implementation issues. *Future Generation Computer Systems*, 101, 843–864.
7. Grover, J. (2022). Security of vehicular ad hoc Networks using blockchain: A comprehensive review. *Vehicular Communications*, 34, 100458.
8. Murugan, S., Jeyalaksshmi, S., Mahalakshmi, B., Suseendran, G., Jabeen, T. N., & Manikandan, R. (2020). Comparison of ACO and PSO algorithm using energy consumption and load balancing in emerging MANET and VANET infrastructure. *J. Crit. Rev.*, 7(9), 2020.
9. Erritali, M., & El Ouahidi, B. (2013, April). A survey on VANET intrusion detection systems. In *Proceedings of the 2013 International Conference on Systems, Control, Signal Processing and Informatics* (pp. 16–19).
10. Ramalingam, M., & Thangarajan, R. (2020). Mutated k-means algorithm for dynamic clustering to perform effective and intelligent broadcasting in medical surveillance using selective reliable broadcast protocol in VANET. *Comput. Commun.*, 150, 563–568.
11. Hussain, R., Lee, J., & Zeadally, S. (2020). Trust in VANET: A survey of current solutions and future research opportunities. *IEEE Trans. Intell. Transp. Syst.*, 22(5), 2553–2571.
12. Rai, K., Guleria, A., & Syamala Devi, M. (2016). Decision tree based algorithm for intrusion detection. *International J. Adv. Netw. Appl*, 7(4), 2828.
13. Al-Heety, O. S., Zakaria, Z., Ismail, M., Shakir, M. M., Alani, S., & Alsariera, H. (2020). A comprehensive survey: Benefits, services, recent works, challenges, security, and use cases for SDN–VANET. *IEEE Access*, 8, 91028–91047.
14. Arif, M., Wang, G., Bhuiyan, M. Z. A., Wang, T., & Chen, J. (2019). A survey on security attacks in VANETs: Communication, applications and challenges. *Veh. Commun.*, 19, 100179.

15. Bariah, L., Shehada, D., Salahat, E., & Yeun, C. Y. (2015, September). Recent advances in VANET security: a survey. In *2015 IEEE 82nd Vehicular Technology Conference (VTC2015–Fall)* (pp. 1–7). IEEE.
16. Amaouche, S., Hazman, C., Guezzaz, A., Benkirane, S., & Azrour, M. (2024). Intrusion Detection Framework Using AdaBoost Algorithm and Chi-Squared Technique. In Blockchain and Machine Learning for IoT Security, pp. 92–111. Chapman and Hall/CRC.
17. Shams, E. A., Rizaner, A., & Ulusoy, A. H. (2023). Flow-based intrusion detection system in vehicular ad hoc network using context-aware feature extraction. *Veh. Commun.*, 41, 100585.
18. Gad, A. R., Nashat, A. A., & Barkat, T. M. (2021). Intrusion detection system using machine learning for vehicular ad hoc networks based on ToN-IoT dataset. *IEEE Access*, 9, 142206–142217.
19. Manderna, A., Kumar, S., Dohare, U., Aljaidi, M., Kaiwartya, O., & Lloret, J. (2023). Vehicular network intrusion detection using a cascaded deep learning approach with multi-variant metaheuristic. *Sensors*, 23(21), 8772.
20. Ghaleb, A. Saeed, F., Al-Sarem, M., Ali Saleh Al-rimy, B., Boulila, W., Eljialy, A. E. M., ... & Alazab, M. (2020). Misbehavior-aware on-demand collaborative intrusion detection system using distributed ensemble learning for VANET. *Electronics*, 9(9), 1411.
21. ALMahadin, G., Aoudni, Y., Shabaz, M., Agrawal, A. V., Yasmin, G., Alomari, E. S., ... & Maaliw, R. R. (2023). VANET network traffic anomaly detection using GRU-based deep learning model. *IEEE Trans. Consumer Electron, 70(1), 4548–4555.*
22. Lihua, L. (2022). Energy–aware intrusion detection model for internet of vehicles using machine learning methods. *Wireless Commun. Mobile Comput.*, 2022, 9865549.
23. Zeeshan, M., Riaz, Q., Bilal, M. A., Shahzad, M. K., Jabeen, H., Haider, S. A., & Rahim, A. (2021). Protocol-based deep intrusion detection for dos and DDOS attacks using unsw-nb15 and bot-IoT data-sets. *IEEE Access*, 10, 2269–2283.
24. Karthiga, B., et al. (2022). Intelligent intrusion detection system for VANET using machine learning and deep learning approaches. *Wireless Commun. Mobile Comput.*, 2022, 1–13.
25. Dina, A. (2023). Deep learning-based intrusion detection methods for computer networks and privacy preserving authentication method for vehicular ad hoc networks. *Theses and Dissertations-- Computer Science*, 137.
26. Guezzaz, A., Benkirane, S., Azrour, M., & Khurram, S. (2021). A reliable network intrusion detection approach using decision tree with enhanced data quality. *Sec. Commun. Netw.*, 2021, 1–8.
27. Slama, O., Tarhouni, M., Zidi, S., & Alaya, B. (2023). One versus all binary tree method to classify misbehaviors in imbalanced VeReMi dataset. *IEEE Access*, 11, 135944–135958.
28. Dhanabal, L., & Shantharajah, S. P. (2015). A study on NSL–KDD dataset for intrusion detection system based on classification algorithms. *Intl. J. Adv. Res. Comput. Commun. Eng.*, 4(6), 446–452.

29. Mohy-eddine, M., Guezzaz, A., Benkirane, S., & Azrour, M. (2023). An efficient network intrusion detection model for IoT security using K-NN classifier and feature selection. *Multimedia. Tools Appl*, 82(15), 23615–23633. doi: 10.1007/s11042-023-14795-2.
30. A. E. M. Eljialy, A. E. M., Uddin, M. Y., & Ahmad, S. (2024). Novel framework for an intrusion detection system using multiple feature selection methods based on deep learning. *Tsinghua Sci. Technol.*, 29(4), 948–958. doi: 10.26599/TST.2023.9010032.
31. Peng, Y., Xu, S., Chen, Q., Huang, W., & Huang, Y. (2024). A novel popularity extraction method applied in session-based recommendation. *Tsinghua Sci. Technol.*, 29(4), 971–984. doi: 10.26599/TST.2023.9010061.
32. Hazman, C., Guezzaz, A., Benkirane, S., & Azrour, M. (2024). Enhanced IDS with deep learning for IoT-based smart cities security. *Tsinghua Sci. Technol.*, 29(4), 929–947. doi: 10.26599/TST.2023.9010033.
33. Wang, P., Zhu, Z., Chen, Q., & Dai, W. (2024). Text reasoning chain extraction for multi-hop question answering. *Tsinghua Sci. Technol.*, 29(4), 959–970. doi: 10.26599/TST.2023.9010060.
34. Mohy-eddine, M., Guezzaz, A., Benkirane, S., & Azrour, M. (2023). An intrusion detection model using election-based feature selection and K-NN. *Microprocess. Microsyst.*, 104966. doi: 10.1016/j.micpro.2023.104966.
35. Hazman, C., Guezzaz, A., Benkirane, S., & Azrour, M. (2023). Toward an intrusion detection model for IoT-based smart environments. *Multimed. Tools Appl.*, 83(22), 62159–62180. doi: 10.1007/s11042-023-16436-0.
36. Meenakshi, N. et al. (2024). Efficient communication in wireless sensor networks using optimized energy efficient engroove leach clustering protocol. *Tsinghua Sci. Technol.*, 29(4), 985–1001. doi: 10.26599/TST.2023.9010056.
37. Attou, H. et al. (2023). Towards an intelligent intrusion detection system to detect malicious activities in cloud computing. *Appl. Sci.*, 13(17), 9588.
38. Li, S., Cui, T., & Viriyasitavat, W. (2024). Edge device fault probability based intelligent calculations for fault probability of smart systems. *Tsinghua Sci. Technol.*, 29(4), 1023–1036. doi: 10.26599/TST.2023.9010085.
39. Liu, W., Zhou, L., Zhang, S., Luo, N., & Xu, M. (2024). A new high-precision and lightweight detection model for illegal construction objects based on deep learning. *Tsinghua Sci. Technol.*, 29(4), 1002–1022. doi: 10.26599/TST.2023.9010090.
40. Attou, H., Guezzaz, A., Benkirane, S., Azrour, M., & Farhaoui, Y. (2023). Cloud-based intrusion detection approach using machine learning techniques. *Big Data Min. Anal.*, 6(3), 311–320.
41. Amaouche, S. et al. (2023). FSCB-IDS: Feature selection and minority class balancing for attacks detection in VANETS. *Appl. Sci.*, 13(13), 7488.
42. Amaouche, S., Guezzaz, A., Benkirane, S., & Azrour, M. (2023). IDS-XGbFS: a smart intrusion detection system using XGboostwith recent feature selection for VANET safety. *Clust. Comput.*, 27(3), 3521–3535.
43. Douiba, M., Benkirane, S., Guezzaz, A., & Azrour, M. (2022). Anomaly detection model based on gradient boosting and decision tree for IoT environments security. *J. Reliab. Intell. Environ.*, 9(4), 421–432.

44. Douiba, M., Benkirane, S., Guezzaz, A., & Azrour, M. (2022). An improved anomaly detection model for IoT security using decision tree and gradient boosting. *J. Supercomput.*, 79(3), 3392–3411 .
45. Bella, K. et al. (2024). An efficient intrusion detection system for IoT security using CNN decision forest. *PeerJ Comput. Sci.*, 10, e2290. doi: 10.7717/peerj-cs.2290.

Chapter 21

A collaborative anomaly detection model using QRNN and blockchain

Chaimae Hazman, Azidine Guezzaz, Said Benkirane, and Mourade Azrour

21.1 INTRODUCTION

Because of the complexity and vulnerability of IT infrastructures on open, dispersed networks, intrusion detection systems (IDSs) have seen substantial technical progress. Since the growth of unauthorized access and cyberattacks, centralized and massive IDSs are no longer appropriate for today's network architecture. A collaborative IDS system in which different parts scattered over the network cooperate to analyze data and generate global and appropriate alarms is an improved method [1–9]. Establishing components that interact to optimize the operation of an IDS in an open, dispersed, and diverse environment is a continuing problem for a variety of factors. To begin, the network's infrastructure is complicated and extensive, and the variety of devices that must collaborate to enable accurate detection of intrusions is large. Furthermore, multiple parts may have distinct designs, arrangements, and working systems, making it challenging to combine them all into a single system. Finally, it is critical to protect the privacy and confidentiality of transmitted data since the system's dependability and accuracy are dependent on the caliber of the information analyzed. Any data modification or tampering can result in biased findings and disturb the overall system's operation [2, 11–17]. Blockchain technology is an appropriate approach for addressing these challenges. Blockchain technology provides a decentralized, tamper-resistant, and searchable platform for effectively conserving and disseminating critical information. As a technology based on distributed ledgers, it enables the establishment of a distributed reliable infrastructure in which every device has a link to similar data and can validate its accuracy. The implementation of blockchain-based systems in IDS enables safe data sharing and builds aggregate confidence among all of the nodes. Furthermore, it permits the construction of a permanent representation of every transaction and information exchange, assuring the confidentiality of the shared data across the entire network [19–27]. The efficiency of an IDS in identifying hostile activity is primarily determined by its analytical section [28–30].

 DOI: 10.1201/9781003587552-21

Machine learning–based analytical approaches make employing methods that may develop from data better over time [3–30]. The aforementioned methods are useful for analyzing and extracting insights from huge and complicated datasets. There are several analytical methodologies, each with a distinct set of advantages and disadvantages. To transcend the limits of each individual analytical approach and capitalize on their benefits, they can be utilized in tandem. Autoencoders and QRNNs, for instance, can be employed in tandem: By generating a reduced form of the data, an autoencoder may be applied to pretrain a QRNN; this can be used as input to the QRNN for classification or other tasks. This method can assist in increasing the QRNN's efficiency, particularly if labelled data is few. Furthermore, autoencoders may be utilized to supplement data for QRNNs. An autoencoder may learn to reconstruct the changed data through performing random modifications to the input data, such as scaling, rotation, or cropping, essentially producing new instances that may be utilized to retrain the QRNN. This technique incorporates both analytical techniques in order to offer greater accuracy detection and lower the risk of false positives and erroneous negative results. It also offers and executes a set of collaborative IDSs based on blockchain technology to assure safe data sharing and communal trust among all nodes. By integrating all of these methodologies, the resultant IDS can detect and prevent disturbances on accessible, large-scale, and indefinitely dispersed networks.

21.2 RELATED WORKS

Researchers have advocated integrating blockchain technology in collaborative intrusion detection systems to improve confidence and security administration across different intrusion detection systems in current research. Sajjad et al. [7] introduced a collaborative detection and mitigation system for the industrial IoT area. The approach is intended to detect abnormal item behavior through contrasting it with predefined regulations. The technology was evaluated and shown to effectively identify all offensive motions performed by hackers, with an excellent rate of identification of 97%. Despite the scientists proving the advantages of utilizing an Ethereum-based collaborative reduction system, their study also highlighted significant drawbacks. The way the system was implemented on Ethereum, in particular, was determined to be quicker to scale than on Hyperledger. But it was also noticed that the evidence of work difficulty of Ethereum is more than that of Hyperledger, which may have an influence on the whole system's efficiency and restrict its efficacy in particular instances. Makhdoom et al. [8] proposed a collaborative intrusion detection system that makes use of blockchain technology to facilitate interaction and exchange of data among different intrusion detection systems. The suggested strategy appears to be a potential option for improving identification of impending attack events. The research managed to identify problems related with maintaining confidence between network peers. The existence of an inside attacker, according to the researchers, could introduce erroneous malware signatures into the network, resulting in efficiency deterioration. This problem emphasizes the need for extra safeguards to protect the system's identity and limit the effect of prospective assaults. The research found that integrating blockchain with IDS may contribute to enhanced trust administration and identification of rogue nodes, thus boosting the system's overall resilience. In addition, the findings revealed that the suggested approach could successfully combine alerts and recognize erroneous data entries, resulting in a decrease in rate of errors. While the work proposes a potential way to improve IDS resilience, it is crucial to emphasize that there may be additional constraints that must be resolved. In particular, the efficiency effect of incorporating blockchain into IDS systems, as well as the possibility for more variables, might cause issues in some cases. Benaddi et al. [9] emphasize the necessity of providing a high standard of protection for IoT gadgets, especially when safely sharing private information between the nodes of a network. Fortunately, the massive volume of data created every day is a problem that needs adequate oversight to ensure security and confidentiality. To overcome these issues, the researchers recommend combining IDSs with blockchain as the primary record for safe storage of information. By exploiting the inviolability and decentralized characteristics of blockchain technology as a whole, this solution can provide more safety and secrecy for IoT devices. The utilization of IDS in conjunction with blockchain offers potential for increasing the safety of IoT devices; however, further study is required to assess its efficacy and applicability in practical applications. Alkadi et al. [2] suggested an integrated intrusion detection approach that enables data stored in the cloud interchange while lowering the cost of overhead. The technology can be employed as well as a decision-making tool for cloud consumers and service providers to help in encrypted information movement. The attack detection approach processes network sequences of data employing a bidirectional long short-term memory (BiLSTM) learning algorithm, and the method's effectiveness was assessed using the UNSW-NB15 and BoT-IoT datasets. But the suggested solution's scalability to massive data sets remained an unanswered question. Liang et al. [2] developed a unique intrusion detection system that combines multi-agents, blockchain, and deep learning to improve protection. The system that is suggested makes use of the NSL-KDD database, and all interaction agent operations are tracked on the blockchain to guarantee security against any attacks. The system's efficacy was evaluated in a variety of circumstances, encompassing networks of differing complexities and different sorts of assaults, yielding excellent results. However, the suggested system's scalability has to be examined, since it may struggle to handle vast volumes of data in real-world contexts. Kolokotronis et al. [10] recommended employing new methods to reduce IDS threats. A trusted chain – a blockchain where private information transferred around collaborative IDS (CIDS) nodes is recorded to avoid fabrication by hostile nodes – is included in the system that has been suggested. Furthermore, each IDS exchanges trust-related information among IDS nodes in order to increase system security. Also suggested was a protocol which combines proof of work (PoW) with proof of stake (PoS). To produce the following block, this method prioritizes reliable IDS sites with greater processing capacity and stakes. Although the suggested technique overcomes certain safety risks, it could run into sustainability challenges as the total amount of nodes increase. Alexopoulos et al. [11] developed a blockchain-based technique centered on CIDS for better harmful detection. Each alarm signal is viewed as a transaction generated by an IDS node, and other participating nodes employ consensus procedures to verify the alert. While the method provides improved security, the reliability of the system remains an issue owing to the possibility of inaccurate results and false negatives. Although the studies yielded encouraging findings, they also revealed several limitations. These limitations involve challenges with scaling when handling massive volumes of data, possible consequences for system efficiency, and the issue of handling trust between system users. The purpose of our proposed approach is to protect smart cities by protecting nodes in the event of an unlawful attack via the implementation of IDS in smart cities. IDS is an effective security technology that may be enhanced with ML and DL algorithms; nevertheless, because smart cities are dispersed, one IDS is adequate to detect many attacks. In fact, we propose interactive distributed smart cities–based IDS that combines DL approaches with the successful Adaboost to create an intrusion detection system that recognizes attacks at every node, as well as Blockchain technology to transfer and safeguard attacks identified by points in complete security as well as to ensure node confidence and dependability. In addition, leveraging the GPU to benefit from the SAE and QRNN model enables quicker capture recognition and processing.

21.3 PROPOSED APPROACH

A collaborative intrusion detection system (CIDS) is a sophisticated method that improves safety by tracking and analyzing information obtained from different networks at the same time. The requirement for CIDS stems from the reality that one IDS node could be unable to identify complicated and sophisticated assaults due to a lack of understanding of prior attacks and other harmful occurrences. CIDS enables all IDS components to interact with one another to exchange data regarding emergent network difficulties, immunizing and prevent assaults from intensifying. Fortunately, organizations are reticent to provide their information owing to concerns regarding privacy. Nonetheless, merging blockchain with CIDS guarantees a reasonable degree of confidence via consensus mechanisms. Blockchain protects data by ensuring its integrity has not been altered while in transit.

21.3.1 Intrusion detection subsystem

This component is in charge of identifying and analyzing suspected network breaches. It intercepts communication over the network and grabs pertinent data for subsequent examination. Machine learning techniques are used to discover and categorize possible security risks.

21.3.2 Blockchain-based communication subsystem

The communication framework makes use of the technology known as blockchain to enable safe and transparent exchange of data across system parts. By utilizing a decentralized and distributed ledger, blockchain secures the confidentiality and permanence of data. It allows IDS stations to communicate with regard to developing problems with the network, cooperate in real time, and prevent assaults from developing. The communication for blockchain feature communicates with the Hyperledger Fabric network, which is made up of many IDS nodes constituted by IDS node (peer) entities. The Hyperledger Fabric's chain code (smart contract) provides the reasoning for IDS node connectivity as well as data exchange. The IDS node functions as another node in the Hyperledger Fabric network, communicating with each other and gaining access to the public ledger and so enabling safe and transparent communication.

- **Intrusion detection subsystem**

The first stage in implementation is pre-processing, which entails changing the raw data retrieved from the BoT-IoT dataset. It has been developed and tagged for prospective multiclass use. The label characteristics denoted an assault flow, a category of attacks, and a subclass. In reality, BoT-IoT has 99.99% more assaults than benign ones (0.01%), and it contains 46 properties, including the target variable.

Missing values are common in datasets, which can be ascribed to recording mistakes or feature extraction difficulties. To remedy this, we opted to remove rows with NaN, Null, or Inf values. Considering the magnitude of the dataset, this has little effect on the outcomes. We utilized a stacked autoencoder and a QRNN to learn from this pre-processed dataset after conducting the pre-processing phase on the BoT-IoT dataset and partitioning it into testing, training, and validation sets.

We used a stacked autoencoder, which is constructed of three autoencoders; every one of them is formed of an encoder network (E) and a decoder network (D). The encoder reduces the source data to produce a lower-dimensional space-time participation, while the decoder D attempts to recreate the initial data provided in this reduced form. The autoencoder was taught from start to finish minimizing reconstruction error, allowing it to learn useful and concise patterns.

21.3.3 Stacked autoencoder structures

- SAE training

On the training set (X_train), we trained the SAE to learn the best implicit forms. The training method entails minimizing the reconstructed loss, measuring the difference between the first input and its reconstructed form. We optimized the encoder and decoder to collect some of the essential aspects of the input information by redistributing the error via the SAE stages and adjusting the variables that are learned.

After learning the SAE, we used the encoder E to get encoded representations of the information that had been processed from the training, testing sets. Z_train denotes the encoded representations of the training set, W_val denotes the one used for validation set, and W_test denotes the one used for testing set.

- SAE output

After training the autoencoder, we used the encoder to get encoded representations of the information that had been processed from the training, testing sets. Z_train denotes the encoded representations of the training set, W_val denotes the one used for validation set, and W_test denotes the one used for testing set.

21.3.4 QRNN structures

For the classification job, we created a quasi-recurrent neural networks (QRNN) architecture using encoded representations as inputting. The QRNN is made up of several layers of linked neurons that allow it to learn intricate structures and generate predictions.

- QRNN training

We trained the QRNN using the encoded representations W_train and the associated labels y_train. Passing the encoded representations into the

QRNN layers and optimizing the QRNN variables to minimize an appropriate loss function are part of the learning phase. Gradient descent or its derivatives are commonly utilized in this optimization technique, with backpropagation employed for determining the gradients.

- **Training and testing**

After training the QRNN, we assessed its generalization capacity by evaluating its efficacy on the validation dataset (W_val). This assessment allows us to fine-tune hyper parameters like the variety of the layers, neurons, and activation processes in order to enhance the algorithm's efficiency. This phase was repeated on multiple occasions to refine the QRNN design. Lastly, we evaluated the QRNN on the testing set (W_test) in order to get an impartial evaluation of its reliability and efficacy. This assessment assisted us in determining how effectively the algorithm generalizes to previously unknown information and gives perspectives on its performance in reality.

We are interested in creating a framework that can successfully categorize and identify breaches in network data by using the SAE to acquire condensed representation and then training the QRNN using these representations. The SAE aids in collecting significant characteristics and decreasing distortion in the information, while the QRNN makes accurate forecasts by using these models.

- **Blockchain-based communication subsystem**

We put Hyperledger Fabric on every single communication node, including IDS and surveillance nodes. This step usually entails installing the binary systems as well as requirements. The network was defined by producing a file with configuration information that describes the variety of endpoints and their duties. Because the system includes triple IDS nodes and two surveilling nodes, the IDS network represents a separate protection part, while the surveillance nodes gather and analyze attack data: ids_nodes.append(node_id), surveillance_nodes.append(node_id). Communication methods and data formats for transferring intrusion detection information are defined by intelligent contracts. For instance, the intelligent contract may define functions for declaring an identified attack or applying for more information from different nodes: context.setContract(attackContract).

We built channels for communication inside the Hyperledger Fabric architecture to allow for targeted data exchange between IDS and surveillance nodes. We established a channel called "AnomalyDetectionChannel" and added three IDS nodes and two monitoring nodes to it: createChannel (AttackDetectionChannel, [ids1, ids2, ids3]). ([surveilling 1, surveillance 2])). Then we built the reasoning inside the intelligent contracts to allow for sharing of information and validation. By activating a function in the intelligent contract and giving essential parameters that include the source IP, destination IP, and attack type, the IDS node can notify a discovered invasion. The information may then be validated per preset parameters by the intelligent contract, confirming the correctness and security of the claimed attack: this.validateAttackData(sourceIP, destinationIP, AttackType) is a function that validates attack information. Employing the provided communication channels, we carried out interactions across the IDS endpoints and the surveillance nodes. By activating a feature in the intelligent contract and supplying an attack ID, the node responsible for monitoring can obtain further information about a reported intrusion. The IDS node that discovered an attack might reply to the query by giving additional details via the intelligent contract: reportAttack(context, sourceIP, destinationIP, AttackType) attackContract. By utilizing a ledger that is distributed, Hyperledger Fabric provides data permanence and consensus. Every legitimate action involving peers is saved in the ledger, resulting in an irreversible and visible background. Compromise between the nodes involved can be achieved by the implementation of an agreed-upon algorithm, practical byzantine fault tolerance (PBFT), which makes certain all of the nodes accept the legitimacy of activities.

Nodes participating in intrusion detection may securely share information, maintain integrity of data, and provide an ethical foundation for cooperation and analysis by utilizing blockchain communication based on Hyperledger Fabric. The decentralized and transparent nature of blockchain technologies improves the overall efficacy and dependability of detection and prevention devices (Figure 21.1).

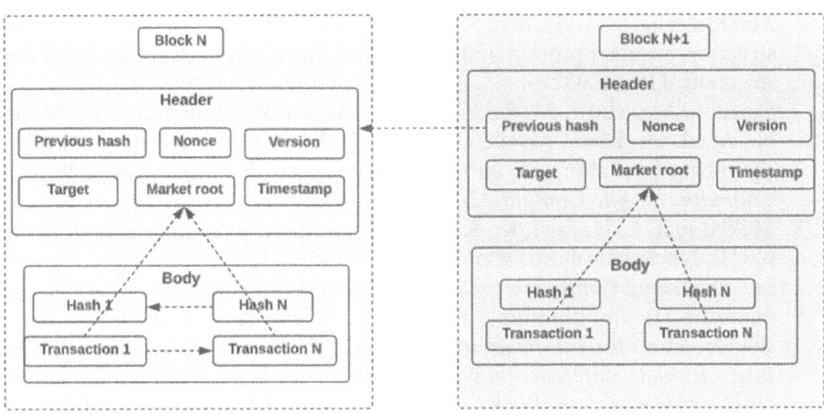

Figure 21.1 Blockchain structure

21.4 CONCLUSION

We proposed in this study an IoT system for protecting the smart cities nodes when receiving a malicious attack event by integrating an efficient IDS enhanced by the learning set QNN for each node, and the collaboration between different nodes is done via a blockchain to exchange attacks detected by each fog node securely. Our study and experiment results confirm the model's effectiveness in accurately detecting attacks and anomalies across various transaction types in binary classification. The experimental dataset utilized in this study comprises samples from the EdgeIIoT.

REFERENCES

1. Aggarwal, S. and Kumar, N. (2021). Hyperledger. In *Advances in Computers*, vol. 121, pp. 323–343. Elsevier.
2. Alkadi, O., Moustafa, N., Turnbull, B., and Choo, K.-K. R. (2020). A deep blockchain framework enabled collaborative intrusion detection for protecting IoT and cloud networks. *IEEE Internet Things J.*, 8(12):9463–9472.
3. El Airaj, Soufian, Fatima Amounas, Mourade Azrour, and Mohamed Badiy (2023). "A Comprehensive Review on the Integration of Blockchain Technology with IPFS in IoT Ecosystem." In The International Conference on Artificial Intelligence and Smart Environment, pp. 78–83. Cham: Springer Nature Switzerland, 2023..
4. Cui, Z., Ke, R., Pu, Z., and Wang, Y. (2018). Deep bidirectional and unidirectional LSTM recurrent neural network for network-wide traffic speed prediction. *arXiv preprint arXiv :1801.02143.*
5. Gadal, S. M. A. M. and Mokhtar, R. A. (2017). Anomaly detection approach using hybrid algorithm of data mining technique. In *2017 International Conference on Communication, Control, Computing and Electronics Engineering (ICCCCEE)*, pp. 1–6. IEEE.
6. Yang, R., Wakefield, R., Lyu, S., Jayasuriya, S., Han, F., Yi, X., Yang, X., Amarasinghe, G. and Chen, S. (2020). Public and private blockchain in construction business process and information integration. Automation in construction, 118, p.103276.
7. Sajjad, S. M., Mufti, M. R., Yousaf, M., Aslam, W., Alshahrani, R., Nemri, N., Afzal, H., Khan, M. A., and Chen, C.-M. (2022). Detection and blockchain-based collaborative mitigation of internet of things botnets. *Wireless Commun. Mobile Comput.*, 2022, p. 1194899.
8. Makhdoom, I., Hayawi, K., Kaosar, M., Mathew, S. S., and Masud, M. M. (2021). Blockchain-based secure CIDS operation. In *2021 5th Cyber Security in Networking Conference (CSNet)*, pp. 103–106. IEEE.
9. Benaddi, H. and Ibrahimi, K. (2020). A review: Col- laborative intrusion detection for IoT integrating the blockchain technologies. In *2020 8th International Conference on Wireless Networks and Mobile Communications (WINCOM)*, pp. 1–6. IEEE.

10. Kolokotronis, N., Brotsis, S., Germanos, G., Vassilakis, C., and Shiaeles, S. (2019). On blockchain architectures for trust-based collaborative intrusion detection. In *2019 IEEE World Congress on Services (SERVICES)*, vol. 2642, pp. 21–28. IEEE.
11. Alexopoulos, N., Vasilomanolakis, E., Iva´nko´, N. R., and Mu¨hlha¨user, M. (2017). Towards blockchain-based collaborative intrusion detection systems. In *International Conference on Critical Information Infrastructures Security*, pp. 107–118. Springer.
12. Hazman, C., Guezzaz, A., Benkirane, S. et al. (2023). Toward an intrusion detection model for IoT-based smart environments. *Multimed Tools Appl*, 83(22), pp. 62159–62180. .
13. Hazman, C., Guezzaz, A., Benkirane, S. et al. (2023). lIDS-SIoEL: intrusion detection framework for IoT-based smart environments security using ensemble learning. *Cluster Comput.*, 26:4069–4083.
14. Mohy-Eddine, M., Guezzaz, A., Benkirane, S., and Azrour, M. (2023). An efficient network intrusion detection model for IoT security using K-NN classifier and feature selection. *Multimed. Tools Appl.*, 82(15), pp. 23615–23633 .doi: 10.1007/s11042-023-14795-2.
15. Eljialy, A. E. M., Uddin, M. Y., and Ahmad, S. (2024). Novel framework for an intrusion detection system using multiple feature selection methods based on deep learning. *Tsinghua Sci. Technol.*, 29(4):948–958. doi: 10.26599/TST.2023.9010032.
16. Peng, Y., Xu, S., Chen, Q., Huang, W., and Huang, Y. (2024). A novel popularity extraction method applied in session-based recommendation. *Tsinghua Sci. Technol.*, 29(4):971–984. doi: 10.26599/TST.2023.9010061.
17. Hazman, C., Guezzaz, A., Benkirane, S., and Azrour, M. (2024). Enhanced IDS with deep learning for IoT-based smart cities security. *Tsinghua Sci. Technol.*, 29(4):929–947. doi: 10.26599/TST.2023.9010033.
18. Wang, P., Zhu, Z., Chen, Q., and Dai, W. (2024). Text reasoning chain extraction for multi-hop question answering. *Tsinghua Sci. Technol.*, 29(4):959–970. doi: 10.26599/TST.2023.9010060.
19. Mohy-eddine, M., Guezzaz, A., Benkirane, S., and Azrour, M. (2023). An intrusion detection model using election-based feature selection and K-NN. *Microprocess. Microsyst.*, 104966. doi: 10.1016/j.micpro.2023.104966.
20. Meenakshi, N., et al. (2024). Efficient communication in wireless sensor networks using optimized energy efficient engroove leach clustering protocol. *Tsinghua Sci. Technol.*, 29(4):985–1001. doi: 10.26599/TST.2023.9010056.
21. Attou, H. et al. (2023). Towards an intelligent intrusion detection system to detect malicious activities in cloud computing. *Appl. Sci.*, 13(17):9588.
22. Li, S., Cui, T., and Viriyasitavat, W. (2024). Edge device fault probability based intelligent calculations for fault probability of smart systems. *Tsinghua Sci. Technol.*, 29(4):1023–1036. doi: 10.26599/TST.2023.9010085.
23. Liu, W., Zhou, L., Zhang, S., Luo, N., and Xu, M. (2024). A new high-precision and lightweight detection model for illegal construction objects based on deep learning. *Tsinghua Sci. Technol.*, 29(4):1002–1022. doi: 10.26599/TST.2023.9010090.

24. Attou, H., Guezzaz, A., Benkirane, S., Azrour, M., and Farhaoui, Y. (2023). Cloud-based intrusion detection approach using machine learning techniques. *Big Data Min. Anal.*, 6(3):311–320.
25. Amaouche, S., et al. (2023). FSCB-IDS: feature selection and minority class balancing for attacks detection in VANETS. *Appl. Sci.*, 13(13):7488.
26. Amaouche, S., Guezzaz, A., Benkirane, B., and Azrour, M. (2023). IDS-XGbFS: a smart intrusion detection system using XGboostwith recent feature selection for VANET safety. *Clust. Comput.*, 27(3), pp.3521–3535.
27. Douiba, M., Benkirane, S., Guezzaz, S., and Azrour, M. (2022). Anomaly detection model based on gradient boosting and decision tree for IoT environments security. *J. Reliab. Intell. Environ.*, 9(4), pp.421–432.
28. Douiba, M., Benkirane, S., Guezzaz, A., and Azrour, M. (2022). An improved anomaly detection model for IoT security using decision tree and gradient boosting. *J. Supercomput.*, 79(3), pp.3392–3411.
29. Bella, K., et al. (2024). An efficient intrusion detection system for IoT security using CNN decision forest. *PeerJ Comput. Sci.*, 10:e2290. doi: 10.7717/peerj-cs.2290.
30. C. Hazman, A. Guezzaz, S. Benkirane and M. Azrour, “Enhanced IDS with Deep Learning for IoT-Based Smart Cities Security,” in *Tsinghua Science and Technology*, 29(4): 929–947, August 2024, doi: 10.26599/TST.2023.9010033.

Chapter 22

Iterated greedy with tabu search solving flow shop scheduling problem

Khadija Mesmar, Maria Lebbar, Said Aqil, and Karam Allali

22.1 INTRODUCTION

In recent decades, production systems have faced intensified competition in meeting client demands within optimal timeframes, as customer satisfaction greatly relies on timely deliveries. One extensively studied scheduling problem is the flow shop problem (FSP), which has garnered significant attention in the literature [1, 2]. In the FSP, a set J = {J1, J2, ..., Jn} consisting of n independent jobs needs to be processed on a set M = {M1, M2, ..., Mm} of m machines. Each job k in J requires a fixed, non-negative processing time Tkh on each machine h in M. Additionally, all tasks (n) must follow the same sequence on machines (m), meaning that the jobs in the shop must adhere to a consistent machine order, starting from machine 1 and ending on machine m. The objective is to determine the optimal order for processing the jobs in the shop, aiming to optimize a specific criterion. The most commonly studied criterion in the literature is the minimization of the total completion time, also known as the makespan (Cmax), of the production sequence. This simplified problem is referred to as the permutation flow shop problem (PFSP) with the makespan criterion denoted as Fm|prmu|Cmax [3]. It is important to note that the standard notation used in scheduling problems consists of three components: $\alpha|\beta|\gamma$, as proposed in [4]. The first component α indicates the problem type, the second component β represents the constraints, and the third component γ denotes the problem's criteria.

Numerous heuristic approaches have been developed for the permutation flow shop problem (PFSP). Constructive methods such as Johnson's algorithm [5], CDS's algorithm [6], and Dannenbring's Rapid Access (RA) procedure [7] are well-known examples. Among the preferable heuristics for PFSP is the NEH heuristic [8]. To achieve optimal results, metaheuristic algorithms have been introduced. Notable examples include the iterated greedy (IG) algorithm, proposed by Ruiz and Stützle [9]; tabu search (TS), presented by Nowicki and Smutnicki [10]; and simulated annealing (SA), developed by Osman and Potts [11]. Furthermore, other metaheuristics based on local search algorithms have been utilized for solving the PFSP.

DOI: 10.1201/9781003587552-22

For instance, the iterative local search (ILS) algorithm has been applied in [12], while the variable neighborhood search (VNS) has been explored in [13]. Nature-inspired algorithms have also found their place in addressing PFSP scheduling problems. Notable examples include the ant colony optimization (ACO) algorithm discussed in [14], the artificial bee colony (ABC) algorithm presented in [15], and the migratory bird optimization (MBO) algorithm highlighted in [16]. It is worth noting that these metaheuristics will continue to be further developed and improved in future research to better align with the evolving needs of industries, as demanded by both customers and managers.

We find that many works show that the hybrid metaheuristics that combine two or more scheduling algorithms can give well desired results. Indeed, when the hybridization is applied to a scheduling problem, a significant enhancement in terms of optimization can be achieved. Therefore, a hybrid metaheuristic can enhance the effectiveness of results given by a single-based scheduling algorithm [17]. In this work, we will implement three variant of metaheuristics; the first is iterated greedy with tabu search (IGTS), the second is iterated greedy with simulated annealing (IGSA) while the last is iterated greedy with both tabu search and simulated annealing (IGSATS). Moreover, we will compare all with the classical NEH heuristic. We will take some instances of different sizes from small-medium to relatively medium-large ones. The objective will be to seek an optimal sequence that gives the best completion time. Numerical tests show that the IGSATS algorithm is relatively more effective in minimizing the makespan than other IGSA and IGTS algorithms.

The rest of the chapter is organized as follows. Section 22.2 provides the permutation flow shop scheduling problem formulation with a makespan criterion. In Section 22.3, we give a detailed description of IGSA, IGTS, and IGSATS algorithms. The effectiveness of three proposed algorithms is verified through numerical experiments and results are discussed in Section 22.4. Finally, a conclusion and perspectives are given in Section 22.5.

22.2 PROBLEM STATEMENT

In the permutation flow shop scheduling problem, all jobs follow the identical order of processing. Our goal is to find a collection of compromise solutions in order that the makespan is minimized. Flow shop scheduling may be a typical line problem where n different jobs must be handled on different machines. All jobs are processed on all machines within the same order. The interval of the roles on the machines is fixed irrespective of the order during which the processing is performed. The issue is to sequence n independent jobs on m different machines. Following the identical notations proposed by Reeves [18], Tkh is the processing time for job k on machine h and employment permutation is represented by the sequence $\beta = \{\beta 1, \beta 2, \ldots, \beta n\}$. When there are n jobs and m machines, the completion time $Q(\beta k, h)$ is calculated as follows:

$$Q(\beta 1,1) = T(\beta 1,1) \tag{22.1}$$

$$Q(\beta k,1) = Q(\beta(k-1),1) + T(\beta k,1),\ k = 2, \ldots, n \tag{22.2}$$

$$Q(\beta 1, h) = Q(\beta 1, h-1) + T(\beta 1, h),\ h = 2, \ldots, m \tag{22.3}$$

$$Q(\beta k, h) = \max\{Q(\beta(k-1),h), Q(\beta k, h-1)\} + T(\beta k, h),\ k = 2, \ldots, n,\ h = 2, \ldots, m \tag{22.4}$$

Essentially, the makespan is defined as:

$$Cmax(\beta) = Q(\beta n,m) \tag{22.5}$$

The next task is to determine a permutation $\beta *$ in the selection of all permutations Π such that:

$$Cmax(\beta *) \leq Cmax(\beta)\ \forall\ \beta \in \Pi \tag{22.6}$$

22.3 PROPOSED ALGORITHMS: IGSA, IGTS, AND IGSATS

We propose three algorithms for solving our problems: the iterative greedy algorithm with tabu research (IGTS), the iterative greedy algorithm with the simulated annealing model (IGSA), and finally the combination of the iterative greedy simulated annealing and tabu research and (IGSATS). This last approach could be a combined hybrid metaheuristic of three resolution algorithms. We note that hybrid metaheuristics show great utility in speed of convergence toward an honest solution for optimization problems. We focus in resolution model descriptions on the last three approaches, i.e., IGSA, IGTS, and IGSATS.

22.3.1 Iterated greedy with simulated annealing (IGSA)

The iterated greedy algorithm is a metaheuristic designed for flow shop scheduling problems, focusing on single-solution optimization. It begins with an initial solution and iteratively perturbs a sequence while searching for the local optimum. The algorithm employs a destructive approach in which several jobs are removed from a permutation β of n jobs during each iteration, chosen randomly and without repetition. These removed jobs form two subsequences: βD, which contains the remaining (n – d) jobs after removal, and βR, which consists of the d jobs that need to be reinserted into βD to form a complete candidate solution. The construction phase starts with βD and iteratively inserts the jobs from βR into βD. Each step involves inserting the first job, βR(1), into all possible (n - d + 1) positions of βD. The optimal position for βR(1) is determined by evaluating the resulting sequence's Cmax, aiming to minimize it. This process continues until βR is empty or a final solution is achieved. Thus, βD is restored to its original size, n, after the destruction-construction procedure. In the local search phase, the algorithm seeks a local optimum for the sequence. The simulated annealing method is employed as the acceptance criterion due to its excellent performance. The criterion utilizes a constant temperature determined by the T0 parameter of the IGSA algorithm.

$$Temperature = T0 \times \frac{\sum_{k=1}^{n} \sum_{h=1}^{m} Tkh}{10 \times m \times n} \tag{22.7}$$

We retain this expression, which clearly shows the characteristics of the instance which are the number of jobs n, the number of machines m, and the processing time Tkh of each job on each machine. The criterion uses a constant temperature that depends on the T0 parameter of the algorithm IGSA.

22.3.2 Iterated greedy with tabu search (IGTS)

The original IG algorithm employs a local search procedure to generate a new sequence, and a decision must be made whether to accept it as the current best solution for the next iteration. In this work, we draw inspiration from the taboo search (TS) method and adopt an acceptance criterion that allows for the acceptance of slightly worse solutions. In the proposed IGTS algorithm, we introduce a tabu list that memorizes a set of sequences that have not been explored in the neighborhood. Throughout the iterations, and depending on the stopping condition, we update the tabu list, which has a fixed size determined at the beginning.

22.3.3 Iterated greedy with simulated annealing and tabu search (IGSATS)

We propose a combined approach of the IGSA algorithm and the IGTS algorithm to solving scheduling PFSP. We consider here a circular tabu list containing sequences of tasks selected in the neighborhood generation process. Before choosing the sequence that will pass the acceptance criterion, we check that it does not appear in the tabu list. The tabu list keeps track of the latest solutions already visited. Each iteration with the a new tabu list will be updated.

22.4 COMPUTATIONAL RESULTS

In this section, we offer a comprehensive experimental evaluation and comparison of the proposed IGSATS algorithm with other powerful methods NEH, IGSA [19], and IGTS [20]. For the comparisons we use randomly generated instances where the processing times of the jobs are uniformly distributed between 1 and 99. The number of jobs is from 20 jobs to 160 and therefore the number of machines is from 5 to 30. Within the simulations, we use the same computational conditions, including the identical computer, the same artificial language, and the same stopping criteria. All considered algorithms are coded in MATLAB and run on a PC with Intel(R) Core(TM) i5-7200U CPU and 4G RAM. For the computational tests, we set the parameters d ∈ and T0 = 0.4. For all algorithms, the run time is restricted to 3,600 seconds or until the iterated number is equal to 100. The performance of all algorithms is evaluated by a percentage deviation ($\Delta C\%$), which is calculated as follows:

$$\Delta C\% = \frac{Cmax(NEH) - Cmax(Algo.)}{Cmax(Algo.)} \times 100 \tag{22.8}$$

We note that Cmax (NEH) represents the value of makespan obtained by the algorithm NEH and Cmax(Algo.), the value of the makespan obtained by IGSA, IGTS, and IGSATS algorithms. To judge the performance of our suggested IGSATS algorithm. We will implement three variant of metaheuristics; the first is iterated greedy with tabu search, the second is iterated greedy with simulated annealing, while the last is iterated greedy with both tabu search and simulated annealing. Additionally, we will compare all of them with the classical NEH heuristic.

Computational results are summarized in Table 22.1 for the number of jobs, which is from 20 jobs to 160 and therefore the number of machines is from 5 to 30, where Cmax and $\Delta C\%$ represent makespan and percentage deviations, respectively.

22.5 CONCLUSION AND PERSPECTIVES

The IGSATS algorithm's success in solving the permutation flow shop issue with a makespan requirement is strongly dependent on its tabu-based reconstruction technique. This reconstruction approach improves the algorithm's

Table 22.1 Computational results for random instances

	NEH	IGSATS	IGTS	IGSA		NEH	IGSATS	IGTS	IGSA
n x m	*Cmax*	*ΔC%*	*ΔC%*	*ΔC%*	*n x m*	*Cmax*	*ΔC%*	*ΔC%*	*ΔC%*
20 X 5	1230	0.99	0.99	0.99	100 X 10	5657	0.96	0.84	0.14
20 X 10	1567	2.42	2.22	1.29	100 X 20	6528	0.38	0.37	0.25
20 X 15	1938	6.66	5.84	4.47	100 X 30	7492	1.34	0.89	0.59
40 X 5	2134	0.14	0.14	0.05	120 X 10	6852	1.30	1.29	0.50
40 X 10	2689	1.20	1.20	0.52	120 X 20	7757	1.68	1.19	0.22
40 X 15	3113	3.66	3.28	2.54	120 X 30	8610	1.57	0.93	0.35
60 X 5	3411	0.24	0.24	0.24	140 X 10	7673	0.97	0.38	0.16
60 X 10	3681	3.81	3.66	1.71	140 X 20	8579	1.65	0.94	0.30
60 X 15	4017	1.95	1.93	0.12	140 X 30	9773	2.46	1.54	0.08
80 X 5	4664	0.09	0.09	0.09	160 X 10	8816	0.54	0.54	0.08
80 X 10	5626	2.07	1.70	0.30	160 X 20	9966	1.37	0.91	0.01
80 X 15	4992	2.82	2.82	0.12	160 X 30	10703	0.77	0.29	0.12

exploitability, resulting in a performance better than other high-performing algorithms. Thus, this study not only gives an appropriate metaheuristic for solving the FSP, but it also proposes a viable technique for improving the IG algorithm's performance in handling additional issues. Several areas require more examination. First, applying the tabu-based reconstruction approach to improve the performance of other metaheuristics would be exciting. Second, investigating more powerful problem-dependent neighborhood search techniques may improve the exploration capabilities of various algorithms while solving the FSP. Third, creating comparable techniques for scheduling issues with other processing setups and/or objective functions might be a promising research path. Finally, coupling tabu-based processes with the IG and SA algorithms to solve other combinatorial optimization problems has the potential to be a promising challenge for future study.

REFERENCES

1. R Ruiz, and C. Maroto, A comprehensive review and evaluation of permutation flowshop heuristics. *European Journal of Operational Research*, 165(2), 479–494, 2005.
2. K Mesmar, S Aqil, and K Allali. Iterated-greedy-based metaheuristic with Tabu search and simulated annealing for solving permutation flow shop problem, in *Proceedings of META'2018 7th International Conference on Metaheuristics and Nature Inspired Computing*, pp. 127–132, Marrakech, Morocco, Oct. 2018.
3. M Pinedo. *Scheduling: Theory, Algorithms and Systems*, 2nd ed. Prentice Hall, New Jersey, 2002.
4. R-L Graham, E-L Lawler, J-K Lenstra, and A-R Kan. Optimization and approximation in deterministic sequencing and scheduling: a survey. *Annals of Discrete Mathematics* , 5, 287–326, 1979.
5. S-M Johnson. Optimal two- and three-stage production schedules with setup times included. *Naval Research Logistics Quarterly*, 1(1), 61–68, 1954.
6. H-G Campbell, R-A Dudek, and M-L Smith. A heuristic algorithm for the n job, m machine sequencing problem. *Management Science*, 16(10), 630–637, 1970.
7. D-G Dannenbring. An evaluation of flow shop sequencing heuristics. *Management Science*, 23(11), 117–1182, 1977.
8. M Nawaz, E-E Enscore, and I Ham. A heuristic algorithm for the m-machine, n-job flow-shop sequencing problem. *Omega*, 11, 91–95, 1983.
9. R Ruiz, and T Stï¿ 12 tzle. A simple and effective iterated greedy algorithm for the permutation flowshop scheduling problem. *European Journal of Operational Research*, 177, 2033–2049, 2007.
10. E Nowicki, and C Smutnicki. A fast tabu search algorithm for the permutation flow-shop problem. *European Journal of Operational Research*, 91, 160–175, 1996.

11. I Osman, and C Potts Simulated annealing for permutation flow-shop scheduling. *Omega*, 17, 551–557, 1989.
12. X Dong, P Chen, H Huang, and M Nowak. A multi-restart iterated local search algorithm for the permutation flow shop problem minimizing total flow time. *Computers and Operations Research*, 40(2), 627–632, 2013.
13. W-E Costa, M-C Goldbarg, and E-G Goldbarg. New VNS heuristic for total flow time flowshop scheduling problem. *Expert Systems with Applications*, 39(9), 8149–8161, 2012.
14. F Ahmadizar. A new ant colony algorithm for makespan minimization in permutation flow shops. *Computers and Industrial Engineering*, 63(2), 355–361, 2012.
15. F-M Tasgetiren, Q-K Pan, P-N Suganthan, and A-H Chen. A discrete artificial bee colony algorithm for the total flowtime minimization in permutation flow shops. *Information Sciences*, 181(16), 3459–3475, 2011.
16. I Benkalai, D Rebaine, C Gagné, and P Baptiste. Improving the migrating birds optimization metaheuristic for the permutation flow shop with sequence-dependent set-up times. *International Journal of Production Research*, 55(20), 6145–6157, 2017.
17. G-I Zobolas, D Christos Tarantilis, and Ioannou George. Minimizing makespan in permutation flow shop scheduling problems using a hybrid metaheuristic algorithm. *Computers and Operations Research*, 36(4), 1249–1267, 2009.
18. CR Reeves. A genetic algorithm for flowshop sequencing. *Computers and Operations Research*, 22, 5–13, 1995.
19. V Fernandez-Viagas, J-M Valente, and J-M. Framinan. Iterated-greedy-based algorithms with beam search initialization for the permutation flowshop to minimise total tardiness. *Expert Systems with Applications*, 94, 58–69, 2018.
20. J-Y Ding, S Song, J-N Gupta, R Zhang, R Chiong, and C Wu. An improved iterated greedy algorithm with a Tabu-based reconstruction strategy for the no-wait flowshop scheduling problem. *Applied Soft Computing*, 30, 604–613, 2015.

Index